FACTORY GIRLS

From Village to City in a Changing China

Leslie T. Chang

Spiegel & Grau

New York

2008

Map designed by Laura Hartman-Maestro

Library of Congress Cataloging-in-Publication Data
Chang, Leslie T.
  Factory girls : from village to city in a changing China / Leslie T.
Chang. — 1st ed.
     p. cm.
  1. Manufacturing industries—Employees—China. 2. Women migrant
labor—China. 3. Young women—Employment—China. I. Title.
  HD9734.C55C53 2008
  331.40951—dc22

                                                          2008012880

ISBN 978-0-385-52017-1

PRINTED IN THE UNITED STATES OF AMERICA

10 9 8 7 6 5 4 3 2 1

First Edition

For my parents

CONTENTS

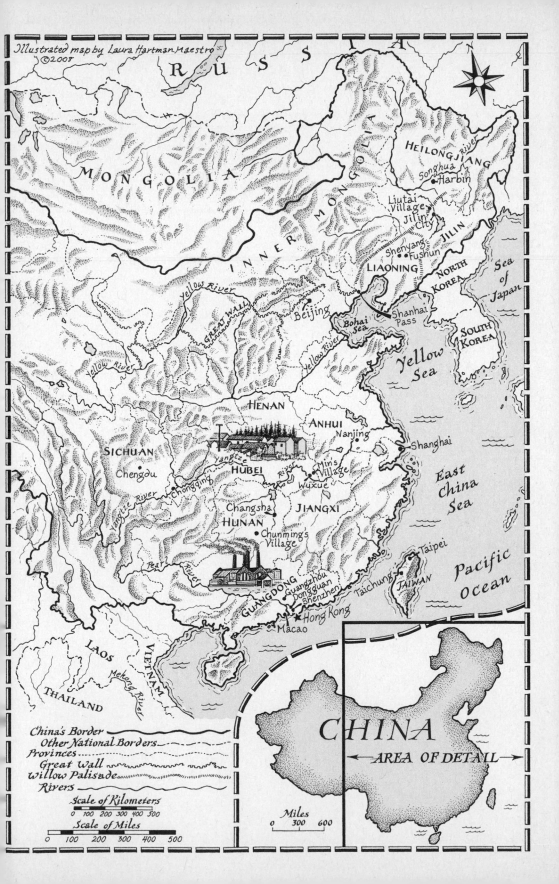

Illustrated map by Laura Hartman Maestro
©2008

RUSSIA

MONGOLIA

INNER MONGOLIA

HEILONGJIANG

Songhua River

Harbin

Liutai
Village

Jilin
City

JILIN

Shenyang · Fushun

LIAONING

NORTH
KOREA

Sea
of
Japan

Yellow River

Beijing

GREAT WALL

Yellow River

Shanhai
Pass

Bohai
Sea

SOUTH
KOREA

Yellow
Sea

Yellow River

HENAN

ANHUI

Nanjing

SICHUAN

Chengdu

HUBEI

Yangtze River

Min's
Village

Wuxue

Shanghai

East
China
Sea

Chongqing

Yangtze River

Changsha

JIANGXI

HUNAN

Chunming's
Village

Taipei

Pearl River

GUANGDONG

Guangzhou
Dongguan
Shenzhen

Taichung

TAIWAN

Pacific
Ocean

Hong Kong

Macao

LAOS

VIETNAM

Mekong River

THAILAND

China's Border
Other National Borders
Provinces
Great Wall
Willow Palisade
Rivers

Scale of Kilometers
0 100 200 300 400 500

Scale of Miles
0 100 200 300 400 500

CHINA

← AREA OF DETAIL →

Miles
0   300   600

PART ONE   *The City*

1 Going Out

When you met a girl from another factory, you quickly took her measure. *What year are you?* you asked each other, as if speaking not of human beings but of the makes of cars. *How much a month? Including room and board? How much for overtime?* Then you might ask what province she was from. You never asked her name.

To have a true friend inside the factory was not easy. Girls slept twelve to a room, and in the tight confines of the dorm it was better to keep your secrets. Some girls joined the factory with borrowed ID cards and never told anyone their real names. Some spoke only to those from their home provinces, but that had risks: Gossip traveled quickly from factory to village, and when you went home every auntie and granny would know how much you made and how much you saved and whether you went out with boys.

When you did make a friend, you did everything for her. If a friend quit her job and had nowhere to stay, you shared your bunk despite the risk of a ten-yuan fine, about $1.25, if you got caught. If she worked far away, you would get up early on a rare day off and ride hours on the bus, and at the other end your friend would take leave from work—this time, the fine one hundred yuan—to spend the day with you. You might stay at a factory you didn't like, or quit one you did, because a friend asked you to. Friends wrote letters every week, although the girls who had been out longer considered that childish. They sent messages by mobile phone instead.

Friends fell out often because life was changing so fast. The easiest thing in the world was to lose touch with someone.

The best day of the month was payday. But in a way it was the worst day, too. After you had worked hard for so long, it was infuriating to see how much money had been docked for silly things: being a few minutes late one morning, or taking a half day off for feeling sick, or having to pay extra when the winter uniforms switched to summer ones. On payday, everyone crowded the post office to wire money to their families. Girls who had just come out from home were crazy about sending money back, but the ones who had been out longer laughed at them. Some girls set up savings accounts for themselves, especially if they already had boyfriends. Everyone knew which girls were the best savers and how many thousands they had saved. Everyone knew the worst savers, too, with their lip gloss and silver mobile phones and heart-shaped lockets and their many pairs of high-heeled shoes.

The girls talked constantly of leaving. Workers were required to stay six months, and even then permission to quit was not always granted. The factory held the first two months of every worker's pay; leaving without approval meant losing that money and starting all over somewhere else. That was a fact of factory life you couldn't know from the outside: Getting into a factory was easy. The hard part was getting out.

The only way to find a better job was to quit the one you had. Interviews took time away from work, and a new hire was expected to start right away. Leaving a job was also the best guarantee of getting a new one: The pressing need for a place to eat and sleep was incentive to find work fast. Girls often quit a factory in groups, finding courage in numbers and pledging to join a new factory together, although that usually turned out to be impossible. The easiest thing in the world was to lose touch with someone.

*   *   *

For a long time Lu Qingmin was alone. Her older sister worked at a factory in Shenzhen, a booming industrial city an hour away by bus. Her friends from home were scattered at factories up and down China's coast, but Min, as her friends called her, was not in touch with them. It was a matter of pride: Because she didn't like the place she was working, she didn't tell anyone where she was. She simply dropped out of sight.

Her factory's name was Carrin Electronics. The Hong Kong–owned company made alarm clocks, calculators, and electronic calendars that displayed the time of day in cities around the world. The factory had looked respectable when Min came for an interview in March 2003: tile buildings, a cement yard, a metal accordion gate that folded shut. It wasn't until she was hired that she was allowed inside. Workers slept twelve to a room in bunks crowded near the toilets; the rooms were dirty and they smelled bad. The food in the canteen was bad, too: A meal consisted of rice, one meat or vegetable dish, and soup, and the soup was watery.

A day on the assembly line stretched from eight in the morning until midnight—thirteen hours on the job plus two breaks for meals—and workers labored every day for weeks on end. Sometimes on a Saturday afternoon they had no overtime, which was their only break. The workers made four hundred yuan a month—the equivalent of fifty dollars—and close to double that with overtime, but the pay was often late. The factory employed a thousand people, mostly women, either teenagers just out from home or married women already past thirty. You could judge the quality of the workplace by who was missing: young women in their twenties, the elite of the factory world. When Min imagined sitting on the assembly line every day for the next ten years, she was filled with dread. She was sixteen years old.

From the moment she entered the factory she wanted to leave, but she pledged to stick it out six months. It would be good to toughen herself up, and her options were limited for now. The legal working age was eighteen, though sixteen- and seventeen-year-olds could work certain jobs for shorter hours. Generally only an employer that freely broke the labor law—"the very blackest factories," Min called them—would hire someone as young as she was.

Her first week on the job, Min turned seventeen. She took a half day off and walked the streets alone, buying some sweets and eating them by herself. She had no idea what people did for fun. Before she had come to the city, she had only a vague notion of what a factory was; dimly, she imagined it as a lively social gathering. "I thought it would be fun to work on the assembly line," she said later. "I thought it would be a lot of people working together, busy, talking, and having fun. I thought it would be very free. But it was not that way at all."

Talking on the job was forbidden and carried a five-yuan fine. Bathroom breaks were limited to ten minutes and required a sign-up list. Min worked in quality control, checking the electronic gadgets as they moved past on the assembly line to make sure buttons worked and plastic pieces joined and batteries hooked up as they should. She was not a model worker. She chattered constantly and sang with the other women on the line. Sitting still made her feel trapped, like a bird in a cage, so she frequently ran to the bathroom just to look out the window at the green mountains that reminded her of home. Dongguan was a factory city set in the lush subtropics, and sometimes it seemed that Min was the only one who noticed. Because of her, the factory passed a rule that limited workers to one bathroom break every four hours; the penalty for violators was five yuan.

After six months Min went to her boss, a man in his twenties, and said she wanted to leave. He refused.

"Your performance on the assembly line is not good," said Min's boss. "Are you blind?"

"Even if I were blind," Min countered, "I would not work under such an ungrateful person as you."

She walked off the line the next day in protest, an act that brought a hundred-yuan fine. The following day, she went to her boss and asked again to leave. His response surprised her: Stay through the lunar new year holiday, which was six months away, and she could quit with the two months' back pay that the factory owed her. Min's boss was gambling that she would stay. Workers flood factory towns like Dongguan after the new year, and competition for jobs then is the toughest.

After the fight, Min's boss became nicer to her. He urged her several times to consider staying; there was even talk of a promotion to factory-floor clerk, though it would not bring an increase in pay. Min resisted. "Your factory is not worth wasting my whole youth here," she told her boss. She signed up for a computer class at a nearby commercial school. When there wasn't an overtime shift, she skipped dinner and took a few hours of lessons in how to type on a keyboard or fill out forms by computer. Most of the factory girls believed they were so poorly educated that taking a class wouldn't help, but Min was different. "Learning is better than not learning," she reasoned.

She phoned home and said she was thinking of quitting her job. Her parents, who farmed a small plot of land and had three younger children still in school, advised against it. "You always want to jump from this place to that place," her father said. Girls should not be so flighty. Stay in one place and save some money, he told her.

Min suspected this was not the best advice. "Don't worry about me," she told her father. "I can take care of myself."

She had two true friends in the factory now, Liang Rong and Huang Jiao'e, who were both a year older than Min. They washed Min's clothes for her on the nights she went to class. Laundry was a constant chore because the workers had only a few changes of clothes. In the humid dark nights after the workday ended, long lines of girls filed back and forth from the dormitory bathrooms carrying buckets of water.

Once you had friends, life in the factory could be fun. On rare evenings off, the three girls would skip dinner and go roller-skating, then return to watch a late movie at the factory. As autumn turned into winter, the cold in the unheated dorms kept the girls awake at night. Min dragged her friends into the yard to play badminton until they were warm enough to fall asleep.

The 2004 lunar new year fell in late January. Workers got only four days off, not enough time to go home and come out again. Min holed up in her dorm and phoned home four times in two days. After the holiday she went to her boss again, and this time he let her leave. Liang Rong and Huang Jiao'e cried when Min told them her news. In a city of strangers, they were the only ones who knew about her departure. They begged her to stay; they believed that conditions at other factories were no better, and that to leave or to stay would be the same in the end. Min did not think so.

She promised she would return for a visit after she got paid at her new job. Min left that same day with a few clothes in a backpack and the two months' wages that the factory owed her. She did not take her towels and bedding with her; those things had cost money, but she couldn't bear the sight of them anymore.

In ten months on the assembly line, Min had sent home three thousand yuan—about $360—and made two true friends.

She should have been scared. But all she knew was that she was free.

*   *   *

In the village where Lu Qingmin was born, almost everyone shared her family name. Ninety households lived there, planting rice, rape, and cotton on small plots of land. Min's family farmed half an acre and ate most of what they grew.

Her future appeared set when she was still a child, and it centered on a tenet of rural life: A family must have a son. Min's mother had four girls before finally giving birth to a boy; in those early years of the government policy limiting families to one child, enforcement was lax in much of the countryside. But five children would bring heavy financial burdens as the economy opened up in the 1980s and the cost of living rose. As the second-oldest child, Min would bear many of those burdens.

She disliked school and did poorly. As long as she could remember, she was in trouble. She climbed the neighbors' trees to steal their plums; if she was caught she got a beating. Once when her mother ordered her to do chores, Min refused. "There are so many people at home. Why do I have to do it?" Her mother chased her for a quarter mile and hit her with a stick.

She was good at having fun. She learned how to swim and to drive a truck; she loved roller-skating and hid her injuries from her mother. "I have fallen every way there is to fall," Min said. "But you can't think about that." She was her father's favorite. One summer, he rented a truck and she traveled the countryside with him, selling watermelons from their farm. They drove during the day and slept in the truck at night; it became one of Min's fondest memories. Most migrants associated the place they came from with poverty and backwardness, and some were even reluctant to say the name of their village. But long after Min came to the city, she still talked about her hometown as if it were something beautiful.

In the late 1990s, both of Min's parents went out to work to earn money for their children's schooling. Her father worked in a shoe factory on the coast, but poor health drove him back. Later her mother went out for a year. Min boarded at a middle school in a nearby town but returned home every weekend to cook and wash clothes for her father and the younger children.

Almost all the young people in her village had gone out. When Min was still in middle school, her older sister, Guimin, went to work in a factory in Dongguan. Soon after, Min failed the national high school entrance exam and her parents considered having her go out, too. Guimin phoned home and urged them to keep Min in school; Guimin's factory wages, she said, would help cover the tuition. Their parents agreed, and Min enrolled in a two-year vocational high school. That made her one of the most educated people in the village—more educated than Guimin, who had sacrificed her own schooling to help the family.

Guimin came home for the 2003 lunar new year holiday and took Min away with her when she left. Min had one more semester of school, but she wanted to save the tuition and get a jump on the job hunt. She was thrilled to be leaving home; she had never ridden on a train or seen a factory. "I wanted to get out early, learn some things, and see the world," she said.

In Dongguan, Guimin rented a cheap hotel room for Min and found her a job in a Japanese factory that made liquid crystal displays. Min worked there for a month and left. She had never been in a place where she didn't know anyone, and she was so lonely she couldn't bear it. She returned to the hotel and found a job at another factory but didn't take it. Her sister offered to continue paying for the hotel room, but Min felt herself becoming a burden. At a bus station, she spotted a help-wanted flyer for a quality-control job on the assembly line of an electronics factory. She dialed the number on the ad—many were just scams to trick migrants out of their money—and the person who answered the phone gave Min directions to the factory. It was a three-hour bus ride to the southeast tip of Dongguan and Carrin Electronics, the place where Min spent her hard year alone.

The minute she entered the factory grounds, Min realized the place was worse than the Japanese factory she had just left behind. But it was too late to turn back, and she did not want to ask her sister's help again. She was getting used to being on her own—it was better that way.

*   *   *

Migrant workers use a simple term for the move that defines their lives: *chuqu,* to go out. *There was nothing to do at home, so I went out.* This is how a migrant story begins.

The city does not offer them an easy living. The pay for hard labor is low—often lower than the official minimum wage, which ranges between fifty and eighty dollars a month. Work hours frequently stretch beyond the legal limit of forty-nine hours per week. Get hurt, sick, or pregnant, and you're on your own. Local governments have little incentive to protect workers; their job is to keep the factory owners happy, which will bring in more investment and tax revenue. But suffering in silence is not how migrant workers see themselves. To come out from home and work in a factory is the hardest thing they have ever done. It is also an adventure. What keeps them in the city is not fear but pride: To return home early is to admit defeat. To go out and stay out—*chuqu*—is to change your fate.

Migrants are the rural elite. They are younger, better educated, and more enterprising than the people they leave behind. The city people's name for them—*liudong renkou,* floating population—

suggests an aimless mob, but most migrants leave home with a work objective in mind, in the company of a relative or fellow villager who already knows the way. And most of today's young migrants don't come from the farm: They come from school. Farming is something they have watched their parents do.

Migration was an accidental consequence of economic reforms. In 1958, the Chinese government set up a household registration system that assigned each person rural or urban residency. City dwellers were allocated jobs, housing, and ration coupons for food and other necessities; residents of the countryside, with none of these privileges, were stuck on the farm.

In the late 1970s, reforms allowed farming households to sell part of their harvest on the market rather than supplying it all to the state. Agricultural production soared. Suddenly, food was available in local markets across the country, and rural residents could survive independently in the cities for the first time. A 1984 government directive permitted farmers to settle in small market towns; to be on the move was no longer a crime. Migration picked up speed, and by 1990, the country had sixty million migrants, many of them drawn to the booming factories and cities of the coast.

Today China has 130 million migrant workers. In factories, restaurants, construction sites, elevators, delivery services, housecleaning, child-raising, garbage-collecting, barbershops, and brothels, almost every worker is a rural migrant. In large cities like Beijing and Shanghai, migrants account for a quarter of the population; in the factory towns of south China, they power the assembly lines of the nation's export economy. Together they represent the largest migration in human history, three times the number of people who emigrated to America from Europe over a century.

Yet the government has been slow to acknowledge the reality of migration. For years, migrants in the cities had to dodge the police; those caught without residency permits were fined or sent home. Finally in 2003, the State Council, China's cabinet, issued a comprehensive document calling migration key to the country's development. It banned job discrimination against migrants and advocated better working conditions for them and schooling for their children. On the brick walls of rural villages, pro-migration slogans appeared: GO OUT FOR MIGRANT WORK, RETURN HOME TO DEVELOP. LABOR FLOWS OUT, MONEY FLOWS BACK.

Migration is emptying villages of young people. Across the Chinese countryside, those plowing and harvesting in the fields are elderly men and women, charged with running the farm and caring for the younger children who are still in school. Money sent home by migrants is already the biggest source of wealth accumulation in rural China. Yet earning money isn't the only reason people migrate. In surveys, migrants rank "seeing the world," "developing myself," and "learning new skills" as important as increasing their incomes. In many cases, it is not crippling poverty that drives migrants out from home, but idleness. Plots of land are small and easily farmed by parents; nearby towns offer few job opportunities. *There was nothing to do at home, so I went out.*

*   *   *

Long afterward Min would remember the first time she went to the talent market, puzzling over its details like a dream she could not interpret. On a Sunday morning in February 2004 after she had quit the Carrin factory, she went to the market and spent four hours there. She was nervous. She carried nothing with her. The whole of her job-hunting strategy could be summarized in two words: Aim low. She interviewed at half a dozen companies that were hiring clerks. A clerk might type, answer phones, fill out forms, file documents, greet guests, and pour tea; a clerk was the lowest person in the office hierarchy. "You don't want to find a company whose standards are too high," she said later. "Then you'll be rejected and quickly lose confidence."

At the booth of a company called Yidong Electronic, a recruiter asked for Min's résumé. She had not thought to prepare one. The woman told her to write her job history on an application form. Min did not even have a pen, so the woman lent her one. And the woman smiled at Min. "I don't know. She smiled at me. Maybe that was it." Thus Min would return over and over to this day, trying to unravel the mystery of the moment when her luck changed.

The woman told Min to go to the factory for a follow-up interview, but Min didn't go. The place was too far away. But at the headquarters of Yidong Electronic, a manager named Li Pengjie was looking over applications, and he stopped at Min's. He noticed that she had good handwriting.

In traditional China, calligraphy was the mark of an educated person. Good calligraphy showed refinement and literary accomplishment; calligraphy could also reveal the subtle weaknesses in a person's character. Li Pengjie had something more mundane in mind: He needed a clerk to keep files on the factory's machines, and the files were written out by hand. In a factory that made connectors and backlights for mobile phones, it was this antique skill that mattered most.

Li Pengjie called Min's cousin on his mobile phone—she did not have one of her own—and asked Min to come in for an interview that would last three hours.

First she flunked the computer test. "The other girls all know computers better than you," Li Pengjie told her.

Next he asked about her work experience.

"I haven't done this work," she said. "I don't have any experience."

Then he gave her a writing test, and she wrote well. Li Pengjie told Min that she was hired, and that he would be her new boss.

He told her to go get her things so she could move into the factory that day.

The offer was so unexpected that Min did not know what to say. But as she got up to leave his office, the words suddenly came. "So many people wanted this job," she said to her new boss. "Why did you choose me? I don't know anything."

"You are very straightforward," he said. "And you are more honest than the others."

Min started work the next day as a clerk in the equipment division. Her department tracked the punches and grinders and roll-plating lines that made the pieces of a mobile phone. A bound book recorded the condition and history of every machine, like the medical file of a giant mute patient. Min's job was to keep these files in order. Workers slept eight to a room; a meal was rice, three meat or vegetable dishes, and soup. A day in the office stretched ten hours, with sometimes a Saturday or Sunday off. Min would make eight hundred yuan a month—one hundred dollars, double the base pay at her old factory.

I MET MIN for the first time three weeks later. She was short and sturdily built, with curly hair and keen dark eyes that didn't miss a thing. Like many young people from the Chinese countryside, she looked even younger than she was. She could have been fifteen, or fourteen, or even twelve—a tomboy in cargo pants and running shoes, waiting impatiently to grow up. She had a child's face. It was round and open to the world, with the look of patient expectation that children's faces sometimes wear.

We met at the apartment of a woman named Lin Xue, who wrote articles for a local magazine that targeted migrant readers. I had told Lin Xue I wanted to write about young migrant women for the *Wall Street Journal*; her younger sister worked in a factory and invited

Min, one of her coworkers, to come. I was meeting many migrants then, and Min's story was already familiar to me.

"I'm from a farming village in Hubei Province, the second of five children," she told me. "Our parents work on a farm. Our conditions are not good.

"I went out with my older sister, who went to work in Shenzhen. We wanted to work in the same place, but we can't work in the same place."

She paused dramatically.

"Why not?" I asked.

"Because we always fight." And then she laughed.

Min was willing to talk about anything; unlike most of the Chinese people I knew, she clearly enjoyed telling her own story. And she was as curious about me as I was about her: She had come to Lin Xue's apartment that day because "I wanted to see what an American looked like," she told me later. My only worry was that she might be too settled—with a stable office job in hand, perhaps the great dramas of her life were already past. But I needn't have worried about that.

On the day we met, Min told me her life plan. She would work in the city for seven years, sending money home all the while to repay her mother and father for raising her to adulthood; that reflected the traditional Chinese view that children should be grateful to their parents for the gift of their existence. When she turned twenty-three, the debt repaid, Min would return home and find someone to marry.

She was in a good mood that day. She had "walked out of the factory," as the migrants say, crossing the class divide between those who work with their hands and those who work with their heads. "God is still fair," she said. "He let me be so tired for a year, but now he lets me have a new beginning." She had just turned eighteen and she was already an expert in new beginnings.

2 *The City*

Long journeys end at the Guangzhou railway station, where the passengers pour off the trains after rides that have lasted twenty or thirty or fifty hours. They are mostly young and they arrive alone, dragging a suitcase or a backpack or a coarse burlap sack that once held rice. The vast plaza in front of the station seethes with travelers, and the first thing you hear is the jangle of announcements for people who, newly arrived, are already lost. *Someone from Henan, your brother is looking for you. Older brother's wife, come to the exit area.* WELCOME TO THE BEAUTIFUL FLOWER CITY: A bus company is offering tours. But the city does not look beautiful and there are no flowers here.

Up a steep ramp and across an overpass is the long-distance bus station, where the express to Dongguan, thirty miles away, leaves every ten minutes. The bus is packed, and it smells of sweat and of clothing that is worn every day and slept in at night—the smell of migrants. The bus races down the elevated highway and the factories emerge below: printing factories, paint and plastic factories, mobile-phone and screw and sofa factories. The buildings, faced in white tile, resemble giant public bathrooms; worker dormitories rise beside them, their balconies blooming with laundry. Chinese factories are named for their auspicious associations, and the journey to Dongguan is a high-speed tour of virtue and fortune: HIGH REFINE-MENT AIR-CONDITIONING. ETERNAL SINCERITY GARMENTS. NEW ERA ZIPPER COMPANY.

Two decades after the first factories were built, development still feels new. The innards of a mountain spill out, red-earthed and raw, where its face was blasted away; exit ramps off the highway disappear in fields of marshy weeds. A brand-new corporate headquarters looks out on rice paddies, fishponds, and duck farms; miraculously, people are still farming here. In the seventeenth century, settlers turned the floodplains of the Pearl River Delta into one of China's most fertile regions, supplying fish, vegetables, and rice to the country and exporting silk to Europe. Today in the land of full-throttle industry, it is these glimpses of nature that are unsettling. The farmers are mostly migrants, the lowest of the low, for they have traveled a thousand miles from home but have still not left the farm behind.

The bus slows for the Dongguan exit, and now the factories appear up close. Red banners stretch across the fronts of buildings in sagging smiles of welcome: SEEKING EXPERIENCED WOMEN WORKERS. At the gate of one factory, migrants have gathered to stare, in mesmerized silence, at a help-wanted sign: MEET 1:30 EVERY AFTERNOON AT THE SIDE GATE. A company called Jobhop Limited is, appropriately enough, seeking workers. The bus passes through another giant construction site—no, this is the bus station—and releases its passengers.

The best way to understand the city of Dongguan is to walk it. Bank headquarters of mirrored glass tower over street-side shops selling motorcycle parts and plastic pipes and dental services. Roads are ten lanes wide, high-speed highways in place of city streets. Migrants walk along the shoulders carrying suitcases or bedding, while buses and trucks bear down from behind. Everywhere is construction and motion, jackhammers and motorcycles, drills and dust; at street level the noise is deafening. The roads are wide and well paved but there are no pedestrian lights or crosswalks. This is a city built for machines, not people.

The offices of the government bureaucracy that appear on almost every block in other Chinese cities are nowhere to be seen. Men on motorcycles accost pedestrians, each one touting a taxi ride, and all of them illegal. Counterfeit college diplomas are for sale at street corners. In Dongguan there is a fake IKEA and a fast-food chain whose name translates as "McKFC" and a ten-story building that calls itself the Haiyatt Hotel, with a marble lobby and a decidedly lax attitude toward copyright violation ("We have an 'i' in our name, they don't," explains a young woman at the front desk). The city is divided into thirty-two towns, and each one specializes in manufacturing. Chang'an produces electronic components, Dalang is famous for sweaters, and Houjie makes shoes. Samsung and Pioneer operate plants in Liaobu; Nancheng is home to the world's largest Nokia mobile-phone factory. All the Nescafé instant coffee that is drunk in China is processed at a plant in downtown Dongguan. Factories are the bus stops and the monuments and the landmarks, and everything exists to serve them. Dongguan's highway network, already the densest in the country, is under constant expansion in hopes of delivering goods to the world faster. Luxury hotels and golf courses have sprung up to pamper factory clients. The buyers of the world stay at the Sheraton Dongguan Hotel, which gives guests a card listing every destination they will ever need:

GUANGDONG INTERNATIONAL EXHIBITION CENTER
DONGGUAN INTERNATIONAL EXHIBITION CENTER
MUSEUM OF OPIUM WAR
TAI PING JETTY

WAL-MART
CARREFOUR
PARK 'N' SHOP
HARBOUR PLAZA GOLF CLUB
HILLVIEW GOLF CLUB
LONG ISLAND GOLF CLUB

No one is sure how many people live here. According to the city government, Dongguan has 1.7 million local residents and almost seven million migrants, but few people believe these official figures, and speculation about the city's true population is rife. *Dongguan has eight million migrants. Dongguan adds one million migrants a year. Dongguan has ten million migrants, but it reports only seven million to avoid paying higher taxes.* The city's mayor might know more, but he's not telling: "Dongguan's population is far more than the publicly announced figure," he told reporters at a forum in 2005. His personal estimate—"conservative," in his words—was over ten million.

Dongguan is unfinished, a city where everything is in the process of becoming something else. A stretch of sidewalk is piled high with stone tiles, under a sign promising EUROPEAN-STYLE PALACE-LEVEL OFFICE BUILDINGS. The central business district yawns with open pits. On the east side of town, a new city center is rising, which will one day have government offices, a library, a science museum, and a theater. For now, the area's wide boulevards are empty of cars and its grassy malls perfectly still, the hedges trimmed in tidy geometries. Dongguan's motto is "One Big Step Every Year, a New City in Five Years."

Molding a new life is even faster. A few computer lessons can catapult a person into a different class, and a morning at the talent market is enough to establish a new career. Twenty yuan at a photo studio buys a package of snapshots, taken against a painted backdrop of picket fences or formal gardens; these prints are mailed home or given to friends or taped to a dormitory wall, a reminder that the person in the picture is already someone new. On walls around the city, next to flyers for job openings and syphilis clinics, are the advertisements for the missing. HE LEFT HOME FIVE YEARS AGO, DARK-SKINNED, WITH A POCKMARKED FACE, SPEAKS RATHER FAST, LIKES TO PLAY VIDEO GAMES. The notices are posted by family members searching for loved ones who have disappeared into the great maw of the city.

On weekends, teenagers take over Dongguan, giving its parks and squares the feel of an open-air high school. Girls roam in cliques, wearing frilly tops and tight jeans, with their arms around one anothers' shoulders. Boys travel in smaller packs, the sleeves of their factory shirts rolled up under their armpits. Couples parade apart, the girls proud in ownership, the boys slouchy and nonchalant. On Monday mornings, the parks and the squares of Dongguan are eerily empty. The long avenues of factories show only blank faces to the world, the packs of girls and boys swallowed up inside. Industry does not require movement and activity, but their opposite—street after street, there is only silence.

At night, the factories lining the highways are lit. Look closely and you can sometimes see shadows moving against a window, erratic as fireflies—as long as there is light, people are still working. Each strip of blue-lighted windows against the dark signals a single factory; one strip is set apart from the next, like stately ocean liners on the sea. From a distance, they are beautiful.

*   *   *

The girls were twenty days out from home, so new to the city they didn't know who owned the factory where they worked. They carried nothing with them: no drinks, no plastic bags of fruit or snacks. They just sat, under the blazing sun, in the public square of a district of Dongguan known for its small shoe factories.

Their names were Tian Yongxia and Zhang Dali. They were sixteen years old and this was their first time away from home. They
had left their farming village in Henan Province on the ninth day
of the lunar new year, which was regarded as an auspicious moment
to depart. A girl from their village worked in a factory here for eight
hundred yuan a month, and they wanted that too. They each paid
four hundred yuan, about fifty dollars, to a husband and wife who
promised them factory jobs and brought them out on a three-day
bus journey. But when they got to the city there were no jobs, and
the couple disappeared.

The girls spent four nights in the bus station and finally got in
touch with someone from home, who found them work in an electronics factory for three hundred yuan a month. It was a poor salary,
but they were in no position to negotiate. "By that time I wanted to
join a factory just so I could get a good night's sleep," said Yongxia,
who had a broad face and small eyes and smiled a lot. She did most
of the talking. Dali was slimmer and prettier, with delicate features
and uneven teeth.

The girls quickly learned the hierarchy of factory life, and that
they were at the bottom. Workers who had joined the previous year
looked down on newcomers and did not talk to them. Theirs was a
smaller subsidiary factory, which paid less, but to work at a company's main facility you needed skills and a proper identity card;
both girls had joined the factory with borrowed IDs because they
had not applied for their own cards yet. The assembly line ran eight
hours a day with weekends off, and that was bad too, because overtime would have meant more money. Shoe factories paid more, but
they were known to work extremely long days, and the girls constantly debated whether the extra money would be worth the ex-
haustion. Soon after Yongxia and Dali arrived in the factory, they
started talking about how to leave.

Before they went out from home, the two girls had made a pact:
If jobs at the first factory fell through, they would go straight home.

But when jobs at the first factory fell through, they stayed. They had come to the city, and already they were changed.

I MET YONGXIA AND DALI on my second day in town. It was a hot February morning, the sky bleached a dingy white and the air humming with heat and motorcycle exhaust; in the Pearl River Delta, summer would begin in another month. I took the girls to a noodle shop and ordered Cokes. They sipped them carefully through straws as they told me the story of how they had left home.

I explained that I was a reporter for the *Wall Street Journal*. Yongxia turned my business card over and over, mulling its unfamiliar Beijing address. "Can we write you letters?" she said suddenly. "We miss our mothers. We are so lonely." Through the restaurant window, one of the girls spotted something outside. Both rose and scattered, like a pair of startled birds. "Sorry, we have to go now."

By the time I caught up with them they were halfway down the block, standing on the sidewalk with a girl in their midst—the prize, the one who had come out from their village the previous year, the one who made eight hundred yuan a month. She was going somewhere, and they weren't letting her get away this time.

I asked Yongxia for the phone number in her dorm, but she was so new to her job that she didn't know it yet. She promised to write me a letter. We agreed to meet in two weeks, on the spot in the square where we had met that morning. And then they vanished. They were sixteen years old, on the loose in one of China's most chaotic boomtowns, raising themselves with no adults in sight. They were prey to all sorts of cons, making life decisions on the barest bits of information. They missed their mothers. But they were also having the time of their lives.

———

I FLEW DOWN FROM BEIJING two weeks later to wait for them on the square. We had agreed to meet at ten o'clock, but there were many reasons they might not come. Perhaps they had found better jobs with overtime and couldn't get away. Possibly they had decided they didn't trust me. Or they simply forgot, or had something more interesting to do; maybe they had already joined the ranks of the disappeared. Why would they come? My only hope came from something Yongxia had said: *We are so lonely.*

I waited until almost noon. By then I knew they were not coming, but I also knew that once I left the square, they would be lost to me forever. They were sixteen years old from Henan Province; that was all I knew about them, and their names. In their frilly tops and jeans and ponytails, they looked just like the millions of other young women who had come to Dongguan from somewhere else. I couldn't bring myself to meet anyone else that day. I wandered under the hot sun for hours, looking at people and talking myself out of approaching them for the pettiest of reasons. If they were in a group, they might be hard to talk to; if they were eating or drinking, they were too well-off. The sight of so many girls I would never know was paralyzing—it seemed inconceivable that any single story mattered at all.

For months afterward, whenever I came to the city, I looked closely into the faces of the young girls on the streets, hoping to find Yongxia and Dali again. Many of the girls looked back at me, wary or curious or challenging. There are millions of young women, and each one has a story worth telling. I had to look into their faces to begin.

I CAME TO DONGGUAN for the first time that February, in 2004. Migration in China was two decades old, and most foreign newspapers, including the *Wall Street Journal*, had done stories about the harsh conditions inside the factories. I wanted to write about something else—how the workers themselves thought about migration. I was especially interested in women, who seemed to have the most to gain in leaving the village but maybe also the most to lose. The assembly lines of Dongguan, one of the largest factory cities in China, drew the young and unskilled and were estimated to be 70 percent female. That seemed a good place to start.

Over the next two years, I spent a week or two of every month in Dongguan. I got to know a few young women well, and I met a great many others who told me their stories and disappeared, like the two girls on the square whom I never saw again. Their tolerance for risk was astonishing. If they didn't like a factory or a boss or a coworker, they jumped somewhere else and never looked back, and when they recounted their stories to me, there were unexplained gaps in time from stays at factories they no longer remembered. Their parents back home were only dimly aware of what their daughters were up to. Existence, to the factory girls, was a perpetual present, which seemed immensely liberating but also troubling. Making it in the city meant cutting ties to everything they knew.

The young women I became closest to had something in common: They understood the drama of their own stories and why I wanted to know about them. I think they also understood me, better than I might have expected. I was from America and I had gone to college; in education and class, I was a million miles away from them. But I knew what it was like to be alone, as a single woman, in the city. I was also bullied by Chinese men, and yelled at by police, and cheated by bus drivers; I also had boyfriend dilemmas and parents who worried that I was still single. When I got married in the spring of 2006, one of the migrant women who knew me best surprised me. "Your mother must be very happy" was the first thing she said. "I have a feeling that she is a traditional Chinese person."

Perhaps my strongest link to the girls was one they never knew:

I, too, had left home. After graduating from college in America, I moved to Prague, Czechoslovakia. Altogether I lived abroad for fifteen years, going home to see my family once every couple of years, as the migrants did. For a long time I resisted the pull of China. In college, I avoided Chinese American organizations and took only one Chinese-language class; I majored in American history and literature and wrote my undergraduate thesis on Larry McMurtry's novels of the American West. In Prague, I reported on Czech politics and society for an expatriate newspaper. One winter day in 1992, a Chinese couple dragging their suitcases along the slushy sidewalk asked me for directions in Mandarin. I waited a long moment before answering, resentfully, in their language—as if they were forcing me back into a world I had already left behind.

Initially, China's appeal for me was pragmatic—in the early 1990s, its booming economy began to attract global attention, and my fluency in Chinese suddenly became an asset. I went to Hong Kong in 1993 to work as a reporter for the *Wall Street Journal* and began to read books on Chinese history for the first time, eventually to the exclusion of everything else; to me, China has always felt like the test I neglected to study for. When I moved to Taiwan two years later, people there frequently asked me what year I had *chuqu*, gone out, to America—their unspoken assumption that everyone in the world had been born in the Chinese nation. Later after I moved to China, I often heard the same question. That was one of the ways that Taiwan and China, which until recently had been technically at war, were more alike than they imagined.

One of the first things most Chinese Americans do when they go to China is to visit their ancestral hometowns, but for twelve years I lived in Hong Kong, Taiwan, and China without making the journey. I worried that I wasn't ready to understand what I would find in my family village; secretly, I was afraid it would mean nothing at all. Either way, I understood the factory girls when they spoke of their complicated feelings for home.

YOUNG WOMEN from the countryside taught me the city. From them I learned which factories were well run; without ever leaving Dongguan, these workers had figured out the global hierarchy of nations. American and European bosses treated workers best, followed by Japanese, Korean, Hong Kong, and then Taiwanese factory owners. Domestic Chinese factories were the worst, because "they always go bankrupt," one migrant explained to me. They also knew when major policies were about to change—in early 2005, some workers told me that the minimum wage would rise, before it was officially announced.

Many things I had read about China's migrants were not true. They no longer lived in fear of being picked up by the police; instead, the authorities just ignored them. Discrimination from local residents was not really an issue, because migrants almost never encountered locals. And I was surprised to learn that job mobility was high. Almost all the senior people I met in factories had started on the assembly line. The young women I knew did not appear destined to return to the farm because they had never farmed before. They often did not know how much land their family had or when the planting season began. My assumptions had come from studies of Chinese migrant workers done in the mid-1990s; almost a decade later, this world had utterly changed, but things were happening too quickly to be written down.

I came to like Dongguan, which seemed a perverse expression of China at its most extreme. Materialism, environmental ruin, corruption, traffic, pollution, noise, prostitution, bad driving, short-term thinking, stress, striving, and chaos: If you could make it here, you'd make it anywhere. I tried to fit in as much as I could. I ate twenty-five-cent bowls of noodles for lunch and took buses everywhere. I dressed, in jeans and sandals, more plainly than many migrant girls who wore embroidered shirts and high heels when they went out. I was invisible in Dongguan, and I liked that too. In other places in China, a person staring at strangers and writing things in a notebook might attract attention; here, people were too focused on their own affairs to notice me. Only once did someone interfere: I was in the talent market, copying down instructions from a sign on the wall. A guard asked me what I was doing. I told him I was practicing my English, and he left me alone.

Dongguan is invisible to the outside world. Most of my friends in Beijing had passed through the city but all they remembered—with a shudder—were the endless factories and the prostitutes. I had stumbled on this secret world, one that I shared with seven million, or eight million, or maybe ten million other people. Living in Dongguan was like arriving in it for the first time, hurtling down the highway at seventy miles an hour, the scenery changing too fast to keep track of it. Dongguan was a place without memory.

*   *   *

Dongguan was also a city of contradictions, because modern Chinese history had begun here. During the nineteenth century, British smuggling of opium into China devastated the country and drained the treasury. In the summer of 1839, a Qing Dynasty imperial commissioner named Lin Zexu ordered the public incineration of twenty thousand cases of opium in the harbor at Humen, a town in Dongguan. That act set the two nations on course for the First Opium War, which was fought in Guangdong Province and ended quickly when British warships overwhelmed Chinese forces. The Treaty of Nanking ceded Hong Kong to Britain, forced open Chinese ports to international trade, and gave foreign nations unprecedented commercial and legal privileges within China. In the history that is taught in Chinese classrooms, the burning of opium in Humen ignited the modern era: the subjugation to foreign powers, followed by the collapse of the Qing Dynasty, revolution, war, and the Communist victory in 1949.

But there was another history of this place. In the autumn of 1978, the Taiping Handbag Factory of Hong Kong opened the first foreign factory in Dongguan. Income in its first year of operation was one million Hong Kong dollars. The factory processed materials from Hong Kong into finished goods, which were shipped back to Hong Kong to be sold to the world. It established the model for thousands of factories to follow. Over the next two years, China set up four "special economic zones" as testing grounds for free-enterprise practices like foreign investment and tax incentives. The largest zone was Shenzhen, about fifty miles south of Dongguan, which quickly became a symbol of a freewheeling China always open for business. Shenzhen was a planned showcase city, willed into being by leaders in Beijing and supported by government ministries and the companies under them.

Dongguan was different. It rose by no one's decree; it simply grew. While Shenzhen aspired to advanced technology and innovation, Dongguan took what it could get, which meant low-tech factories from Hong Kong and Taiwan that made clothing, toys, and shoes. All they needed was cheap land and labor, as well as local officials who left them alone. What they initially built could not be called modern industry. Many of the early factories were two- or three-story houses where workers sat at desks, fifty to a room, engaged in simple tasks like sewing cloth for a stuffed animal or attaching artificial hair to a doll. Some of the factories were housed in makeshift structures of sheet metal because their owners did not want the expense of real buildings.

In the early days, there was no train service from Hong Kong. Businessmen traveled to the British colony's border with Shenzhen, crossed on foot, and caught a taxi to their Dongguan factory on the other side, passing farms on the way. "There were no roads around here, no cars, no TVs, not even curtains," recalled Allen Lee, a Taiwan shoe industry executive who moved to the city in 1989. "You couldn't buy stuff like that here." In June 1989, he bicycled forty minutes to watch the news on TV about the shooting of protesters around Tiananmen Square.

The local labor supply was soon exhausted and migrants began arriving from neighboring provinces. Lin Xue, the woman I knew who wrote for a migrant magazine, had come to Dongguan from rural Sichuan in 1990. "We came here blind," she told me. "I would go to someone selling tickets and ask, 'Where should I buy a ticket to?' and we would do what they said." Lin Xue got a factory job that paid seventy yuan a month, and her younger sister pressed plywood in a lumber factory.

In the 1990s, the city's manufacturing shifted to electronics and computer parts. Today Dongguan makes 40 percent of the world's magnetic heads used in personal computers and 30 percent of its disk drives. Economic growth over the past two decades has averaged more than 15 percent a year. Some things have not changed. The migrants are still arriving. Labor-intensive factories still dominate, and though their products have gotten more sophisticated, the work itself has not. There are still a great many apartment buildings where workers sit at desks engaged in simple tasks with their hands.

So Dongguan was a place with conflicting versions of its past—one a high-profile rejection of the foreign presence in China, the other stealthy embrace of it. Every Chinese schoolchild learns about the burning of opium. But from the Taiping Handbag Factory, which did not appear in any textbook, I could trace a direct line to everyone I ever met in Dongguan, from the migrants studying Microsoft Word to the self-help gurus to the Mercedes salesman who told me that the priciest S- and E-Class cars sold best in Dongguan, because "for a boss to improve his image, this is a good product." For all of them, modern history began with the handbag factory.

* * *

I went for months without meeting a native of Dongguan. The world of the factory, from the top managers to the assembly line, was the exclusive domain of migrants, though the top boss was sometimes from Hong Kong or Taiwan. Local residents spoke the Cantonese dialect, but the factory world functioned in the official dialect of Mandarin, because that was the only way people from different provinces could talk to one another. Migrants held the local residents in low regard: They were uneducated farmers who made a living renting out farmland to factories, and they could not survive a day in the factory's demanding environment. "It's mutual contempt," my friend Lin Xue said, to describe relations between locals and migrants.

Six months after I started coming to Dongguan, I interviewed the deputy mayor. His name was Zhang Shunguang and he was a Dongguan native: my first. We sat in a big reception room in a city government building and drank tea out of tiny paper cups. Several of his assistants gathered, speaking to one another in Cantonese. I had never met a Dongguan person and here they all were, inside the government.

"Do you speak Cantonese?" one assistant asked me.

"Sorry, no," I said. No one in the city had ever asked me this question before.

"Is this your first time in Dongguan?"

"No, I've been here many times."

"Oh, were they all secret trips?"

"Is it a secret if you don't know about it?"

We already disliked each other. In the middle of the interview, I looked over at the assistant and he stared blankly back at me. The young woman next to him had fallen asleep. The phrase *mutual contempt* popped into my mind.

The interview was useful: Without seeing for myself, I never would have believed how completely the government ignored the migrants. The deputy mayor did not have an accurate count of the migrant population—that was up to the national census, not his department. He admitted that the local government lacked the resources to check conditions in the factories. "If I inspected one factory a day," he said, "it would take me fifty years to inspect all the factories. So we must rely on the companies to police themselves."

The deputy mayor then talked of a plan to "lift the quality of the Dongguan people," but the effort excluded those who were not native-born. Like all city people, he had a reflexive contempt for *waidiren*, outsiders, the common term for migrants. "The quality of migrant workers is not high," he said, "but this is the responsibility of the companies. They should be running classes for workers."

I asked the deputy mayor why there were no Dongguan people in the factories, even at the highest levels, and he contradicted what he had just said without missing a beat.

"The people from outside," he said, "have higher quality and lower wages."

After the interview, the deputy mayor shook my hand and praised my knowledge of the city. I didn't tell him my informants were all teenage girls—migrants of low quality and even lower wages.

AFTER A YEAR of visiting the city, I rented a one-bedroom apartment downtown for $160 a month. The high-rise complex was called Dongguan City Holiday, and it targeted single women; hot-pink billboards around town advertised ONE PERSON'S HOUSE, ONE PER-

SON'S SPLENDOR. I thought I would meet young women and hear their stories, but no one ever said a word to me in the lobbies and elevators, and I never saw a single person in the common room. People were too busy with their own lives to bother with anyone else's. I got most of my news from the bulletin boards in the apartment complex, which portrayed a community of petty crime and round-the-clock construction.

FOR THE PEACE OF RESIDENTS, RENOVATION WILL STOP ON JANUARY 1. IT WILL RESUME ON JANUARY 2.

WHEN A PERSON KNOCKS ON YOUR DOOR, DO NOT CASUALLY OPEN IT UNTIL YOU HAVE CONFIRMED THE PERSON'S IDENTITY.

ANYONE WITH INFORMATION ABOUT THE THEFT RING IN THE NANCHENG AREA SHOULD CONTACT THE POLICE.

My landlady had moved to the city years before from rural Guangdong. She often showed up at my apartment in pink pajamas and house slippers to collect the rent, and I once heard her say "Fuck your mother" on the phone to her husband because he had just told her he was returning late from a business trip. She worked the night shift at a hotel, doing sales. I wondered what kind of sales had to be done between midnight and six o'clock in the morning, but I never found the courage to ask. My landlady had a way of deflecting questions.

"How did you have two children?" I asked her once. Most urban families were limited to one.

"How do you think I had two children?" she answered.

The retail environment outside my apartment was in constant flux. On the day I moved in, I was excited to see a BRICK OVEN PIZZA sign beside the entrance to my building, a welcome taste of home. By my next visit, that had morphed into the GREAT AMBITIONS MO- BILE PHONE DIGITAL SUPERMARKET. Just what China needed: an- other store selling mobile phones. Over the following two weeks, the space below my apartment transformed from an empty shell with cables dangling from the ceiling into a full-on mobile-phone store, with robotic salespeople and music blasting from giant speak- ers into an empty parking lot. On my next stay, marketing had be- gun, in the form of a young woman who stood at the store entrance and read phone model numbers and prices into a microphone, one after another. Another sign had materialized in front of my building: HAVE KFC AS YOUR NEIGHBOR! EARN 8% ANNUAL INTEREST WITHOUT DOING ANYTHING. I wasn't thrilled to have KFC as my neighbor. The only constant in the neighborhood was the Nescafé plant across the street. On summer days, the smell of coffee en- veloped me as soon as I walked outside, a warm bath at once sweet and bitter.

When you lived in Beijing, you were shielded from many things, but in the hinterland cities you could see the strains of China's de- velopment up close. Public buses often diverged from their routes to fill up on gas; fuel shortages were common, so an open station was worth a stop even with a load of passengers. Full-day power stop- pages were regular events, and factories had to juggle their produc- tion schedules because of government rationing. Among the notices on my apartment bulletin board was one that never varied: THE ORIGINAL POWER SUPPLY TRUNK LINE CANNOT KEEP UP WITH THE NEEDS OF DEVELOPMENT AND MUST BE CHANGED.

During the summer of 2005, the power went off for at least one day on each of my trips to Dongguan. With some advance notice I could plan ahead, but sometimes the power went dead without warning, consigning me to a day indoors in ninety-degree heat and as little movement as possible. I would call the building's manage- ment office, fuming, but it was not their fault. It was not anyone's fault. China's economy was growing by 10 percent a year, faster in the south, and it was a miracle that things were holding together as well as they were.

*   *   *

I took the bus everywhere. In part this was to see as much of the migrant world as I could, but it was also practical. Taxi drivers were some of the biggest cheats around—more than once I found myself speeding down a dark highway while a cabbie threatened to leave me by the side of the road if I didn't give him more money. Another high-speed negotiating tactic was to offer to take a passenger partway to his destination for a smaller fare; drivers were such short-term thinkers that they would rather earn less money but get paid sooner. Even honest cabdrivers suffered the shortcomings of peasants: Once they left the patch of turf they knew, they were as lost as I was.

The employees of the bus system worked in pairs: The driver was usually a local man, the ticket seller a female migrant. Sometimes they shouted conversations the length of the bus over the heads of passengers, and sometimes there was a small television screen mounted in the dashboard so the driver could watch TV as he drove. When approaching a stop, the ticket seller leaned out the door while the bus was still moving and called out destinations in a hoarse voice. The waiting people were usually susceptible to pressure; if they were yelled at long enough, some would get on.

The young men on the bus smelled of gamy sweat, the scent of people who walked long distances outdoors and never enjoyed the luxury of air-conditioning. The young women were immaculate: They never smelled, and their hair was always sleek and shiny. On every bus there were several migrants holding plastic bags to their mouths and throwing up quietly. Motion sickness was the terror of people from the countryside, who were not accustomed to car travel. Brown plastic bags hung from bus ceiling hooks in bunches, like overripe bananas beginning to go bad. Passengers on buses carried an amazing variety of things; in the way of the countryside, nothing was ever thrown away. On different journeys, I saw people carrying an ancient TV set, a wicker basket of electric cables, a mud-encrusted bucket of stonemason's tools, and a murderous-looking wrench a yard long. Once I saw a young woman with a six-foot-long broomstick handle.

Bus stops were unmarked, and there were never signs showing the routes. You had to ask: Information was conveyed by word of mouth, as if we lived in ancient times before the invention of writing. Twice I bought city maps with bus schedules but both times the routes were already out of date; things were happening too quickly to be written down. The other passengers were as confused as I was, often calling out the names of stops that had already passed and making panicked departures. Wherever I went, I was asked directions. One afternoon, I puzzled over routes with a migrant woman, who asked me after a while, "Are you from Hubei?" Was that an insult or a compliment? I just wanted to get home.

At night the buses stopped running early, an injustice to everyone who could afford no other form of transportation. After eight o'clock, people arranged to spend the night in friends' dorms, even though most factories banned overnight visitors and getting caught would mean a large fine.

I never saw old people on the bus.

ONE NIGHT I caught a bus from Shenzhen back to Dongguan. About halfway to our destination, the bus stopped and the driver yelled at the passengers to switch to another vehicle. This was common, though illegal: Late at night, half-empty buses preferred to pool their passengers rather than continue on money-losing journeys alone. The driver of one bus would pay another a set price for each passenger taken off his hands.

After the second bus was on the highway, the new ticket seller announced that we weren't going to Dongguan after all. This was common, too: Once the second bus had been paid for taking passengers, its sole purpose was to get rid of them as soon as possible.

The bus stopped. "All passengers for Houjie get off here." The ticket seller was a skinny Cantonese man who yelled everything in a nasal voice. He walked down the aisle, pointing at certain people and ordering them off. He pointed at me.

A passenger ahead of me got off the bus and disappeared into the night. I walked to the front of the bus and leaned out from the bottom step. We were on a pitch-black highway beside a deserted construction site.

"There are no taxis here," I said to the ticket seller. "I'm not getting off."

"There are taxis," he yelled in snarling Cantonese.

"I'm not getting off."

He came up behind me and put his hand on my shoulder.

"Don't touch me!" I climbed back up the stairs and sat in a front-row seat. None of the other passengers had budged.

And then the bus started driving again. It had failed to dispose of its cargo, so it kept going. Passengers continued to get off at their stops as if nothing had happened. "These buses are very black," said a young woman with a slender dark face who was sitting next to me. "You should only take buses where the driver is wearing a uniform." Yet she was on this bus, just like me.

"The people who work on this bus are evil," she said loudly, "and every word out of their mouths is an obscenity." I felt safe just being next to her, but then she got off too.

The bus pulled to the side of the road and stopped again. "Okay, everyone off," the ticket seller yelled. This time he walked up and down the aisle, giving two yuan to each person.

I walked down the aisle to where he was. "I paid twenty-five yuan to get to Dongguan, and I want my money back."

He turned around to face me. Of course, he was taller than I was, and he was a man. At that moment, I realized how powerless I truly was.

"If you paid a hundred, should I give you a hundred?" he yelled. "If I take my pants off, will you give me a hundred?"

It didn't make sense and it wasn't funny, but he liked the sound of it and he said it again. "If I take my pants off, will you give me a hundred?"

"Fuck you," I said in English. "Asshole. Prick." That broke my cardinal rule about living in China—never play the American card—but sometimes only cursing in English will do. The man looked at me with newfound respect.

I pushed past him to the front of the bus and looked for something to throw. I wanted to grab his money belt and toss it out the window, but of course he kept that close to him. There was a dirty towel on the dashboard, and I flung it in the driver's face. Then I got off the bus and ran. My heart was pounding; I thought he might come after me. Then I stopped running, and I realized how stupid I must have looked.

On a side street, I saw a taxi and asked the driver how much to Dongguan. Eighty yuan—ten dollars. I got in. I was so mad I was shaking. I thought of all the young women I knew who lived here, and how every single one had been cheated, abused, and yelled at by someone just like the skinny Cantonese man, who probably woke up in the morning already angry at the world. There was no recourse but tears and fury at your own impotence. In a confrontation, everything boiled down instantly to brute force, and a woman would always lose. I had money, and with money I could buy my way to comfort and safety. They didn't have that.

And yet there were also people who were kind, like the woman on the bus who had cursed out the driver on my behalf. You had to focus on that or you would never survive.

* * *

Dongguan might feel like a place without a past, but city officials did not see it that way. In the new downtown, they had erected a museum of history—an immense building of gray stone, as squat and permanent as the mausoleum of a dead dictator. Cabdrivers didn't know the place—invariably they took me to a commercial exhibition center down the street—and the museum was deserted all three times I went in the summer of 2005.

Chinese history museums are troubled places. Ancient civilization was great, or so the official narrative went, but it was feudal and backward. Modern China was ravaged by foreigners, but the Chinese people were heroic in humiliation and defeat. China stood up in 1949 when the Communists came to power, but there were other years since—1957, 1966, and 1989 in particular—that went prominently unmentioned. Everything that was jumbled and incoherent and better left unsaid must be smoothed into a rational pattern, because the purpose of history from the time of Confucius has been to transmit moral lessons to later generations.

In Dongguan, the museum's yawning lobby was a monument to wasted real estate and powerful air-conditioning. Signs pointed to History, straight ahead, and Economy, second floor. On my initial visit, I entered History. The first room stretched from prehistoric marine fossils to the Qing Dynasty, with glass cases displaying what looked like piles of rocks. On closer inspection, they were piles of rocks with incomprehensible English captions: *Whetstone appearing from Haogang shell mound remains.* A room-size diorama of women weavers illustrated Dongguan's early talent in handicrafts. A tape of the scraping sound of the loom played in a continuous loop and haunted me through the rooms.

More piles of rocks followed, and then history lurched forward with startling accuracy. *The population increased and reached 150,378 by the sixth year of the Tianshun reign of the Ming Dynasty (1462 A.D.).* Markets developed; the salt industry flourished; agriculture thrived. In a large open room, a fake tree cast its shadow over a fake lake, a fake rowboat, a fake arched footbridge, three fake geese, and two fake ducks. The continuous loop quacked.

That was another difficulty of telling about the past. Every place had to reflect the continuity of five thousand years of Chinese history, but in most places little had been recorded and nothing concrete remained. Valuable artifacts would have been claimed by Beijing or lost in wars and political campaigns, so museums were forced to invent the rest. They forged cannons and bells and suits of armor, and printed texts of old documents on Formica tablets and hung them on the walls. Dioramas occupied whole rooms—a favorite display method, probably because they took up lots of space. The only authentic artifacts in the Dongguan museum were the piles of rocks.

Once modern history began with the nineteenth-century Opium Wars, things got really confusing. A display entitled "Fury Against the British" featured mannequins of British naval officers and an angry Chinese mandarin. *The defeat in the Opium Wars has always been a deep-rooted humiliation and agony to China.* But perhaps in a city of thriving commerce it was impossible to summon the necessary fury against the British, because the adjoining display had already moved on. *In 1878, the governor of Hong Kong suggested founding the Inferior Protection Bureau to protect Chinese women and children.* The exhibit marched quickly through the Second World War and straight to Communist victory, a blurry photo of happy faces. *Millions of people rejoiced at the liberation.*

In the next room, a title stretched across one wall: "A Vision Made Real: From Agricultural County to IT City." A light board showed photos of the Communist Party meeting at which Deng Xiaoping set forth his program for economic reform and opening to the West. That was in 1978. From one room to the next, the exhibit had jumped thirty years, skipping over the founding of Communist China, the land reform and the execution of counterrevolutionaries, the attacks against "class enemies" and the establishment of the communes, the Great Leap Forward and the famine that killed at least twenty million people, and the decade of the Cultural Revolution.

I had exited History and entered Economy, and now the exhibit came to life. A vast diorama showed the Taiping Handbag Factory with four women bent over a table sewing shoes. A mock-up of the government office where businesses applied for licenses featured the familiar figure of Dongguan Man: a businessman with a potbelly and a pleather briefcase. History picked up speed—*Decades passed in a wink*—and giant photographs featured highway overpasses and sewage-treatment plants and investment conferences.

A BENIGN CIRCLE OF INPUT-OUTPUT-INPUT

FIRST PREFECTURAL CITY TO HAVE ONE MILLION
MOBILE-PHONE SUBSCRIBERS

BUILD ROADS, BRIDGES, AND POWER PLANTS TO
GENERATE FUNDS FOR MORE ROADS, BRIDGES, AND
POWER PLANTS

An interactive demonstration showed the city's GDP, exports, balance of deposits, and tax revenue. The final display was a photo of the signing ceremony of China's accession to the World Trade Organization in 2001.

A NEW TIME IS COMING!

AS I WAS LEAVING THE MUSEUM, third- and fourth-graders on a field trip were lining up in the lobby in jostling rows. The students wore school-issue sweatpants with Young Pioneers scarves tied around their necks. A museum guide, a young woman with a stern face and sticklike legs, picked up a megaphone. I braced for the Opium War and 150 years of humiliation.

"On the third floor, you will see a model of the city," she began. "I want you all to find your own house on this model. Do you all know Songshan Lake?"

"Yes," the students replied in chorus.

"Songshan Lake is our high-tech industrial zone. Dongguan has a motto: 'One Big Step Every Year, A New City in Five Years.' We are now in Year Three of that plan."

She paused. "Do you all know 'Build the City, Construct the Roads, Renovate the Mountains, Harness the Rivers'?"

Silence. Nobody knew that one.

"It is government policy. Dongguan also has a harbor that is open to foreign ships . . ."

In the seventh century, the emperors of the Tang Dynasty ordered court historians to compose a chronicle of the previous reign. Every dynasty since has written the history of the preceding one, slanting or omitting facts to bolster the ruling regime; since 1949, the Communist Party has done the same, presenting modern history as a heroic struggle to resist the will of foreign powers. But here in Dongguan, the past contained a startlingly different lesson: History was openness, markets, and foreign investment. History began with a handbag factory, and schoolchildren must be indoctrinated in the merits of good infrastructure.

The museum guide urged the children to be "civilized spectators," and the third- and fourth-graders filed into History in ragged lines. Soon the huge lobby was deserted, and I was left alone to ponder the unlikelihood of a Chinese history museum that did not make a single mention of Mao Zedong.

3 *To Die Poor Is a Sin*

May 25, 1994

After I was fired from the Yongtong factory, fortunately my wages were fully paid. I had more than one hundred yuan on me and I was not frightened at all. Still I was a little worried, since after all I did not even have an identity card. But with no way out I could only take an ID card that said I was born in 1969 and try my luck. Who knew my luck would be pretty good? I made my way into this factory's plastic molds department.

Since I have come to Guangdong, I have jumped factories four or five times, and each factory was better than the last. More important was that at each instance, I relied on myself. I never begged for help from anyone. Although I have a few good friends, not one helped me at the time when I most needed it.

I remember when I fled back from Shenzhen. At that

time, I truly had nothing to my name. Other than my own self, I had nothing else. I wandered outside for a month, completely penniless, once even going hungry for two days, and no one knew . . . Although older cousin and his wife were in Longyan, I did not want to go find them, because they could not really help me. I often wanted to rely on others, but they cannot be relied on. You can only rely on yourself.

Yes, I can only rely on myself.

The first time Wu Chunming went out she did not tell her parents. It was the summer of 1992 and to migrate was something bold and dangerous. In her village in Hunan Province, it was said that girls who went to the city would be tricked into brothels and never heard from again.

Chunming was seventeen years old that summer. She had finished middle school and was peddling fruits and vegetables in a city near home; she migrated with a cousin who was still in school. The two girls borrowed money for train tickets to Dongguan and found jobs in a factory that made paint for toys. The smell of the chemicals gave them headaches, and they returned home after two months as broke as before. Chunming went out again the following spring. Her parents objected, and argued, and cried. But when she decided to leave anyway, with a few friends from nearby villages, her mother borrowed money for her train fare.

Guangdong in 1993 was even more chaotic than it is today. Migrants from the countryside flooded the streets looking for work, sleeping in bus stations and under bridges. The only way to find a job was to knock on factory doors, and Chunming and her friends were turned away from many doors before they were hired at the Guotong toy factory. Ordinary workers there made one hundred yuan a month, or about twelve dollars; to stave off hunger, they bought giant bags of instant noodles and added salt and boiling water. "We thought if we ever made two hundred yuan a month," Chunming said later, "we would be perfectly happy."

After four months, Chunming jumped to another factory, but left soon after a fellow worker said her cousin knew of better jobs in Shenzhen. Chunming and a few friends traveled there, spent the night under a highway overpass, and met the girl's cousin the next morning. He brought them to a hair salon and took them upstairs, where a heavily made-up young woman sat on a massage bed waiting for customers. Chunming was terrified at the sight. "I was raised very traditionally," she said. "I thought everyone in that place was bad and wanted me to be a prostitute. I thought that once I went in there, I would turn bad too."

The girls were told that they should stay and take showers in a communal stall, but Chunming refused. She walked back down the stairs, looked out the front door, and ran, abandoning her friends and the suitcase that contained her money, a government-issued identity card, and a photograph of her mother. Footsteps came up behind her. She turned in to one alley and then another, and the footsteps stopped. Chunming ran into a yard and found a deserted chicken coop in back. She climbed into the coop and hid there, all day and all night. The next morning, her arms laced with mosquito bites, Chunming went into the street and knelt on the sidewalk to beg for money, but no one gave her anything. A passerby brought her to the police station; without the name or address of the hair salon, the police couldn't help her either. They gave her twenty yuan for bus fare back to her factory.

The bus driver dropped her off only partway back to Dongguan. Chunming started to walk, and a man on the street followed her. She spotted a young woman in a factory uniform and asked if she could sneak into her factory for the night. The young woman borrowed a worker's ID card and brought Chunming in, where she hid that night in a shower stall. In the morning, Chunming stole clean pants and a T-shirt that were hanging out to dry in the bathroom and climbed the factory gate to get out. By then she had not eaten in two days. A bus driver bought her a piece a bread and gave her a lift back to Dongguan, where her cousin and his wife worked.

Chunming did not tell them what had happened to her. Instead she wandered the streets. She befriended a cook on a construction site who let her eat with the other workers, and at night she sneaked into friends' factory dorms to sleep. Without an ID card, she could not get a new job. After a month of wandering, Chunming saw an ad for assembly-line jobs at the Yinhui toy factory. She found an ID card that someone had lost or left behind and used it to get hired. Officially she was Tang Congyun, born in 1969. That made her five years older than she really was, but no one looked closely at such things.

Chunming worked at the Yinhui factory for a year, mixing vats of plastic that was poured into molds to make toy cars, planes, and trains. She was bold and she liked to talk, and she made friends easily. Her new friends called her Tang Congyun. She had become, quite literally, someone else.

For years after she left the factory, she received letters addressed to Tang Congyun. Chunming never found out who she was.

I HAD KNOWN CHUNMING for two years before she told me this story. It was a Sunday afternoon at the end of 2006, and she was sitting in a Dongguan juice bar after a day of shopping for birthday presents. "I've never told anyone about what happened to me then," she said, sipping her mixed-fruit juice. "When I tell this story it's like it happened yesterday."

"Did you ever find out what happened to the friends you left behind in the hair salon?" I asked.

"No," she said. "I don't know if it was a truly bad place or just a place where you could work as a massage girl if you wanted. But it was frightening that they would not let us leave."

Chunming's best friend had been among the ones she left behind. They had met in the city on the assembly line, so Chunming didn't know the name of her friend's village or how to find her again. Years later, Chunming met a girl who had known the friend; she said the friend had gone home and had later come out to Dongguan again. Chunming had to conclude from that brief account that her friend had turned out fine. But there was no way of knowing for sure; perhaps she had been tricked into a brothel and was never heard from again, just as the people in the village had said. Chunming's good friend was lost to her, like so many people she had met along the way. A year in Dongguan is a long time, and Chunming had lived in the city for thirteen years.

*   *   *

May 24, 1994

We start work at seven in the morning and get off work at nine at night. Afterward we shower and wash our clothes. At around ten, those with money go out for midnight snacks and those without money go to sleep. We sleep until 6:30 in the morning. No one wants to get out of bed, but we must work at seven. Twenty minutes to go: Crawl out of bed, rub your swollen eyes, wash your face, and brush your teeth. Ten minutes to go: Those who want breakfast use these ten minutes to eat breakfast, but I have seen many people not eat. I don't know if it's because they don't want to eat, or to save money, or to stay thin . . .

I certainly would not ignore my health for the sake of

thinness or saving money. After all, what is the point of doing migrant work? Can it be that it is just to earn this bit of money?!

Soon after she came to the city, Chunming began to keep a diary. In notebooks with pastel-pink covers she described life in the factory, the tyranny of the timekeepers, and the rare moments of leisure that were given over to gossip, snacks, and crushes on boys. *You must record every day the things you have seen, heard, felt, and thought,* she wrote. *In this way, you can not only raise your writing standards but also see the traces of your own growing up.* In these same pages, she plotted her escape from this world through a relentless program of self-improvement: reading novels, practicing her handwriting, and learning to speak—both to erase her Hunan accent and to master Cantonese, the language of the factory bosses. Her greatest fear was of getting stuck where she was. Time was Chunming's enemy, reminding her that another day had passed and she had not yet achieved her goals. But time was also her friend, because she was still young.

The diary entries were often undated and out of order. Chunming wrote quickly, describing her days, drafting letters to her parents, copying inspirational slogans and song lyrics, and goading herself to work harder. Sometimes her sentences marched in diagonal formation across two pages, growing until each character was an inch high. Inside her head she was shouting.

I HAVE NO TIME TO BE UNHAPPY BECAUSE THERE ARE TOO MANY THINGS I WANT TO DO.

"TIME IS LIFE"

WE CAN BE ORDINARY BUT WE MUST NOT BE VULGAR. —*WU CHUNMING*

*RIGHT NOW I HAVE NOTHING. MY ONLY
CAPITAL IS THAT I AM STILL YOUNG.*

It is almost one o'clock! I cannot bear to put down this issue of *Migrant Worker* but I must work at seven tonight again. I might as well go to sleep.

Ai! I truly hate that there is too little time. Every day I work for twelve hours; in the remaining twelve hours I must eat, shower, wash my clothes, and sleep. How much time is there left to read? Working on the night shift, time is even more fragmented: After I get off work and eat, I must wait an hour to shower. I sleep in the afternoon until six and then must get up. Dinner is another hour wasted . . . I read at night until midnight; that leaves not even six hours for sleep. There is one hour left for other things.

I HAVE BEEN DEFEATED, DEFEATED

*CAN IT REALLY BE THAT ON THIS ROAD
OF LIFE I AM DESTINED TO BE DEFEATED?*

I DON'T BELIEVE IT

I ABSOLUTELY DON'T BELIEVE IT

Wu Chunming, you cannot go on living every day like this! Think about it: You have already been at this factory an entire half year, but what have you really gained? You know that to do migrant work in the plastic molds department for your whole life does not have any prospects, so you want to job-hop and find a satisfactory job. First you must learn to speak Cantonese. Why are you so useless? Are you truly so stupid?

Why can't you learn the things other people learn?

You are also a person, Wu Chunming. Can it be that you are a useless thing?

You have already had more than two months but made no progress in Cantonese. Do you remember your goal when you entered this factory was to learn Cantonese? If you cannot learn Cantonese in this year, then you are a dumb pig, a dumb ox, and you need not do migrant work in Guangdong anymore. With this two or three hundred yuan a month, you would be better off at home.

March 23

Ai, there are really too many things I want to do, and too little time. Some people say they are annoyed to death, *hai!* Other people are annoyed, but I have no time to be annoyed.

One, I must exercise my body. To be fat is not acceptable.

Two, I must read a lot and practice my writing, so that I can live happily and richly.

Three, I must learn to speak Cantonese. This must not be hurried but slowly learned.

As for sleep time, six hours at most is enough.

March 29

We were paid today. I got 365 yuan. After repaying a fifty-yuan debt, I still have three hundred yuan. I want to buy a watch, clothes, and personal items. How will I have any left over? . . . Summer is here and I don't have any clothes . . . and I must buy a watch. Without a watch, I cannot make better use of my time.

As for sending money home, that is even less possible. Next month after we are paid, I will register at the Shorthand Secretarial Correspondence University. I must get a college diploma. I certainly did not come to Guangdong just to earn this two or three hundred yuan a month . . . This is merely a temporary stopping place. This is definitely not the place I will stay forever.

No one will understand me, and I don't need others to understand me.

I can only walk my own road and let other people talk!

May 22

A lot of people say I have changed. I don't know if I have changed or not . . . I am much more silent now and I don't love to laugh the way I used to. Sometimes when I laugh it is forced. Sometimes I feel I have become numb. "Numb." Numb. No! No! But I really don't know what word I should use to describe the me that I am now.

Anyway, I am so tired, so tired.

Really, really, I feel so tired.

My body and my spirit feel so tired.

Too tired, too tired.

I don't want to live this way anymore.

I don't want to live this way anymore.

Never to live that way anymore.

How should I live?

*   *   *

Even as Chunming plotted her rise in the factory world, in her letters home she struggled to be a good traditional daughter.

Mother, I have knit you a sweater . . . If I weren't knitting a sweater, I could have used this day to read so many books. But

Mother, sometimes I think: I would rather be Mother's obedient daughter, a filial daughter, and even throw away those books I want so much to read.

Mother, I have knit my love for you into this sweater . . . Mother, remember when I was still at home, you always said other people's daughters knew how to knit sweaters but that I lacked perseverance. But today, do you see that your daughter also knows how to knit? Remember, your daughter will never be dumber than other people!

The expectations of family weighed on her. Young women from the countryside felt particular pressure from home. If they didn't progress quickly, their parents would urge them to return home to marry.

I finally got a letter from home . . . Other than Father, who else can write me a letter? Mother did not include even a single line to tell me that she misses me . . . In the last letter, she added on a line telling me not to find a boyfriend outside. Although it was only one line, it made me happy, as if Mother were at my side teaching me.

How badly I want to pour out to my mother all the words in my heart, but I cannot. Mother! My mother, why are you an illiterate? It's all right that you are an illiterate. Why can you not even write a letter? It's all right that you cannot write a letter. It would be fine if you could write a few words. Even if you made up a few words to say what you wanted to tell me, I would understand your true thoughts.

Mother, I know you have many things to say to me, only that Father did not write them . . .

Father and Mother, it looks like we cannot communicate between us. You will never know and never understand what is really in your daughter's heart. Maybe you think

that I have already found my ideal factory, with three hundred yuan a month. Maybe you think that I will never again
jump factories. Maybe your wish is that I never jump factories again, that I work at this factory for two years and then
come home to get married, to have a family like all the girls
in the countryside. But I am not thinking any of these
things . . .

I want to carve out a world for myself in Guangdong . . .
My plan is:

1. To study at correspondence university
2. To learn to speak Cantonese
3. With nothing to my name and without any accomplishment, to absolutely not marry

During her first three years in the city, Chunming did not return
home once. She told friends that the factory break was too short,
but in her diary she wrote: *Who knows why I am not going home for
the new year? The main reason: I really do not want to waste time. Because I must study!* She also rejected her mother's advice and wrote
love letters to a good-looking young man who worked on the factory floor. Young men in the workplace were a rarity, and the better-
looking ones were spoiled by the attentions of multiple girls. This
one was not interested in Chunming, and he passed her letters
around for others to read.

After six months on the assembly line, Chunming learned that
her factory was hiring internally for clerks, and she wrote a letter
to the head of her department expressing interest. The boss had
heard of her boy-chasing reputation and ordered her transferred
to another department. But his order was somehow misstated,
and Chunming reported to work as a clerk. She performed well
and the boss changed his mind about her. The new job paid three

hundred yuan a month—triple what Chunming had made a year before.

THE STORIES OF MIGRANT WOMEN shared certain features. The arrival in the city was blurry and confused and often involved being tricked in some way. Young women often said they had gone out alone, though in fact they usually traveled with others; they just felt alone. They quickly forgot the names of factories, but certain dates were branded in their minds, like the day they left home or quit a bad factory forever. What a factory actually made was never important; what mattered was the hardship or opportunity that came with working there. The turning point in a migrant's fortunes always came when she challenged her boss. At the moment she risked everything, she emerged from the crowd and forced the world to see her as an individual.

It was easy to lose yourself in the factory, where there were hundreds of girls with identical backgrounds: born in the village, badly educated, and poor. You had to believe that you mattered even though you were one among millions.

April 1, 1994

Yes, I am a person so ordinary that I cannot be more ordinary, so plain I cannot be plainer, a girl like all the other girls. I like to eat snacks, I like to have fun, and I like to look pretty.

Don't imagine that I can be superhuman.

You are just a most ordinary, most plain girl, attracted to anything that is pretty or tasty or fun.

So from being ordinary and plain I will make my start.

*   *   *

Inside a Dongguan factory, the sexes were sharply divided. Women worked as clerks and in human resources and sales, and they held most of the jobs on the assembly line; the bosses felt that young women were more diligent and easier to manage. Men monopolized technical jobs like mold design and machine repair. They generally held the top positions in the factory but also the dead-end occupations at the bottom: security guards, cooks, and drivers. Outside the factory, women were waitresses, nannies, hairdressers, and prostitutes. Men worked on construction sites.

This gender segregation was reflected in help-wanted ads:

GAOBU HANDBAG FACTORY SEEKS TO EMPLOY

SALESPERSON: FEMALE ONLY, GRADE FOUR ENGLISH
RECEPTIONIST: FEMALE ONLY, CAN SPEAK
    CANTONESE
SECURITY GUARDS: MALE, UNDER 30, 1.7 METERS
    OR ABOVE, EX-MILITARY, KNOWS
    FIREFIGHTING, CAN PLAY BASKETBALL A PLUS

The divide implied certain things. Young women enjoyed a more fluid job situation; they could join a factory assembly line and move up to be clerks or salespeople. Young men had a harder time entering a factory, and once in they were often stuck. Women, in the factory or out, came into contact with a wider range of people and quickly adopted the clothes, hairstyles, and accents of the city; men tended to stay locked in their outsider worlds. Women integrated more easily into urban life, and they had more incentive to stay.

Women make up more than one-third of China's migrants. They tend to be younger than their male counterparts and more likely to be single; they travel farther from home and they stay out longer. They are more motivated to improve themselves and more likely to value migration for its life-changing possibilities. In one survey, men cited higher income as the chief purpose of leaving home, while women aspired to "more experience in life." Unlike men, women had no home to go back to. According to Chinese tradition, a son was expected to return to his parents' house with his wife after he married; a son would forever have a home in the village where he was born. Daughters, once grown, would never return home to live—until they married, they didn't belong anywhere.

To some extent, this deep-rooted sexism worked in women's favor. Many rural parents wanted a grown son to stay close to home, perhaps delivering goods or selling vegetables in the towns near the village. Young men with such uninspiring prospects might simply *hun*—drift—doing odd jobs, smoking and drinking and gambling away their meager earnings. Young women—less treasured, less coddled—could go far from home and make their own plans. Precisely because they mattered less, they were freer to do what they wanted.

But it was a precarious advantage. If migration liberated young women from the village, it also dropped them in a no-man's-land. Most girls in the countryside were married by their early twenties, and a migrant woman who postponed marriage risked closing off that possibility for good. The gender imbalance in Dongguan, where 70 percent of the workforce was said to be female, worked against finding a high-quality mate. And social mobility complicated the search for a husband. Women who had moved up from the assembly line disdained the men back in the village, but city men looked down on them in turn. Migrants called this *gaobucheng, dibujiu*—unfit for a higher position but unwilling to take a lower one.

The migrant women I knew never complained about the unfairness of being a woman. Parents might favor sons over daughters, bosses prefer pretty secretaries, and job ads discriminate openly, but they took all of these injustices in stride—over three years in Dong-guan, I never heard a single person express anything like a feminist sentiment. Perhaps they took for granted that life was hard for everyone. The divide between countryside and city was the only one that mattered: Once you crossed that line, you could change your fate.

*   *   *

Moving up came easily to Chunming. In 1995, she jumped to a fac-tory in a remote part of Dongguan that made water pistols and BB guns. She finally learned to speak Cantonese. Within a year, her monthly salary increased from three hundred yuan to six hundred and fifty, then eight hundred, then one thousand yuan. She discov-ered that the department heads above her made more money though she did the same work. *If you don't increase my salary to 1,500 yuan a month*, she wrote her boss, *I refuse to do this anymore.* She got what she wanted; no one in the factory had ever received a five-hundred-yuan raise before. But the promotion did not satisfy Chun-ming. It cast her into a new world where there was so much to learn.

Her dealings with other people immediately became more com-plicated. In the village, relations between people were determined by kinship ties and shared histories. In school and on the assembly line, everyone was in the same lowly position. But once a person started to rise in the factory world, the balance of power shifted, and that could be unsettling. A friend could turn into a boss; a young woman might be promoted ahead of her boyfriend.

March 26, 1996
My promotion this time has let me see the hundred vari-eties of human experience. Some people cheer me, some

envy me, some congratulate me, some wish me luck, some are jealous of me, and some cannot accept it . . .

As to those who envy me . . . I will only treat them as an obstacle on the road to progress, kicking them aside and walking on. In the future there will be even more to envy!

Making a good impression on strangers became important. Chunming studied the higher-ups in her factory, as intent as a biologist with her specimens. She observed that when the head of the human resources department gave a speech, he was so nervous that his hands trembled. Around the new year holiday, a manager on the factory floor ignored her until she boldly wished him a happy new year; he responded warmly and gave her ten yuan in a red envelope, a traditional gift. *From this incident, I understand: Some people who have always seemed unapproachable may not really be so. You just need to make yourself a little more approachable.*

Her plan to remold herself kicked into high gear. In her diary, Chunming no longer recorded the details of her days but copied the rules for becoming someone else, a task for which she read widely if not always coherently.

Self-confidence, dignity, and elegance are the image that professional women should have.

Benjamin Franklin's Thirteen Rules of Morality
1. Moderation: Do not eat to saturation or drink to excess.
2. Silence: Do not engage in unimportant talk.
3. Order: Place things in fixed positions and do tasks at fixed times.
4. Decisiveness: Decide what you want to accomplish, be unyielding.

5. Thrift: Do not waste money. Spend money on
   things that benefit yourself and others . . .

Receiving Criticism
1. When other people criticize you, you must be calm
   and dispassionate and show that you are listening
   attentively.
2. Look at the person who is speaking to you.
3. Do not criticize someone who has just criticized you.
4. Do not be dejected.
5. Do not make jokes . . .

The ideals in Chunming's diary bore an inverse relationship to the
world she lived in. One of her lists, entitled "The Fifteen Traits of
Unqualified Leaders," could easily have been called "How to Be a
Dongguan Boss," including trait three:

Busies himself over small things and participates in everything.

and trait fifteen:

When the group is given bonuses or awards, he appears first
on the name list; among the executive members, he sits in
the front row.

She enrolled in a correspondence course to learn secretarial
skills, but gave up because the textbook looked too complicated. An
effort to learn public relations also foundered.

How do you plan to learn public relations studies?
Answer: To learn public relations properly, you must first
learn how to behave as a person.

At one point, Chunming decided to learn English on her own. She made a list of vocabulary words—

ABLE

ABILITY

ADD

AGO

ALWAYS

AGREE

AUGUST

BABY

BLACK

BREATH

—but gave up before she got to C.

So many things would have to be learned, and the rules for getting ahead bled together in her diary. *Sixty percent of people do not have a goal. For a look of "Gorgeous Radiance," blend black, gray, golden yellow, sapphire blue, and bright red eye shadow. Ⓐ Can be dry-cleaned; "A" means any detergent can be used. The exchange of greetings is the catalyst and lubricant of conversation. When you drink soup, don't let the soup spoon rattle against the plate. People who don't read books will find their speech dull and their appearance repulsive.*

* * *

With their mothers far away, migrant workers looked elsewhere for advice. Magazines for migrant readers appeared in the mid-1990s, particularly in the factory cities of southern China. They were published on cheap newsprint and sold for about four yuan, or fifty cents, an issue. The magazines investigated migrant work conditions and gave advice on legal questions, job-hunting, and relationships. In first-person stories that traced the lives of individual migrants, life followed one of two trajectories: A young woman went to the city, endured hardship, and triumphed, usually by starting her own business and buying an apartment. Or a young woman went to the city and was brought low, typically by a man who turned out to be lazy, faithless, or married with a child. These could have been the heroines of Theodore Dreiser, Edith Wharton, and Henry James, for upon such narratives was built the modern Western tradition of the novel. But in the pages of the migrant magazines, the moral was always the same: You can only rely on yourself.

Every success story ended with a personal triumph that could be tallied on an accountant's ledger: the monthly turnover of a business, the square-footage of an apartment. In "Ambition Made Me Who I Am," a teenage nanny taught herself to read and write and put herself and her brother through college by selling Popsicles, delivering goods, cutting hair, and peddling insurance. At the story's end, she headed an insurance company's sales department and owned a 1,300-square-foot apartment. In "Be Your Own Master," a young woman worked as a hairdresser for two years without pay in order to learn the trade and set up her own shop. *Turnover is more than three thousand yuan a month, six hundred yuan for rent, and one hundred yuan for taxes, and the rest is all hers.* In "The Girl Who Wanted to Make Television Dramas," a young woman worked diligently at a menial office job—*she often typed for ten hours without interruption*—and rose to be vice-president of an entertainment company with an eight-hundred-square-foot apartment.

The path to success was long and hard, and many strayed from it. A young woman might dream of finding a man who would love and support her. But this was always the wrong way.

When I got home, I burst into loud sobbing, not daring to believe that my own true love was a fraud.

What he saw in me was how easy it would be to deceive me.

If I leave him the way I am now, who will still want me?

Articles described the indignities of daily life as a migrant. A young woman sneaked into the bathroom at McDonald's because her own building's facilities were so poor: *The environment inside a McDonald's bathroom is so good. It is not only very clean, but there is toilet paper and there are hand dryers.* A migrant worker was ashamed to tell his boss that he couldn't afford a mobile phone. Those lucky enough to land office jobs found an environment as ruthless as anything described by Darwin:

> Because some of my clients are behind in their payments, the company says I am responsible for collecting these debts and will withhold 30 percent of my salary every month until all the money is paid. Is this reasonable?

> Our company rule is that every month the person with the worst sales record is fired. Is this legal?

Sometimes the message of self-reliance went too far. An article about a physically abused maid did not address the vulnerabilities of domestic workers but celebrated her daring escape from her employer's apartment. *The only person who could rescue Wang Li was Wang Li herself.* An account of a deadly department store fire skirted the bigger issues—poor construction and prevention measures—to focus on fire survival tips: *When the fire burns your body, take off your clothes or roll around on the floor to extinguish the flames.*

Against the staid and preachy Chinese media, the migrant magazines broke new ground. They did not insist on upbeat endings; many of the stories ended in anguish or confusion. They described a world in which people cheated one another and did nothing to aid the lonely and the lost. They did not preach about laws that must be amended or behaviors that must be improved, and they never mentioned the Communist Party. They wrote about how to live in the world just as it was.

*   *   *

In the summer of 1996, Chunming wrote in her diary:

> Friends, we were born into the world poor through no fault of our own. But to die poor is a sin.
>
> In the course of life, have we not worked hard and persisted in the struggle? To be a success in network sales, we must honestly achieve these four points:
>
> 1. Have determination.
> 2. Have a clear goal.
> 3. Deeply study and thoroughly understand the company's products and plans.
> 4. Study the techniques of network selling.

That summer, a friend from the factory took Chunming to a lecture that changed her life. The speaker worked for a company called Wanmei Daily Use Products. Wanmei, which means "perfect," sold health supplements, but what it really offered was a dream of wealth and personal fulfillment encapsulated in the magical word *chuanxiao*. The Chinese phrase, which translates as "network sales," does not distinguish between legitimate direct sales and fraudulent pyramid schemes. Corruption, which sometimes seemed to be in the air people breathed, had also seeped into the language they used.

Chunming started selling Wanmei health products to supplement her income, mostly to fellow factory workers. She bought

Wanmei tapes and attended Wanmei lectures, and her diary turned into a Wanmei sales manual mixed with some bizarre health claims.

THE SUCCESS OF A SALE LIES IN THE FIRST THREE
    SECONDS OF MEETING.
WHEN YOU SPEAK, LOOK INTO THE OTHER PERSON'S EYES.
GET TO KNOW THREE PEOPLE A DAY.
THE ALOE MINERAL CRYSTAL CAN REGULATE THE HUMAN
    BODY'S FIVE SYSTEMS.
A PERSON LOSES HIS HAIR BECAUSE HE LACKS COPPER.

By the end of 1996, Chunming had an influential job in the factory as head of its general affairs department, but she quit to sell Wanmei products full-time. She spent ten thousand yuan in savings to rent out meeting rooms and equipment for training sessions. She recruited former colleagues from the factory to join her network, with the promise that they would all get rich together. In the back pages of her diary, Chunming listed the salespeople she had recruited. Many of them were still in their teens; the oldest person in her network was twenty-five years old.

Why have we come together today? Simply to let everyone discuss the topic: "How should a person live one's entire life?"

Think about it: Why are we still so ordinary? Why are so many people who have worked hard their entire lives still not living the lives they imagined? We all had dreams once. We all once struggled and worked hard. But why is there such an imbalance between what we spent and what we have gained? How many regrets have been played out upon us!

We have gradually understood one truth: A person who

wants to develop must grasp opportunity. Merely to have a dream and determination is not enough . . . If the choice of vehicle is not good, you will be bustling about your whole life. Just as our mothers and fathers chose farming: They have been busy their whole lives, but when the hair on their heads is white, they must still scrape together money for oil and salt.

My friends, do we want to follow the road of our mothers and fathers?

No!

Give yourselves a round of applause!

Direct-sales companies had taken off in the United States during the economic boom that followed the Second World War. Unlike traditional retailers, companies like the Amway Corporation and Avon Products sold their goods through independent distributors rather than stores. These distributors made money in two ways: through selling goods themselves and through recruiting a network of salespeople and receiving bonuses based on their sales.

In the mid-1990s, a craze for network sales swept China, with some of the *chuanxiao* companies copying the American sales model. Others simply charged new recruits a hefty fee to join, with the promise of riches when they recruited additional members. These were pyramid schemes: Their money came not from selling actual products but only from the high entry fees they charged. The schemes made money for the earliest entrants but collapsed when they ran out of new members, defrauding many people out of their savings.

The network-sales model was ideally suited to a Chinese society in which traditional morality had broken down and only the harshest rules—trust no one, make money fast—still applied. The companies relied on traditional networks of extended family and friends; the first thing a *chuanxiao* salesman usually did was to browbeat every friend and relative into buying something. They promised wealth and fulfillment. And they offered a clear road map to success: *Get to know three people a day.* The industry flourished in the small towns and migrant communities of the Pearl River Delta. Here where rural and urban worlds met, people envied the success of others and were hungry to have it themselves. If someone they knew promised instant wealth and a miracle cure, they were easily swayed.

The rise of *chuanxiao* companies worried the central government. Some of the companies traded in fake, smuggled, or shoddy goods; their training meetings, where charismatic leaders drove members into an evangelical selling frenzy, came to look disturbingly similar to cults. The more extravagant operations even threatened the social order; in 1994, the police were called out to disperse hundreds of angry distributors after the collapse of a Taiwanese diamond-selling scheme. Beijing passed many regulations to bring the network-sales industry under control, but local governments rarely enforced its orders. This was partly because the companies brought welcome tax revenue and employment to local areas, and partly because moonlighting as a *chuanxiao* distributor was a popular sideline for government officials.

*   *   *

For Chunming, the sales meetings were a training ground for learning how to speak. In traditional China, the art of oratory was not an important skill—to write an elegant essay in beautiful calligraphy was what mattered—and speeches in China have always been dismal affairs. Speakers often read directly from a script, and the script is usually tedious. A person like Chunming—young, rural, and female—would have many reasons to stay silent in the presence of her betters. But in a modern China driven by commerce and competition, knowing how to speak had become a necessary skill.

The network-sales companies imported the ethos of America direct to the Chinese lower classes. Their style of speaking combined the call-and-response of old-time preachers with the tireless haranguing of motivational speakers. They spread the news that the individual was important and that everyone was a winner. And they brought with them the very American faith that wealth and virtue could go hand in hand.

In her diary, Chunming collected drafts of her speeches:

> My name is Wu Chunming, a very plain and ordinary name. But I believe that someday in the future I will make my name no longer ordinary . . .
>
> Friends, what kind of person do you want to become in the future? This is a question worth thinking about. What kind of person are we today: Is that important?
>
> Not important!
>
> What's important is: What kind of person do you want to become in the future? For what purpose have we traveled thousands of miles and left our homes behind to come out to work?
>
> To earn money!
>
> Correct, to earn money. But until today, have we earned the money we wanted?
>
> No!
>
> Is the life we live today the one we want to live or the one we can live?
>
> Correct, the one we can live . . .
>
> Friends, what kind of person do you want to become? That is all up to you. If you never dare to want to succeed, then you will never succeed . . . What is important is that you must dare to think, dare to want . . .

Really, each of us is unique in the world. When we are born, we are not doomed to failure. Because we are all born winners.

Friends, please believe me! But more important, believe in yourself! Because you can!

At Wanmei, Chunming rose quickly from trainee to manager. In 1997, she quit to join a Taiwanese company called Tangjing Soul Pagoda Garden Development Company. Its business was constructing high-rise buildings to store the ashes of the dead. The buildings were known as "soul pagodas," and the company's sales pitch married the spiritual, the practical, and the Chinese passion for real estate. For the dead, the Tangjing Soul Pagoda Garden promised an eternal resting place with excellent feng shui. For the living, the pitch focused on the garden's prime location, its limited number of spaces, and the burgeoning population of the Pearl River Delta. An investor could purchase an entire soul pagoda and then flip individual spaces to buyers at a profit.

Chunming's job was to run training sessions for the company's salespeople. She had learned to talk, and now she taught others how to do it—as with the factories, what was actually being sold was the least important facet of the enterprise. Chunming's pitch blended Buddhism, the environmental benefits of cremation, and the near-certainty that a soul pagoda would appreciate 300 percent. Death, in other words, was the best long-term investment there was.

Let our ancestors take life's last journey in the most civilized, dignified, and stately way.

Guangdong alone has more than one million dead each year.

For our company's regular pagoda spots, the July 1995 price of 3,500 yuan has grown to 5,600 yuan today.

We offer a full line of services (from cremation to entering the pagoda, including the expiation of sins of the dead and so on).

Our operating time is from July 11, 1994, to July 10, 2044.

Chunming was on a more abbreviated schedule. In late 1997 she jumped again, to a *chuanxiao* company that charged new members one thousand yuan for a box of traditional Tibetan medicine. It was a pyramid scheme, pure and simple, and Chunming got in early enough to make some real money. She recruited a dozen people, all proven earners, and within a few months she headed a network of ten thousand people. By then Chunming was making forty thousand yuan a month—about five thousand dollars, an astronomical sum in the Pearl River Delta in 1998. The company began laminating her weekly pay slips in sheets of clear plastic so she could show them to recruits as a motivational tool. On a visit home, Chunming gave her parents thirty thousand yuan to renovate the family house, install tile floors, and buy new appliances and a twenty-nine-inch television set. Her success in the city had made her famous beyond her village. "Everyone living in our area had heard about me," she said.

But the industry was getting out of control. In a town called Danshui, about forty miles from Dongguan, a Taiwanese scheme to sell foot vibrators had become all the rage. To join the enterprise, a participant had to buy a foot vibrator for 3,900 yuan, or almost five hundred dollars—about eight times the market price. Participants were told they would receive 40 percent of the admission fees of anyone they recruited. Migrants flocked to Danshui; some sold their houses, furniture, and oxen to pay the admission fee. But it turned out that selling 3,900-yuan foot vibrators in a poor town was not easy, especially when thousands of other people were doing the same thing.

When the scheme collapsed, some defrauded members assaulted the people who had recruited them, while others demonstrated in front of government offices to get their money back. Police were called in to quell the crowds, restore order, and send migrants home. By then, the organizers had moved inland to a town in Hunan Province, where they set up the same operation and recruited about thirty thousand participants before that scheme, too, fell apart.

In April 1998, the cabinet of Premier Zhu Rongji ordered all *chuanxiao* companies to cease operations. More than two thousand companies shut down, and an industry that had resisted government regulation for years collapsed in an instant. Chunming found herself out of a job; her life as a wealthy person had lasted exactly two months. She took the blow hard, and she knew who was to blame. "After Zhu Rongji came on," she said, "he wouldn't allow network sales anymore, so I stopped." In the freewheeling Pearl River Delta, where Chunming had learned to talk, where commerce was king and everyone was a winner and to die poor was a sin, the long arm of the government had touched her life, astonishingly, for the first time.

4 *The Talent Market*

In the evenings after Min got off her shift, I would take the bus to meet her at the front gate of her factory. Dongguan came to life after the sun went down; as the day's wearying heat evaporated, the darkening streets would be flooded with young people getting off work—changelings, turning before my eyes from dutiful workers back into eager teenagers again. Min and I would walk the few blocks around her factory and choose a cheap restaurant for dinner. She always ordered a meat dish, stir-fried greens, a whole fish for the two of us that invariably turned out to be mostly bone; if we met up around payday, she would insist on treating me. Min ate like someone starved for good food. Long after I had finished, she would continue picking at the dishes, extracting flavor from the tiniest morsels like a discerning gourmet.

Once when her cousin was in town, he took us to McDonald's. Min took a long look at her Big Mac, lowered her face down to the table until it was eye-level with the sandwich, and ate through it layer by layer—bun, tomato, lettuce, beef. She had never been to McDonald's before. When I gave her two small picture frames one birthday, I had to show her how to open the back to slip a photograph inside. Once she asked me what a stock was. She was completely uninterested in the affairs of the nation. During a meal with two older coworkers from her factory one afternoon, the conversation turned to growing up in the 1970s under Mao Zedong. "We were always hungry," one of the men recalled. "It wasn't until the 1980s that we stopped being hungry."

"Who is Chairman Mao now?" Min asked suddenly. "I don't even know."

"Hu Jintao," one of the men said.

A hint of recognition. "Then it isn't Jiang Zemin anymore?" she said.

I said no, that Jiang Zemin had retired and Hu Jintao had taken his place.

"Oh. I thought Jiang Zemin was dead." Then she said, "These people seem very far away from me."

The details of her own life crowded out everything else; almost every time I saw Min, she had something new to tell me. It sometimes felt as if the laws of the physical world did not apply to her, that she had only to think of something—a job switch, a breakup—to make it so. If I didn't see her for a while, she might forget to tell me that she had quit a factory or gotten a raise, because in her mind she had already moved on. She rarely stopped to take stock of everything she had done since coming out from home, a common trait in Dongguan. Maybe people worried that they would lose momentum if they stopped moving long enough to look backward.

When my first article about Min was published in the *Wall Street Journal*, I brought her a translated copy when we met up one night in a pastry shop near her factory. Her pound cake and iced mungbean shake sat untouched while she read. On page three, she gig-gled—"You remember it in great detail," she said—and again on page four. She read the story through to the end and flipped the last page over, looking for more. "That's it?"

"That's it," I said.

"It leaves you wanting more," she said.

"There will be more."

"Really?" she said. "Are you writing it now?"

"You're living it," I said. "It's happening now." Min gave me an odd look, as if she weren't sure whether I was joking with her.

She read the article several more times, and afterward she sent me an e-mail. *Seeing the self I used to be*, she wrote, *I realize that I have really changed.*

One thing Min never forgot was how hard her year on the assem-bly line had been. In the factory world, it was common to hear peo-ple speak almost nostalgically about their days on the assembly line, a time of few worries and responsibilities. Min did not do that. "Nothing is as hard as being an ordinary worker," I often heard her say. She never forgot where she had come from. That was one of the things I liked most about her.

*   *   *

In April 2004, Min got her first two weeks' pay at her new job, but she did not send the money home. Instead, she went to the mall and she bought a fitted black shirt and white capri pants. She was keep-ing a promise to visit old friends, and to visit old friends required new clothes. The next morning at eight o'clock, Min and I boarded the bus for a remote district of Dongguan, where she had worked her first year out from home. The bus was packed with migrants on their weekend outings. Young women sat in pairs wearing their Sunday best—white shirts, clean jeans, sleek ponytails—and the overflow passengers in the aisle snaked merrily, like a conga line, with every lurch of the bus. A few carsick young women clutched the railings, their heads bowed and their eyes squeezed tightly, as if to shut out the suffering.

Min talked the entire two-hour ride. She was hoping to convince her friends to jump factories, as she had done. She kept up a running commentary on the places we passed.

Zhangmutou: "They call this Little Hong Kong. It is very luxurious here. I came here many times looking for jobs but couldn't find one."

Qingxi: "There are a lot of computer factories here, but you need more skills to get in."

Fenggang: "This isn't as developed as the place I am now, right?"

To me, every town looked the same. Construction sites and cheap restaurants. Factories, factories, factories, the metal lattices of their gates drawn shut like nets. Min saw the city through different eyes: Every town was the possibility of a more desirable job than the one she had. Her mental map of Dongguan traced all the bus journeys she had made in search of a better life.

MIN'S FRIENDS WAITED for us at the bottom of a highway overpass, looking anxiously in the wrong direction. Liang Rong was tall with a pretty face; Huang Jiao'e was short and plump, with bright eyes and cheeks still soft with baby fat. Both were a year older than Min. The three girls held hands and squealed and jumped up and down, like game-show contestants who had just won a big prize.

"Wow! You lost weight!"

"You've grown taller!"

"You cut your hair!"

"I just bought these clothes," Min said urgently. "Are they pretty?" Her friends agreed that they were.

Next to the highway was a small park with a concrete plaza. Its stone benches had baked white in the sun, like ancient tombs; they were shaded by a few skinny saplings that looked like they were drawing their final breaths. The girls found a vacant bench and sat down and played with one another's hair. They admired Min's new clothes and she told them what each item cost.

"So, have I changed?" Min demanded. She had been gone exactly two months.

"Yes, you've changed," Huang Jiao'e said.

"How have I changed?"

"You look more mature."

Liang Rong and Huang Jiao'e shared the news from the factory: who had found a new job, who had cut her hair. This was their first day off in a month, because the factory's power had been cut. The pay was still the same and often late, depending on the boss's mood.

Min couldn't help boasting a little about the place where she worked now. "The people in this factory are really low-quality," she said. "My factory now is much better. The boss has a lot of money."

"Come on over to where I am," Min said suddenly. "I'll invite you out to dinner. When will you come?"

"But if we come," said Liang Rong, "you might not have a day off."

"You come visit me and I'll introduce boyfriends to you," Min said boldly. "There are many boys in my factory."

The two girls' eyes opened wide. They said "Ooh!" at the same time, and then all three of them laughed.

A beggar with a cane walked up, and the girls stopped talking. Liang Rong hesitated and then gently placed an apple in the old man's bowl, like a scene out of a fairy tale. Dongguan was a hard place to live in, and maybe because of that people could be surprisingly kind to one another. I saw more charity toward beggars in Dongguan than I ever saw in another Chinese city. The factory workers had compassion for the elderly or anyone with a physical handicap, but toward people their own age they showed no pity. If you were young and healthy, there was no excuse for not working.

MIN'S OLD FACTORY was a half hour's walk from town, where industrial China broadened into open farmland. A stream flowed sluggish and shiny black, like a river of gasoline. The road turned from pavement to packed dirt, a dusty strip lined with noodle stalls and pool tables set out in the open air. Knots of young men in factory shirts and slippers shot pool. Min walked along with a friend on either side, her head held high like a centurion returning from battle. Teenage boys and girls called out to her: "When did you get back?" "Where are you now?" They were impressed that she was working in downtown Dongguan.

"Have I changed?" Min asked of everyone who came up to her.

"You're thinner and darker," one young woman said.

Min was disappointed. "I want you to say I'm more mature than I used to be."

Liang Rong and Huang Jiao'e went into the factory to pick up their wages; apparently the boss was in such a good mood that he had consented to pay his workers that day. Min waited outside the gate, peering in at the tile buildings and a mountain of dirt in the middle of the yard. The factory was expanding.

"How do you think it looks?" Min asked me.

"It looks okay," I said.

"It looks all right from the outside," she said, "but you never see the inside until you've agreed to work there. And then you have nowhere else to go."

IN THE AFTERNOON, the girls met up with two other friends from the factory and went to a nearby park. Part of being a migrant worker was having no idea how to spend leisure time. At Tangxia Park, they watched a girl of about six aiming pebbles at the head of a turtle squatting in a shallow pool. But most entertainments at the park cost money. Visitors could use air rifles to shoot fish in a pond; Min looked at the few skinny fish awaiting execution and said solemnly, "This is what happens when you don't have freedom." A cable car brought passengers to a nearby hilltop, but that cost fifteen yuan. The girls sat at a picnic spot far below and watched the cars pass overhead.

Huang Jiao'e had enrolled in a computer class. She wanted to leave the factory, go to the talent market, and find a better job, as Min had done. "I have already made plans," she said shyly.

"Do you know how to go online yet?" Min asked.

"I haven't been online yet."

"I'll teach you." Min looked at her watch; it was four o'clock. "Maybe not today, though—next time.

"Just try to learn what you can," Min advised. "If you learn something, you can always take it with you to your next job. At least that has been my experience," she concluded modestly. Somewhere during the course of the day, she had realized she could do little to help her friends. Finding the courage to leave a factory was something a person had to do alone. It was as the migrants always said: *You can only rely on yourself.*

At five o'clock, the girls parted with the most casual of goodbyes. "I'm not tired yet," Min said as we found seats on the bus. "I'll be tired later. Right now I'm too excited." But as the bus passed through the towns of her job searches, now falling into evening, Min's mood darkened. She had visited her old life and knew it was past. Yet her new life, too, was somehow wanting. On the street outside, the lights in the factories started to come on, and shadows moved soundlessly against the windows; even on Sunday night, people were going to work. "If I only go to school, come out and do migrant work for a few years, then go home, marry and have children," Min said, "I might as well not have lived this whole life."

IN THE BLUE LIGHT OF EVENING, Min and I stood outside the gate of her factory. An electrician friend of hers was joining us for dinner, and we waited while he changed his clothes. A good-looking security guard in camouflage pants—1.7 METERS OR ABOVE, CAN PLAY BASKETBALL A PLUS—passed by with the flash of a smile and tossed Min a bunch of keys; she had given them to him for safe-keeping. People trickled back to the factory from their Sunday outings. Min called out to a young woman, who peered into the shadows and barked roughly, "I'm starving to death!" She went into the factory without coming by to say hello.

Min seemed taken aback by her rudeness. The woman had recently tried to abort a pregnancy using herbal medicine, Min told me, but it didn't work. Min had gone with her to the hospital for surgery. "She's one of the people I pretend to have good relations with, but really we are not friends," she said.

An older man with glasses and a potbelly walked past us into the factory. "Was it you who left the office door open?" he asked.

"I've been out all day," Min shot back.

That was Min's boss; she hated him. "He is very proud," she said. "Not a single person in the factory likes him." Her boss passed by again a few minutes later, going out, and glared at her. Min stood her ground and glared back. Neither of them said anything.

"Tomorrow he'll ask me who you are," Min said. "I know he will. I'll tell him you're a friend, that's all." Privately she called him *Liu Laotou*, "Old Fogey Liu."

In ten minutes by the factory gate, I felt as if I had seen Min's world: the easy friendship with the guard, the young woman's coldness and her botched abortion, the gratuitous cruelty of bosses. The fact that she stood her ground.

MIN'S ELECTRICIAN FRIEND APPEARED—he had muscular arms, an open face, and a shy smile—and we went to a street-side restaurant for grilled beef, braised fish, and beer. At the end of a long day, Min's discontent poured out all at once. "In my old factory, I cried once for half an hour and my friends tried to console me but couldn't," she said. "Since I've been at this factory I've cried twice, but no one even knew."

The electrician looked into his bowl of rice and didn't say anything.

Min's fury turned to the two friends who had gone to the park with us that afternoon. "We're not close. We just pretend to be friends," she said. "The fatter one? All she cares about is trying to find a boyfriend. When she gets paid, she doesn't send any money home. She'll just pay her boyfriend's mobile-phone bill or invite boys out to dinner. And she isn't even good-looking! The other one had a boyfriend but she broke up with him when she found out he was cheating on her. He gave her a watch and she still wears it.

"Do you see how they are all unhappy when they get their month's pay? They are all thinking: I work so hard and this is all I get? To work every day in the factory is so hard."

And then she turned on me. "You can't know what it feels like," she said. "Only someone who has experienced it knows."

*   *   *

Min tired of things she had so recently wanted. The thrill of joining an office gave way quickly to the realization that she was the lowest person in it. Everybody dumped work on their newest and youngest colleague, and Min's only workplace ally had disappeared: Two weeks after she arrived, the kindly man who had hired her decamped to a better job in Beijing. Left on her own, Min learned about the complicated politics of the white-collar world. Her new boss, the man with the potbelly, had been fired from the factory the previous year for keeping a mistress—because no one respected him, it made things harder for Min. Her coworkers appeared eager to see her fail: When she entered a room, conversations stopped, and no one helped her in her new job. She discovered that a person could say one thing and mean another, and that she must learn this skill too. "In the office, they may be very friendly to you, but they say things behind your back," Min told me. "You can't have a single friend in that factory."

Crossing the class divide added to her loneliness. The workers on the assembly line were closest to her in age and background, but she was no longer of that world. Her office colleagues were older, many of them married, and they had nothing in common with her. The dorm room emptied out on weekends when the others visited their boyfriends or husbands. Min pretended not to care, and she never let anyone see her cry.

In April, her former boss called from Beijing to offer her a job. He was assembling computer parts to sell in the provinces, and he needed someone to mind the store. He was in his thirties, had attended elite Tsinghua University, and was the only adult in Dongguan who had shown her any kindness: That was all she knew. She decided to go.

She phoned her older sister in Shenzhen.

"What will you do there?" her sister asked.

"Mind the store," Min said.

"How much is the salary?"

"I don't know. But it must be better than here."

"Do you trust him?"

"Yes."

"Be careful."

Min sent me a letter about her plans:

> I have decided to go to Beijing after all, to give myself an
> opportunity. I will handle these feelings between "Big
> Brother" and "Little Sister" well. But having gotten used to this
> work here at last, I am really loath to leave . . .
>
>   A person cannot grow up through happiness. Happiness
> makes a person shallow. It is only through suffering that we
> grow up, transform, and come to a better understanding of life!

But in a place with no moorings, Min was prone to wild changes
in mood. She decided it wouldn't be proper to join her boss in Beijing. He was a man, he was not family, and she didn't trust him after all. She would stay where she was.

Production in the factory was picking up; her dorm room now
housed nine people, up from six. With so many people working different shifts, it was hard to sleep at night, and Min thought again
about leaving. Next door to her office was the human resources department, where Min sometimes saw people lined up for job interviews. Ten people were interviewed for every one hired, and many
of them had college diplomas. Min felt lucky then to have the job
she did.

The assembly-line workers in Min's factory made 320 yuan a
month. That was low for Dongguan, and it bothered Min. She always said hello to the workers but she never got to know them better. "Some of the people in the office won't even speak to the
workers, because they look down on them," Min said. "But I used to
be a worker too."

*   *   *

In late May, Min sent me a message from her mobile phone. *I have a pleasant surprise for you. I won't tell you now. Ha ha.*

I was on my way to see her, and I raced through the possibilities in my mind. She had quit her job. She had found a boyfriend. She was going to Beijing after all.

I answered her: *I'm very curious.*

Maybe you'll think it's not good, she wrote back. *Ha ha. I hope you won't be disappointed.*

She was waiting for me at the factory gate, and I saw that she had straightened her hair. It was sleekly cut in an asymmetrical line; her girlish long curls were gone. The chemical treatment had taken three hours and cost one hundred yuan at a salon, Min told me. She had just gotten her first full month's pay.

She shared the gossip from work. Her immediate superior, who was a few years older than Min, had fought with his girlfriend. She was smart and made twice as much money as he did, a fact that everyone in the office knew and relished. She had saved eighty thousand yuan; everyone knew that too. If they were going to split up, the girlfriend demanded ten thousand yuan in compensation for the seven years she had spent with him. That was a breakup, Dongguan style: Emotional hurt gave way to financial calculation, and everyone in the factory knew every last detail. Now her young boss was quitting the factory, Min said, and several others with him. There was no reason to stay, so she had resigned yesterday.

"You've decided to leave?" I asked. The swiftness of her decisions took my breath away.

"I handed in my resignation letter yesterday," Min said.

Her boss, the one she disliked, had asked why she wanted to leave.

"I want to go home," Min had lied.

"Have you found another job?" he asked.

"No," she said. "I just have things to take care of at home." Another lie.

"You're doing well here," her boss said. "Why do you want to leave?" For once he was not rude to her. But he didn't approve her departure either; he told her he would decide within a month.

This was Min's surprise: She had straightened her hair. She had also made a move to quit her job and jump back into the unknown, but apparently she did not consider that news.

THAT AFTERNOON, we went to a small park near Min's factory. It was ringed by apartment buildings, with a pond of greenish yellow water the color of Mountain Dew. Children waded up to their knees, filling shallow pans and glass jars. "At home the ponds where we go swimming are deep and the water is clear," Min said.

"In the summers when I was a child," she continued dreamily, "we would plant watermelons. About ten minutes' walk from home, the adults would build a shed with tree trunks for posts and put a plank of wood with grass on top. We would sit under it all day guarding the watermelons and my father would sleep there at night.

"My older sister, my cousin, my two younger sisters, and I would go there during the day. We'd play cards, fish, and swim. We had schoolwork during the summer and our mother would tell us to do it but we wouldn't.

"We would put a few watermelons in the fast-rushing river. We'd tie them to the bank with a rope so they wouldn't float away. When we ate the watermelon, it was really cold."

I had never heard a migrant speak of the countryside as Min did.

"If I were you, if I had your qualifications and your money," she said then, "I would work very hard while I was young. But when I was older I would go to the countryside and find someone to marry and live in a small house there. You could live in a hut and raise a few chickens." She was silent for a while, spinning out in her mind a fantasy that we both knew would never come true.

*   *   *

In early June, a newly hired worker in Min's factory lost four fingers of his left hand on the single-punch machine. A week later, the same machine ate the tips of three fingers of another recent hire. Neither employee had been properly trained. On the city's factory floors, injuries hewed closely to the demands of production. During the slow winter months, factories could afford to train new workers; when orders picked up in the spring, such training was often cut short even as inexperienced people flooded in. Because the assembly line paid by the piece, working faster during busy times meant a bigger paycheck—spending time training others brought nothing. That was the zero-sum logic of the Dongguan factory, where helping someone else meant hurting yourself.

Later that month, Min was unexpectedly promoted to her factory's human resources department. Her job was to stand on the sidewalk under a scorching sun and convince people who passed by to join her factory; she signed up ten workers her first day. She also ran orientation sessions for the new workers, most of whom were older than she was. Min had no weekends now, so we met one Friday night in late June when her overtime shift ended at nine, at a fruit-drinks shop outside the factory gate. Her friend from the old factory, Huang Jiao'e, arrived just after I did with a small suitcase. She had come to work on the assembly line.

Min told us about her new job. "I stand by the side of the road and convince people to come work at our factory."

"What do you say to them?" I asked.

"I tell them, 'You may think that other factories look better. But every factory has its own difficulties that you may not be able to see. Isn't it better to stay here and be more stable? Save some money, get some experience, and then decide what you want to do.' " The words were familiar; this was what her parents always told her.

"But that's the opposite of what you have done," I said.

"Yes." She nodded and smiled. "It goes against what I believe in."

"I've never heard you speak in such an exaggerated way!" Huang Jiao'e said.

"This is my responsibility," Min said defensively. "You would do the same if you were in my place." Though the conversation was teasing, there was an edge to it. The two girls had been friends and equals, but now Min worked in the office, far above assembly-line workers like Huang Jiao'e.

Min went to the stall next door to buy me some noodles for dinner. "If it weren't for Min, I wouldn't have come here," Huang Jiao'e confided after she had gone. Two days earlier, she had visited the factory but had not liked the conditions. Originally she was to move over yesterday, but she hesitated; finally today she had left her factory without asking anyone or getting her two months' back pay. There were many ways to quit a factory. A worker might resign with her boss's permission and receive all of her back pay. She could take a temporary leave that guaranteed a position upon her return. Some departing workers negotiated with their employers for a portion of the money they were owed. But nothing was worse than *kuangli*—literally, "crazy leaving"—which was what Huang Jiao'e had done.

I asked her how long she planned to stay.

"We'll see," she said. "I am testing them, and they are testing me."

Min returned to the table. "If you do well, you will move up." She added, still defensively, "Our salary is not high either: eight hundred yuan. If you have overtime, you may get more than me."

"But I would be tired to death!" Huang Jiao'e said.

"There are different ways of being tired," Min said. "In my job now, my body is tired and my heart is tired." She was moving up in the world. Her new responsibilities included pouring tea for visiting clients, and she had enrolled in a weekly English class for the factory's managers. "Do you know what 'pardon' means?" Min asked Huang Jiao'e, saying the single word in English. She looked disappointed when her friend said yes.

MIN'S OTHER NEWS did not emerge until after repeated prodding from Huang Jiao'e. A boy from home had come out to Dongguan and found a job as an assembly-line worker. He and Min had dated briefly in middle school, but she had not seen him in three years. The previous week, he had come to visit.

"There is still feeling between us," she announced. Then, immediately—"But he is very short: only 1.65 meters." She reported the details: "He smokes, he drinks, and he gets into fights. His family situation is not good. He has a stepmother."

"What does his family do?" I asked.

"I don't know," she said. "I don't want to know. In the end we must rely on ourselves."

The two of them had spent the day together. At lunch, Min poured tea for her former boyfriend while he stared at the television set mounted somewhere above Min's head. In cheap Chinese restaurants, there is always a television playing at top volume, and the eyes of the patrons and wait staff are usually glued to it.

"Why don't we talk?" Min prodded him. "Why do you keep looking at the television?"

After he left, Min sent him a message on his mobile phone. *How did you feel about our day together?*

I feel a lot of pressure, he wrote back. *My feelings are very complicated.*

They had talked on the phone the night before. Min got right to the point. "Do you think we have a future together?"

He told her he needed three days to think about it.

"So I will have my answer in two days," she said. "Whatever he answers is fine with me." But she was already spinning her dreams around the boy, who had some training as a cook. "We could go home and start a small restaurant," she said. "There is no future in this migrant work."

"Do you want to get married?" I asked her. The entire conversation astonished me.

"That's not what this is about," she said impatiently. "I'm eighteen years old now. I don't want to waste my time. If he's not serious about me, I want him to tell me now."

IN THE END, everything was decided for Min. Three days after the conversation with her former boyfriend, she got a message on her mobile phone at seven in the morning: *I'm here at the factory gate*. She didn't believe it and ran downstairs to see. He had gotten off the night shift and taken the bus straight to her factory. Min had to work, so the boy waited outside from eight o'clock until noon. The two of them ate lunch together, then he left and Min returned to work.

"Did he say you have a future?" I asked.

"No," said Min. "But because he came, I knew."

She had recently taken the bus—a two-hour ride—to spend an afternoon with him. "He is not tall, he is not handsome, he has no money, his job is not good," Min said.

I waited for something to follow this declaration of shortcomings.

"But you like him," I said at last.

Min didn't say anything, but she smiled.

Now the boy was leaving Dongguan because his father wanted

him to work closer to home. No sooner had Min found a stable prospect than he was disappearing too, but she was unfazed. "We will keep in touch by mobile phone," she said. She was not staying put either. Later that month, her boss approved her departure and returned her two months' back pay. Min went to the talent market again. She had worked in her factory's human resources department for exactly twenty-four days, and on that she could build a new career.

* * *

In an unforgiving city, the Dongguan talent market was the toughest place of all. For ten yuan, about $1.25, anyone could enter and interview for the hundreds of jobs on offer at the company booths inside. But going in required courage—to talk to strangers, to sell yourself, to face rejection while everyone within earshot listened. Min hated the talent market because it made her feel "replaceable." The job listings reduced human beings to the only characteristics that mattered, and rarely did these essentials require more than twenty words:

RECEPTIONIST. SWEET VOICE. GOOD APPEARANCE
AND DISPOSITION. KNOWS OFFICE SOFTWARE AND
CANTONESE.

LATHE WORKER. 18- TO 22-YEAR-OLD MALE,
EXPERIENCE AT A FOREIGN FACTORY. NOT
NEARSIGHTED. NO SKIN SENSITIVITY.

SALES SPECIALIST. CAN EAT BITTERNESS AND
ENDURE HARDSHIP. OPEN TO MEN AND WOMEN
WITH RURAL RESIDENCY. NO ONLY CHILDREN.

On a busy Saturday, Dongguan's biggest job fair might draw seven thousand visitors. By midmorning, all these people would have congealed into a single bloated mass, making individual movement all but impossible; occasionally, a group would break off and swamp a certain booth, though it was unclear what suddenly made one job more desirable than all the others. The most popular booths featured airbrushed posters, usually of long, windowless buildings set in concrete landscapes; a simple booth consisted of a man or a woman with a clipboard. The talent market stretched a full city block and filled a four-story building that had once housed a karaoke lounge and a bowling alley. Trading in the futures of people, it turned out, was a more lucrative business than entertainment.

SECRETARIES. 18 TO 25, 155 CENTIMETERS OR
TALLER, REGULAR FEATURES.

SECURITY GUARDS. 20 TO 26, 172 CENTIMETERS OR
TALLER.

Discrimination was the operative rule. Bosses liked their clerks female, pretty, and single, and they would only consider men for certain technical jobs. One factory might impose a blanket ban on people from Henan Province; another could refuse to hire anyone from Anhui. Sometimes an applicant's entire family would come under scrutiny, because people who had siblings were deemed more likely than only children to *chiku nailao*, eat bitterness and endure hardship. Being less than 160 centimeters tall, or about five feet three inches, guaranteed a frustrating day at the talent market.

Height was a universal Chinese obsession. In a country that had experienced malnutrition and even famine in living memory, height signaled fortune, and it functioned as a proxy for class: On any construction site, the armies of peasant workers were a head shorter than the city people whose homes they were building. Manual laborers in the West might be larger than their white-collar counterparts, but in China the opposite held true—the educated could literally look down on the lower classes. For women, height requirements were attached to the more glamorous trades. "If I were only ten centimeters taller," a young woman who worked in a hair salon told me once, "I could sell cars."

Age was another liability—in the talent market, that meant anyone over thirty-five, which was the upper age limit for many positions. "People over thirty-five are inferior in their thinking and drive," explained a factory manager in a promotional newspaper put out by the company that operated the market. The paper's advice to this demographic: "Don't always talk about your past experience. You must have a mentality of starting from zero." In a perverse way, age limits were evidence of upward mobility. At the booth of a company that made headboards for beds, the list of jobs and target ages seemed to be a timetable for career advancement:

COST ACCOUNTANT: 25
MARKETING DEPARTMENT MANAGER: 30
PRODUCTION DEPUTY MANAGER: 35

The most common openings were for clerks, receptionists, salespeople, security guards, and cooks, with mold design and machine repair also in high demand. One company was looking for people "skilled in operating Mitsubishi and Fujitsu machinery." Job titles were specific and sometimes bewildering: PATTERN GROUPERS. APPLIQUE WORKERS. PRESSURE VESSEL WELDERS. Here the industrial might of modern China was broken down into pieces, and the pieces were people.

Interviews at the talent market were brief and brutally honest. Recruiters did not pretend that jobs were anything to write home about; candidates freely admitted their ignorance. It was the rare interview that lasted more than five minutes. Hiring was usually done on the spot, and no one checked references.

At the booth of the Hengfeng Molds factory, a young woman sat down.

"Our pay is not high," the recruiter said immediately. Then: "Have you worked with computers?"

"Yes, I learned computers in school."

"Well, our pay is only six hundred."

Another booth, another woman: "What can you do?"

"I keep in touch with customers, mostly through e-mail, and if they come to the office, I can receive them. If the job is more technical, I don't know anything about that."

What can you do? In most Chinese cities, where finding a job required a college diploma, money, and connections, that was a rare question. At the Dongguan talent market, you never heard: *Where did you go to school? Whom do you know?* Or least of all, *Are you from around here?* It was always: *What can you do? Do you know computers? Do you know English?* Job listings, which were usually written out by hand on preprinted cards, mocked the standard categories that were provided. In the space for residency, an employer usually specified the sex of the person sought: instead of profession, a company might list height requirements instead.

Not everyone who came to the talent market dared to go inside. Throngs gathered on the sidewalk before a giant electronic job board, like people fated only to look upon a promised land they would never enter. The listings moved upward in a continuous crawl, like stock prices, and the crowd stared, mesmerized.

*   *   *

Her second time at the market, Min knew exactly what to do. She aimed high, approaching only those companies with jobs in the human resources department. "Clerk is a very low position, so I didn't look for that." In her interviews, she asked about employee turnover and company size; she was looking for a smaller factory with fewer superiors to please. She sidestepped questions about why she had left her old job. That was a personal matter, Min said, that she would rather not discuss.

And this time she was not more honest than the others. At the booth of the Shenxing Rubber Products Company, she told the recruiter that she had worked in human resources for a year. "If you say less," she explained to me afterward, "they think it's not enough experience." She was hired with a six-dollar-per-month raise above the salary of the person she was replacing.

Min started work two days later in the human resources department of the company, which made rubber components for mobile phones and computer keyboards. Her workday lasted eight hours, with every Sunday off. Workers at her level slept four to a room, and her room had its own bathroom and phone. She made eight hundred yuan a month, including room and board—the same as her last job, with a chance of a raise if she did well.

In her new job, Min kept track of the employment records, performance, demerits, and salaries of the factory's four hundred workers. Where she had once looked after machines, now she was in charge of people, and it seemed a better fit. When workers came to the factory gate, she screened them for hiring. *Do you have an ID? How long do you plan to stay?*

Thank you, she told those who did not answer to her liking. *We don't have jobs right now.*

On the tenth of every month, the Taiwanese wife of the factory owner came to pay the workers and seek the Buddha's blessing. Min would follow the boss's wife around the factory—to the canteen, the front gate, and each of the dangerous machines—and the two of them would ask the Buddha to protect the workers and let business prosper. Min would silently seek blessings for her family and friends and for her grandparents in the next world, but she didn't tell the boss's wife that.

She was getting better at office politics. Not long after she arrived, the top boss called Min into his office. The previous person in Min's position, he told her, had been talkative and made mistakes. "You don't like to talk much," he observed.

"No," she agreed.

The boss smiled. "When you have to speak," he said, "you should speak. If you don't have to speak, don't speak." That was the secret rule of Chinese workplace survival, but no one had ever shared it with Min.

This time she handled her parents more adeptly. She didn't tell them she was quitting her job. Instead she found a new one, wired home $120, then called her parents with her news; the cash transfer was a preemptive strike that stunned them into silence. "They don't know how things are outside," Min told me. "So I do something first, and then I tell them about it."

Everyone she knew was in flux, and many were on their way up too. Her sister in Shenzhen had been promoted to executive secretary; her cousin was now a manager in Guangzhou. Her two friends from the old factory had scattered. Liang Rong had gone home to marry someone of her parents' choosing. Huang Jiao'e, who had moved over to Min's factory, quit the same day Min did and landed a job as a production clerk elsewhere in the city. And Min's old boss was back in Dongguan. He had returned from Beijing to work in a Taiwanese socket factory, but Min refused to see him. Workers in her old factory said he was romantically interested in her. She went through his old phone messages to her—*Your big brother misses you*—and decided it was true. The only adult who had been kind to her was not to be trusted, after all.

Small factories had their own problems, and Min soon discovered what they were. The workplace was disorganized, and her own responsibilities were never made clear; she scrambled to keep up with all the tasks thrown her way. Her new boss, like her old one, was insecure and status-conscious. Min was learning that many Chinese men had this flaw. He didn't like it that Min did not get his approval for everything she did. He didn't like it that she was friendly with the security guards. His response was to begin interviewing candidates for her position—a colleague, rival, or replacement for Min— without telling her. She heard about it from the office receptionist.

In August 2004, two months after she arrived, Min collected her pay and left without telling anyone. A former colleague had joined a factory in Shenzhen and invited her to go work for him, and she decided to go. She spent the night in a hotel near her factory; while she slept, someone broke the lock on her door. The thief took nine hundred yuan and Min's mobile phone, the only place where she had stored the numbers of everyone she knew in the city: the ex-colleague who was her only link to her new job, the friends she had made since going out, and the boyfriend who had gone home.

*   *   *

The mobile phone was the first big purchase of most migrants. Without a phone, it was virtually impossible to keep up with friends or find a new job. Letters between factories often went missing, and calling up a worker in her dorm, where a hundred people might share a single hallway phone, was difficult. Office phones inside factories were often programmed not to allow outside calls or to cut off automatically after several minutes. Anyway, people jumped jobs so often that dorm and office numbers quickly went out of date. In a universe of perpetual motion, the mobile phone was magnetic north, the thing that fixed a person in place.

I learned all of this painfully. In my early days in Dongguan, I befriended many new arrivals who did not have mobile phones yet, and I lost track of them, one by one. When I met Min, I decided to buy her a pager, but that industry had collapsed so suddenly and completely in the past few years that salesmen in electronics stores just laughed at me when I said I wanted one. I gave Min a mobile phone so I would not lose her too.

In the migrant world, the mobile phone was a metaphor for the relentless pace of city life. An executive at a shoe factory summed up the disjunctions of migration this way: "At home they have no phones, then suddenly they are here and it is Nokia 6850." A young woman who sold insurance said to me, "At home they hand down a mobile phone from one person to another" to describe rural life. People referred to themselves in the terminology of mobile phones: *I need to recharge. I am upgrading myself.* The parents of migrant girls instinctively distrusted the phones, and some forbade their daughters from buying one. The mobile phone, which allowed and even encouraged private contact with strangers, was everything that communal village life was not.

A girl might signal her interest in a young man by offering to pay his mobile-phone bill. Couples announced their allegiance with a shared phone, though relationships sometimes broke up when one person secretly read text messages intended for another. The migrants I knew spent a great deal of time managing their phones—changing numbers constantly to take advantage of cheaper calling plans, and switching phone cards when crossing to another city to save on roaming fees. That was the short-term mentality of Dongguan: Save a few pennies, even if it meant losing touch with some people for good.

Migrant workers are a major reason the Chinese mobile-phone market is the world's largest, yet the industry has mixed feelings about them. Migrants were behind the market's poor economics, one friend in the telecommunications industry told me; they supposedly drove down prices because they were willing to pay for only the cheapest services. Popular culture also felt their negative impact: The quality of Chinese pop music had deteriorated in recent years, I was also told, because migrants chose the least sophisticated songs for the ring tones of their phones.

Hundreds of Dongguan factories made parts for mobile phones, and every third retailer in the city seemed to be a mobile-phone store. The city also did a thriving trade in stolen phones. Certain districts were known for a high incidence of phone theft; one tactic was to speed down a sidewalk on a motorcycle and rip a phone from a pedestrian's ear, mid-sentence. The stolen phones might be fitted with new covers and then sold as new. Manufactured, sold, stolen, repackaged, and resold, the mobile phone was like an endlessly renewable resource at the heart of the Dongguan economy.

It was also Min's link to the city. With the theft of her phone, the friendships of a year and a half vanished as if they had never been. She was alone again.

5 *Factory Girls*

It takes two hundred pairs of hands to make a running shoe. Everything begins with a person called a cutter, who stamps a sheet of mesh fabric into curvy irregular pieces, like a child's picture puzzle. Stitchers are next. They sew the pieces together into the shoe upper, attaching other things—a plastic logo, shoelace eyelets—as they go. After that, sole-workers use infrared ovens to heat pieces of the sole and glue them together. Assemblers—typically men, as the work requires greater strength—stretch the upper over a plastic mold, or last, shaped like a human foot. They lace the upper tightly, brush glue on the sole, and press the upper and the sole together. A machine applies ninety pounds of pressure to each shoe. Finishers remove the lasts, check each shoe for flaws, and place matched pairs in cardboard boxes. The boxes are put in crates, ten boxes to a crate, and shipped to the world within three days. Every shoe has a label on its tongue: MADE IN CHINA.

If you wear athletic shoes, chances are you have worn a pair that was made at the Yue Yuen factory in Dongguan. The Taiwanese-owned factory is the biggest manufacturer for Nike, Adidas, and Reebok, along with smaller brands like Puma and Asics, all of whom stopped making shoes years ago and farmed out production to factories that could do it more cheaply. Yue Yuen's secret is vertical integration: It controls every step of the manufacturing process—from initial design to making glues, soles, molds, and lasts to cutting, stitching, and assembling the finished products. One-third of the world's shoes are made in Guangdong Province, and the Yue Yuen plant is the biggest of them all.

Seventy thousand people work at its Dongguan factory. Imagine the entire population of Santa Fe, New Mexico, under the age of thirty and engaged in making athletic shoes. Inside the compound's brick walls, workers sleep in factory dorms and eat in factory cafeterias and shop at factory commissaries. Yue Yuen runs a kindergarten for employees' children and a hospital with a 150-member staff; it has a movie theater and a performance troupe, volunteer activities and English classes. It operates its own power plant and fire department, and sometimes the city of Dongguan borrows Yue Yuen's fire-truck ladder, the tallest one around, to put out fires. Yue Yuen bottles its own water. Locals will tell you that it grows its own food, which is not true, although the company at one point contracted with farmers in the area to guarantee its food sources. Nothing short of apocalypse could cut off the world's supply of what the industry calls "branded athletic footwear."

For young migrants, Yue Yuen offers stability. An assembly-line job brings only an average salary—about seventy-two dollars a month in take-home pay, in line with the city's minimum wage—but it is paid every month, on time. Work is capped at eleven hours a day and sixty hours a week with Sundays off, rare for an industry in which laboring through the night is not unheard of. Yue Yuen workers sleep ten to a room in metal bunks, and this too is better than average. Young women typically pay middlemen one hundred yuan to procure a job here; men pay several times that. Eighty percent of the workers at Yue Yuen are women, most between the ages of eighteen and twenty-five.

A migrant who lands a job at Yue Yuen may never work anywhere else. Over the years, she may quit and go home—to see a sick relative or settle a marriage engagement, to have a rest or a child—and then return to Yue Yuen. A worker may introduce a sibling or a cousin or a fellow villager into the factory, and the company encourages this; in one instance, ten members of an extended family all worked inside the factory. Employee turnover is high—5 percent a month, meaning that more than half the workforce changes in a year—but that does not take into account the many workers who quit only to return again. Zhou Yinfang joined Yue Yuen in 1991, when she was seventeen. She met her husband in the factory, took time off to have two children, talked her way into a promotion, and now manages 1,500 workers as a factory chief. "I would like to work here until I retire," she told me; she was thirty years old, but her voice was already the harsh whisper of an old woman. All of the Yue Yuen bosses, the workers say, have raspy voices from years of shouting orders over the din of the machines.

Upward mobility is possible; the demands of production are so intense that Yue Yuen must promote from within. Almost all of the company's managers, from supervisors of single lines to the heads of whole factories, are rural migrants who started out on the assembly line. An intricate hierarchy orders this world. Managers are divided into thirteen grades, from trainee to managing director; they typically address each other by title and not by name. One cafeteria is reserved exclusively for production line leaders, while another caters to supervisors, the next step up from them. A child is a status symbol: Only line leaders and above are allowed to live inside the factory as a married couple with a child. Ordinary workers usually leave their children at home in the village, to be minded by grandparents.

Factory society divides along provincial lines. Workers from the same province stick together, speaking dialects that outsiders cannot understand. Those from provinces with large migrant populations further segregate based on which county they come from. Natives of the adjoining provinces of Anhui, Henan, Shaanxi, and Shandong can speak to one another in their own dialects; they call one another "half-fellow provincials," which brings a sense of closeness. The company doesn't fight these regional prejudices: Its cafeterias offer workers a choice of Hunan, Sichuan, or Cantonese dishes. Provincial stereotypes color hiring, and a boss can ban an entire province if he believes that a hundred million people from one place can share a personality trait. *Henan people get into fights. People from Anhui are hardworking but untrustworthy.*

Workers can spend their days without venturing beyond Yue Yuen's guarded gates, and many of them do, saying the world outside is *luan*—chaotic, dangerous. Yet life inside Yue Yuen's walls can be turbulent too. Petty theft is rampant; workers are banned from dorms during work hours in an effort to reduce such crimes. Factory-floor quarrels carry over into the dorms, where workers on the same production line are required to room together for the sake of efficiency. Gangs thrive inside Yue Yuen. Some rob workers of their wages on payday; others focus on stealing shoe parts. The gangs practice a vertical integration of their own. One group may spirit shoelaces out of the factory, while another smuggles out soles. The parts are assembled into shoes and distributed in other parts of the city. In the universe of Chinese counterfeiting, theirs is a distinctive sub-specialty—the illicit assembly of authentic parts. The gangs are organized along provincial lines, and the ones from Hunan are most feared.

Love triangles and extramarital affairs are common, as are out-of-wedlock pregnancies and abortions. A few years ago, a young woman committed suicide over a failed love affair; another gave birth in her dorm bathroom and threw the baby into the toilet. The baby died, and the young woman was sent home. "We have seventy thousand people. It is a city," says Luke Lee, a Yue Yuen executive who oversees worker health and safety. "Whatever problems a city has, we have in the factory."

*   *   *

On weekends when the production lines shut down, the mood inside the Yue Yuen compound changes. Girls who walked with purpose and poker faces during the week turn slow and languorous. They stroll hand in hand with girlfriends, their factory IDs on straps around their necks or on chains linked to their belts, like American school janitors. They talk loudly in their native dialects; they show skin. They wear tank tops and jeans, or black party dresses with high heels; sometimes several friends step out in identical outfits, announcing their shared loyalties to the world. They eat ice-cream cones and sit barefoot on patches of grass in twos and threes, reading magazines or sharing confidences. Sometimes one girl sits alone staring dreamily at nothing.

The dorms offer no privacy. Girls stand in doorways combing their shampooed hair in hand mirrors; girls in shorts and flip-flops lug buckets of water to mop the dormitory floors. Residents of the upper floors lean on bare arms over balcony railings, checking out the goings-on at ground level and calling out to friends many stories below. A pop ballad blasts from a tape deck into the muggy morning. *I love you, loving you, as a mouse loves rice.* The air smells of laundry hanging out to dry; bleach, detergent, and damp are the perpetual scents of the Yue Yuen factory.

On a Sunday morning in June 2004, several young women lay chatting in their bunks in Building J, Room 805. The room had the disheveled feel of the last stage of a slumber party, and the girls lounged in their pajamas although it was already eleven o'clock.

"When you meet a man outside the village," one girl said, "you don't know his real character and you don't know about his family."

"If you get a boyfriend while you are outside, your parents will have no face at home."

"You may make friends with someone, then you go home and lose touch."

"When you go home, you find out people know all sorts of things about you."

Ten girls lived together in J805, an eighth-floor room measuring two hundred square feet with two rows of metal bunk beds. The room smelled, like everywhere else at Yue Yuen, of wet laundry. Each girl was assigned a wall cabinet that held clothes, snacks, makeup, and jewelry; they decorated the insides with magazine pictures of movie stars, like the lockers of American high school girls. The spaces under the bunks were a graveyard for shoes: high heels, sneakers, Hello Kitty flip-flops. Room J805 was on a long hallway of identical rooms, with toilets and showers at each end. The building housed two thousand workers.

Back home on the farm it was the busiest season of the year, the time for the summer harvest and the summer planting. But the global cycle of shoe manufacturing was slowing down. The girls in J805 worked in the Yue Yuen Number 8 factory, which made shoes for Adidas and Salomon. Now they were working only ten and a half hours a day plus half or full days on Saturdays; in the world of Dongguan manufacturing, that was considered the slow season. Some of the girls were planning to go home on leave, but their paths diverged depending on which part of the shoe they made. The ones who worked on shoe soles could leave. Cutters and stitchers had to stay on.

Jia Jimei, a twenty-one-year-old Henan native who worked in the sole department, rushed into the room from a shopping trip and showed off her purchases: snacks for the train ride and a cassette player for her family. She had just been granted a one-month home leave. "I haven't been able to sleep these past two nights," she said. "Once you know you're going home, you can't think about anything else." She had a snub nose and wide-set eyes in a round face that turned softer when she smiled. She sat down on her lower bunk, clutching a stuffed panda bear to her chest.

Zhang Qianqian, a young woman from Anhui Province who was visiting from down the hall, watched the going-home preparations. She was solidly built, with broad shoulders and a hard unsmiling face; she wore jeans and a black sports watch that made her look tough. She was a cutter, so she was staying. "When I go home, I'm bored to death," Qianqian said. "There's no TV and no cassette player. And almost everyone from home has gone out, so I'm all by myself all day.

"My grandmother gets up at dawn to make breakfast," she continued, "and calls me to come eat, and sometimes I'm still sleeping. Then my father says, 'You're lying in bed and won't even come to eat breakfast your grandmother has made for you.' At home they are always criticizing you."

"When you go home, you can't stay," agreed Li Xiaoyan, a roommate from Hunan who was also a cutter. The girls had a complicated relationship with home. Out in the city, they were tired and lonely and talked constantly of going home; once home, they quickly grew bored and longed to go out again. If a girl decided to leave the factory, it sent ripples of shock and uncertainty through everyone around her. To be a migrant was to be constantly abandoned by the people closest to you.

Qianqian was a veteran of departures and returns. She had come out from home three years before, worked at Yue Yuen for a year and a half, quit because of conflicts with her boss, and gone home for a while. Back in Dongguan, she joined a small electronics factory where conditions were much worse than at Yue Yuen. She quit and went home again, this time for her grandmother's eightieth birthday. Four months ago, she had rejoined Yue Yuen. "I've moved here and there, and I always seem to end up in this factory," she said.

Jia Jimei was less certain. "I may return to Yue Yuen but I'm not sure yet," she said. She left for home a week later without telling her roommates if she was coming back.

*   *   *

China is a quarter century into the largest migration in human history, and the profiles of the people on the move are changing. Those who came out from their rural villages in the 1980s and early 1990s were heading into the unknown, often driven by a family's need for cash and the desire to build a house back home. It was considered risky, even shameful, for a single woman to go out on her own. These early migrants often found seasonal work, and the seasons were those of the farm. They returned home to help out during the sowing season and again at harvest time. When they had made enough money, they returned to the village for good.

The new generation came of age when migration was already an accepted path to a better life. Younger and better-educated than their predecessors, they are driven out less by the poverty of the countryside than by the opportunity of the city. There is no longer any shame attached to migration. The shame now lies in staying home.

Newer migrants have looser ties to their villages. Their trips home are no longer dictated by the farming calendar or even by the timing of traditional holidays like the lunar new year. Instead, younger migrants come and go according to their personal schedules of switching jobs or obtaining leaves, and these are often tied to the demands of the production cycle. It is the seasons of the factory, rather than the fields, that define migrant life now.

Migrants increasingly look and act like city people. Migrant magazines launched in the 1990s have folded or are struggling to find readers now. Songs about the migrant experience are no longer heard in the factory cities of the south; the workers on the assembly line now listen to the same pop tunes as urban teenagers. Today's migrants spend money freely on themselves—on clothes, hairstyles, and mobile phones—and may send home cash only in instances of need. The newer migrants are more ambitious and less content than their elders were. One survey found that 12 percent of migrants who had left home in the 1990s were satisfied with their situations in life, compared with 27 percent of the generation that had come out a decade earlier. That does not necessarily mean that the newer migrants want to return to the village. But it suggests that their basis of comparison is already the city, and perhaps these greater expectations promise a greater chance of success. Or it may mean that this new generation is only bound to be disappointed.

GETTING TO KNOW the factory girls of Yue Yuen was not easy. Girls would make dates to meet me and not show up; if I found them later, they gave no explanation or apology. No one was willing to accept the mobile phone I offered so we could stay in touch, perhaps not wanting the responsibility. They might be friendly to me one day and cold the next, and if I struck up a conversation with one girl in a dorm, the others in the room would shun me. One girl instructed her roommates to lie and tell me she had left the factory, because her friends had told her I was not to be trusted. The company granted me free access to its dormitories, but winning the trust of those who lived there was the hard part. In the shadow of the giant shoe factory they flitted, insubstantial as moths, and more elusive than anyone I met in the city.

The girls were equally wary with one another and often spoke roughly among themselves. They frequently knew nothing about the people with whom they lived and worked; as I got to know them better, they often asked me for news of one another. Most girls seemed to have one or two true friends who lived far away, perhaps in another factory, preferring to confide in them rather than in the many close by. Maybe this was their defense against living in a colony of strangers: They took it for granted that someone who slept in an adjoining bunk one night would disappear the next.

It took willpower for any migrant worker to change her situation. But inside a factory as large as Yue Yuen, the pressure to conform felt especially intense. The girls all claimed in front of one another that they didn't approve of finding a boyfriend in the city, although many of them already had one; they disparaged further education as useless even as some quietly took classes in an effort to improve themselves. Yue Yuen was a good place to work—everyone who worked there said that. But if you wanted something different, it took all your strength to break free.

*   *   *

In July, the hottest season of the year in the farmer's calendar, work at Yue Yuen slowed to a crawl. Dorm rooms gaped empty as more workers went home on leave. Those who stayed behind were working only eight hours a day, five days a week. The normal work schedule of the Western white-collar world was paradise here.

Qianqian woke up past ten o'clock one Sunday just as I arrived to see her. She yawned, stretched, and slowly swung herself out of her top bunk. She pulled on a green tank top, jeans with floral embroidery stitched down one leg, and scuffed high heels with pointy toes. "In the whole year, only these few months are a bit more fun," she said. Two bunks over, a roommate sat in bed practicing English phrases under her breath. She took a weekly class run by the factory. The sentences in her well-thumbed book were strange.

THIS IS LOO. HE'S FROM PERU.

One made sense:

DON'T LOSE THE OPPORTUNITY.

Qianqian walked downstairs, past the other dormitory buildings, and through the factory gate. Out on the sidewalk, the sun's glare was so strong that the street appeared blinding white, like an over-exposed photograph. Qianqian entered a department store and gravitated toward the racks of sequined high-heeled shoes. She fingered a yellow platform shoe whose strap had three glittery pink hearts, like Valentine's Day candy. "This is very fashionable this year," she said. In the gifts section, she pointed out a picture frame with fake roses embedded inside; she had given one to a friend for her birthday.

Back on the near-deserted street, she shouted at a girl walking past. "Qu Jimei! Where have you been?"

A girl with dyed red streaks in her hair stopped walking. She was carrying a nylon Nike backpack. "I'm going home," she said.

"You're going home? Now?"

"Now."

Qianqian held the girl's hand for a moment. "Well, goodbye then," she said. She watched the girl walk away. "You meet so many friends in the factory like this, and then they go home."

"Do you keep in touch?" I asked her.

"It's hard. Sometimes we exchange addresses." Her closest friend in the city was someone she had met during her first stint at Yue Yuen. They had quit the factory at the same time, gone home to their respective villages, and arranged to come out again together. Qianqian frequently visited the friend on her days off. The effort required to keep in touch explained why the factory girls had so few true friends. The easiest thing in the world was to lose touch with someone.

We sat down in a sunbaked plaza outside a department store and ate ice-cream cones. A girl in a blue-and-white striped factory shirt who appeared to know Qianqian sat down with us. She idly fanned herself with a postcard she was on her way to mail. "I have left the factory," she announced. It was so hot that no one responded. The two girls sat in silence and watched me writing in my notebook.

"Do you read English?" Qianqian asked the girl.

She laughed harshly. "I didn't even finish elementary school!"

After the girl left, Qianqian explained that they had worked together at a small factory nearby. "Yue Yuen is better," she said. "The welfare benefits are better. There is a library and an activities center. You can play chess or join the Hula-Hoop club." I asked her if she took part in any of those activities, and she said no.

She walked down the street, encountering other friends who were going home, saying hello and goodbye to people who in all likelihood she would never see again. From afar, Qianqian's parents were pressuring her to go home too, and yet they wanted her to send more money. She had given them almost five thousand yuan in her first two years out but nothing since. In her village, parents traditionally built a house for a grown son to live in after his marriage; Qianqian's younger brother was only fourteen, but her parents were already worrying about the expense.

"All the other people in the village have built their houses," her father had said to her. "How come mine hasn't been built yet?"

"I was going to ask you the same question," Qianqian retorted.

From their homes in the village, families tried to influence their daughters. *Send money home. Don't get a boyfriend outside. Get mar-*

ried sooner. Come back. For the most part the girls did as they pleased. Qianqian's parents didn't even know her phone number inside the factory—when she wanted to talk, she would call them. They were always home.

*   *   *

The streets around the Yue Yuen factory teemed with opportunities for spending or self-improvement. On weekend afternoons, the Hopeful Computer Training Center was crowded with workers sitting at computers learning Word and Excel. (A sign outside advertised, in English, MICROSOFT WORB.) A shop sold men's white dress shirts for twenty yuan, and a photo studio offered a choice of aspirational backdrops: Pastoral Landscape, Corinthian Columns, Suburban Villa. Retailers catered to the homesick with geographically specific offerings. HENAN ZHOUKOU SESAME CAKES. WUHAN BARBER. One store consisted of a row of plastic phone booths crammed along the wall, an enterprise that existed only in migrant towns. Pasted to the opposite wall was a train schedule to cities all over China: twenty-five hours to Ningbo, forty to Chengdu. The Shangjiang City Health Station advertised one-minute pregnancy tests, venereal disease cures, and abortions. The hospital inside Yue Yuen also performed abortions, but almost no one went there. The sidewalk clinics offered the same procedures and no one had to know.

Outside the gates of Yue Yuen, I once saw a man speaking rapidly, like an old-time carnival barker, into a microphone headset. "If you have stomachache, if you have backache, if you have rheumatism, this is for you." The air reeked sourly of alcohol, and a blanket spread out on the sidewalk displayed preserved snakes, a starfish, and bottles of brownish liquid the color of strong iced tea. Several snakes, apparently dead, were entwined in a plastic bucket; the man stirred them with a stick, like a stew. He was a chain-smoker with a hacking cough, and he did not look in the least qualified to be giving out medical opinions. Yet a crowd of young men and women clamored for the flyers he was handing out.

SNAKE WINE TO NOURISH KIDNEYS

Prescription: This product's main components are king cobra, krait, silver-ringed snake, and so on, in all seven types of poisonous snakes and many kinds of herbal medicines. Usage: Mornings and evenings take half or one *liang*.

Another day on the same stretch of sidewalk, a man lay on his stomach with his crippled legs curled under him, writing on the pavement with a stub of chalk. A crowd of young migrants gathered to read his story: His wife had died, his son was sick, and he had traveled far from home to beg for money. The man had some bills in his cup already, and two more people gave money as I watched.

From the main street in front of the Yue Yuen factory, alleys ran straight back at intervals between the stores. These passages were strewn with garbage and the walls of the buildings were plastered with ads for gonorrhea and syphilis clinics; in China these flyers broke out like rashes wherever prostitution thrived. Down one of these alleys, I once looked through the window of a single-story building. Young women were sitting in the shadows with their heads bent over, sewing. That was a factory too, the worst kind.

The girls who worked at Yue Yuen seldom ventured down this way. The alleys did not open onto more streets of computer schools and hair salons: They ended in farmland. Just beyond the border of the factory world, men and women past middle age worked in fields of leafy green vegetables, under a cloudy sky that did not protect them from the glare of the sun.

THE TRADITIONAL CHINESE calendar divides the year into twenty-four segments and gives farming instructions for every two-week interval. The year begins with *lichun,* the start of spring on February 4 or 5 and the time for spring sowing. The calendar dictates when to plant melons, beans, coarse cereals, beets, and grapes and when to harvest rice, wheat, apples, potatoes, radishes, and cabbage. It predicts heat and heavy rains. It sets the proper time to protect crops from the wind, to kill pests and collect manure, to weed and to irrigate, to fix fences for livestock and to welcome in the new year. The calendar was standardized during the Former Han Dynasty—with regional variations, it has governed the rhythms of life on the farm for two thousand years.

The girls at Yue Yuen know nothing of the farming cycle. When they go home, their parents don't usually want them to work; if they help out in the fields, they suffer sunburns and blisters from the unfamiliar labor. One migrant worker described to me a typical day at home: She kept farmers' hours with the rest of the family but spent most of her day watching television.

> I get up at 6:30. I watch TV—*News Focus,* then the serials.
> I watch TV until one or two in the afternoon. I take a nap
> and walk around a bit. I eat dinner and go to bed at ten.

The global calendar of shoe manufacturing also picks up in the spring. The machines gear up in March and quicken in April, May, and June, turning out footwear ahead of the summer shopping season in the United States and Europe. In July—when the farmer's calendar urges moving fast to bring in the summer harvest before the rains come—the shoe industry falls into a lull. Orders drop to their lowest in August, with production lines sometimes running at only 20 percent of capacity. In September and October, business picks up and the machines run full-time in anticipation of the production crunch to come. November and early December are the go-for-broke periods, with everyone clocking lots of overtime to meet the Christmas rush. After the holidays, the cycle slows until spring comes again.

The girls know the seasons of the shoe intimately, and also its daily rhythms. On the cavernous factory floors of Yue Yuen, making sneakers is a science measured with stopwatches. A plastic sign in front of every station on the assembly line displays how many seconds a worker needs to complete a given task. It takes a Yue Yuen assembly line ten hours to make a shoe, down from twenty-five days four years ago, and the number of shoes produced per worker has gone up 10 percent.

The factory floor has its own hierarchy. The best jobs are in the development department, where workers produce small quantities of shoes for samples and don't have much production pressure. Cutters and sole-workers are next: As the first people on the assembly line, they set the pace and enjoy more freedom. The highest-stress jobs are in stitching and assembly, where workers are locked into the middle of the production chain. Pressure bears down on them from both ends—people up the line push work on them, while those farther down implore them to move faster. There is little room for error here: Quality inspectors and customers alike zero in on these lower sections of the assembly line, because it is easier to spot flaws in a finished shoe. The workers have a saying:

> *Those in stitching are scolded to death,*
> *Those in shoe assembly are worked to death,*
> *Those in cutting play to death.*

When Yue Yuen set up its first factory in China in 1989, South Korea dominated the global sneaker market. In its first decade here, Yue Yuen often worked employees through midnight and gave them a single day off each month. "As long as you gave the brands the goods at a certain price, they didn't care how you ran your factories," says Allen Lee, the head of Yue Yuen's manufacturing operation for Adidas in Dongguan. "We didn't talk about whether to pay overtime, or whether to put toilet paper in the bathrooms, or whether workers should wash their hands, or how many slept in each dorm. We used repressive management methods: This is your task and if you have to stay up three days and nights, you do it."

China's cheap, motivated workforce was suited to the labor-intensive business of sewing shoes, and in the 1990s China became the global leader. After the big American brands came under attack from unions and workers' rights groups for harsh conditions in their factories, Nike and Adidas began pushing their suppliers to improve the working environment. Yue Yuen changed to an eleven-hour workday and gave employees every Sunday off; many workers quit, complaining that the overtime pay was no longer enough. The company set up a business unit to oversee working conditions and a counseling center where workers could seek help and file complaints. It improved safety measures, banned hazardous chemicals, and abolished military-style calisthenics. Yet even as the brands have pushed factories to treat workers better, they are also pressuring them to cut costs. At times these goals work at cross-purposes. The Yue Yuen plant for Adidas used to issue workers' uniforms free of charge. Because of cost-cutting pressure from Adidas, Yue Yuen started charging workers for uniforms, but Adidas objected to this practice too. Yue Yuen abolished uniforms altogether, and workers now wear their own clothes on the job.

In 2001, Adidas initiated a program called Lean Manufacturing to increase efficiency and reduce waste at Yue Yuen. Workers say that while they work shorter hours now, the time on the line is more stressful; tasks are parceled out precisely and there is almost no downtime. Assembly lines have been restructured into small teams so workers can switch tasks every few days, whereas before they might have done the same thing for a month at a time. This makes production more flexible, but it is exhausting for the workers. Also in the name of efficiency, living arrangements have been reshuffled so workers live with their assembly-line colleagues rather than with their friends.

The accelerating pace of the global fashion cycle increases the pressure. A decade ago, the big athletic-shoe brands gave factories ninety days from receiving an order to delivering a product; several years ago it was sixty days, and now it is thirty days. Orders are getting smaller, to allow for a rapid response when fashions change, and workers live inside this unpredictable cycle. Only on Thursday does their boss tell them if they must work overtime on Saturday. During busy times, the sole department runs double shifts; employees take turns working the day shift one month and the night shift the next, their internal clocks scrambled and their bodies struggling to catch up.

Executives say that the demands of the market have only made Yue Yuen better. "If we didn't have pressure, we wouldn't improve," says Allen Lee. "As Darwin said, only the strongest survive." An Adidas study found that workers initially felt stress from the Lean Manufacturing program, but over time, the study said, they got used to it.

*   *   *

August is the time to irrigate corn and prepare to plant the winter wheat. Inside the Yue Yuen factory, a new season was starting earlier than expected: the long approach to Christmas. After the easy pace of summer, the girls were working overtime every weekday and all day Saturday. On the assembly line, they worked faster and talked less. But their bodies rebelled.

"I have the worst headache," complained Qianqian one morning in early August. "This is supposed to be the low season, but we have so many orders." The day before, she had turned twenty-two; she had planned to visit her best friend to celebrate but spent her birthday working overtime instead.

Down the hall in Room J805, Jia Jimei had returned to the factory from her visit home. She sat on her lower bunk, listless and unsmiling.

"How was home?" I asked her.

She smiled briefly. "It was good."

"What did you do?"

"Nothing. I thought about not returning," she said slowly, as if she were just waking from a dream. "But there is nothing to do at home. If there were something to do near home, it would be better to be close to home. But there isn't. I feel very uncomfortable being back here. I don't really want to go back to work again."

In the bunk above, Wu Yongli was more cheerful. She was nineteen years old, with pretty features in a slender face, and on this summer morning she wore an elegant black dress with spaghetti straps and a choker with a heart-shaped locket. "Don't mind her," Wu Yongli said. "She hasn't adjusted to being back yet." More jarring change was on the horizon: Once a year, the factory reassigned workers to new dorms. The purpose was to take into account people who had left or arrived during the year and to ensure that production teams were living together, but it turned everyone's lives upside down. "We already have friends here," said Jia Jimei. "Now there is a chance we will all be scattered again."

LATER THAT MONTH, the workers were transferred to new dorms. In a factory the size of Yue Yuen, girls who had seen one another every day suddenly did not know how to find their friends again. Many lost touch for good.

After the move, Qianqian disappeared, and I searched for her through September. I visited her new dorm many times—it was four floors down from her old one—but her roommates did not know where she had gone. They asked me for news of other workers they had lost touch with as well. I called Qianqian's family in a farming village in Anhui; her father told me she was still working at Yue Yuen. According to the factory, Zhang Qianqian, employee 28103, Number 8 Factory, Building B, Second Cutting Group, was still registered as an employee. On paper she was living in the dorm, working on the assembly line, cutting materials for the uppers of Adidas shoes. But in person she had vanished, a disappearance that mocked the rule of schedules and stopwatches that had seemed to order factory life so well.

*   *   *

From the gate of the Yue Yuen factory, down the main street, and through a maze of dirt roads lined with restaurant stalls and shops, there is a neighborhood of low red-tiled apartment buildings. The doors to the apartments are pieces of sheet metal. The area is pockmarked with vacant lots and half-finished buildings, and it feels at once overcrowded and abandoned. In the relentless delta summer, neighbors sat outside in their undershirts or pajamas playing mahjong, as chickens pecked in the dirt underfoot.

On a Sunday afternoon in mid-October, I was brought here by a young woman I had met in Qianqian's old dorm. She led me through the alleys, into a red-tiled building, up a flight of stairs, and through a sheet-metal door. We entered a one-room apartment with a double bed, and a poster hanging on the wall above it.

SUCCESS

Success feels very, very far from you, while failure in contrast seems to always follow you. You must bravely vanquish one failure after another, and then success will walk toward you.

Next to this poster was a picture ripped from a calendar of a topless woman holding a Grecian urn. Sitting on the bed, in a T-shirt, cut-off shorts, and bare feet, was Qianqian. When she saw me, she gave me a smile that was fleeting but also reluctant, as if she were not entirely happy at being found.

After payday in August, she had quit the Yue Yuen factory, walking off the line without permission and without the back pay that the company owed her. Since then she had stayed with various friends, including a young woman named Ge Li who shared this apartment with her boyfriend. She was thinking of going home or joining another factory.

"Why did you leave Yue Yuen?" I asked Qianqian.

"It isn't fun anymore," she said. And though I asked her several different ways, she would not say anything more.

IN THE WEEKS THAT FOLLOWED, production pressure in the factory continued to build as Christmas approached. In the country-side it was *lidong*, the beginning of winter, the time to fix fences for livestock. On a Sunday afternoon in November, I went by the red-tiled apartment building with the sheet-metal doors and asked Ge Li if she had news of Qianqian.

She hadn't seen her friend in a while. "She's still trying to decide between going home and rejoining the factory," Ge Li said.

"What exactly is she trying to decide?" I asked.

Ge Li shook her head. "I don't know what she's thinking in her heart. We haven't spoken about it." Ge Li had recently quit Yue Yuen and was planning to go home soon to introduce her new boyfriend to her parents. Once she left, there would be no way for me to find Qianqian anymore. Maybe this was what failure in the migrant world meant—not any incident or tragedy you could name, just a gradual drifting away, until a person was lost from view.

THE LAST TIME I went to Yue Yuen was in January 2005. The factory girls wore thin cotton jackets, their shoulders hunched against the cold. Being cold appeared to be a pragmatic decision: Winter in Dongguan did not last long enough to justify spending money on a warm coat. Jia Jimei was just returning to her room when I stopped by, and she smiled when she saw me. She had dyed her hair with dark crimson streaks.

Work in the factory had slowed once Christmas passed, and now the traditional calendar took over, filling the streets with festive crowds returning home for the new year. Migrants who had just arrived in the city often wandered solitary and lost, but the ones heading home were different. They walked with purpose, in groups; they looked happy, and they knew the way. They carried cash in their pockets and shopping bags of gifts for their families—CD players, comforters, candy for the younger children. At home on the farm it was *dahan*, the Great Cold, the season to welcome in the new year, but by the Dongguan calendar it was time to reap the rewards of a year's hard work. This was the only harvest that mattered now.

The parents of migrants had terrible instincts. At every stage, they gave bad advice; they specialized in outdated knowledge and conservatism born out of fear. Some initially forbade their children, especially their daughters, from going out at all. But once a migrant got to the city, the parental message shifted dramatically: Send home money, the more the better. Some parents pressured their daughters to marry, though only someone from their home province—which seemed as unreasonable as telling a person living in New York to date only natives of Ohio. On the job front, their advice was invariably bad: They warned against jumping factories, which was usually the best way to get ahead.

Migrants learned quickly how to deal with their parents: They disobeyed, they fought, and they lied. They kept their distance; Chunming did not go home during her first three years in the city. The girls were matter-of-fact about such transgressions. "They don't know how things are outside, so I do something first, and then I tell them about it," Min said. A new life began the day they arrived in the city, and they would do what they needed to protect it. The past did not matter, and the present was everything. Family was a trap that would pull you backward if you weren't careful.

After I moved to China, I had always resisted the pull of my own family, and perhaps some of the reasons were the same. My parents' China was fifty years out of date; the Chinese have always respected scholars and disparaged merchants, they had taught me as a child, but the people I was meeting now contradicted all of that. I didn't try to find relatives who were still living here. I wanted to learn about this country on my own terms. And family history seemed like a trap—a ready-made way to see China in tragic terms, a view that had little to do with how things were now.

Around the time I started meeting migrant workers in Dongguan, I began to investigate my own family history. Initially these were separate projects, a study in contrasts—there could be no common ground between the teeming chaos of the south China factories and the sober gray cities of the Northeast, with their steel mills and stone monuments aging and proud. I enjoyed the rhythms of these journeys as I shuttled south and then north, from the future to the past and back to the future again.

But the more I learned, the more I saw connections. Almost a hundred years ago, my grandfather had been a migrant too. He had left his village, changed his name, and tried to remake himself for the modern age. In his youth, China was emerging from a long, self-imposed isolation to rejoin the world—and so it is again today. My grandfather left home for good when he was sixteen years old— although he probably did not know it then, just as today's migrants might not know it now. *Chuqu*, to go out: This is how the story of my family also begins.

*   *   *

When I was growing up in America, my parents rarely talked about the past. There is a mode of exile that dwells on everything that was lost—the twilit boulevards of the capital city, the large house and the servants, the shaded garden with the persimmon trees where we will return one day when the regime falls and we reclaim what is rightfully ours. But the Chinese who fled the Communists seldom indulged in such reveries. Their way was to move forward and make a new life; to linger on loss was pointless. The migrants and immigrants I have known have shared this pragmatism, which seems so deeply ingrained in the Chinese character. The present is everything, and the past recedes.

As a child I heard only fragments of our family history from my father, and I turned them over and over in my mind until each fragment became its own story, mysterious and complete. The stories never connected, or they connected in a secret way I did not know.

The four best mining schools in America are in Michigan, Colorado, New Mexico, and West Virginia.

We carried the gold bars in our belts when we traveled.

We left our stamp collections behind when we fled the Communists. We left everything behind.

Every day I went to the American consulate in Taipei and waited for the officer to call my name.

China came in pieces, too. China was the sweaters that my maternal grandmother sent us from Taiwan, wrapped in mothballs and emerging from their cardboard boxes smelling like the insides of attics. Wearing one to school, I felt acutely that I looked different, *smelled* different, from everyone else. China was the Kuomintang newspaper that arrived in our mailbox from Taiwan, folded into tight bands that would spring open, as if in their eagerness to tell the news from afar. It was the Chinese Ping-Pong players with rubbery limbs and pasty faces whom my parents rooted for—to me, inexplicably—when the Olympics came around. China was, thrillingly, the vinyl records my father brought back from his first trip to the People's Republic of China in 1975, when Mao was still alive.

> *The sun in the east is rising,*
> *The People's Republic is growing;*
> *Our supreme leader Mao Zedong*
> *Points our direction forward.*
> *Our lives are improving day by day,*
> *Our future shining in glorious splendor.*

The song is called "In Praise of the Motherland." When I first heard it I was six years old, and the sunny Communist paradise it celebrated had disintegrated long ago. Yet even now the song's opening bars make me shiver.

I knew many of these songs by heart. Chinese was my first language, and its lullabies and ballads threaded through my childhood from its earliest days, like the memory of a life I had lived before this one. My father's family was from Manchuria, the region that the Chinese call simply Dongbei, the Northeast, and many of my earliest songs came from there. I did not feel a strong tie to China when I was growing up, but I knew I was from Dongbei.

> *My home is on the Songhua River in the Northeast*
> *Where there are forests and coal mines*
> *And soybeans and sorghum over slopes and fields.*
> *My home is on the Songhua River in the Northeast*
> *Where there are my compatriots*
> *And also my aging father and mother . . .*
> *I have fled my home village,*
> *Forsaken its inexhaustible treasures.*

Wandering, wandering,
Wandering all my days inside the pass.

The pass was the Shanhai Pass, an imposing stone fortress on China's east coast where the Great Wall runs into the sea. Built during the Ming Dynasty to guard China's northern frontier, it marked the point at which civilization ended and Manchurian wilderness began.

To me, the saddest song was about the Great Wall, sung by a Northeasterner exiled from home after the Japanese invasion. The wall's watchtowers and battlements had been constructed over centuries to protect China from its northern enemies. After the Japanese army overran Manchuria in 1931, the wall took on a different meaning—it delineated the lands that were under the Japanese yoke. The song was a tacit admission that the Great Wall had failed, because the enemy was already in Dongbei.

The Great Wall is ten thousand miles long
Outside the Great Wall is my hometown.
The sorghum is fat, the soybeans fragrant
Gold is everywhere, and calamities rare.
Ever since the great catastrophe started suddenly
Rape, plunder, and capture, miseries too bitter to bear
Miseries too bitter to bear, fleeing to unknown lands
Family pulled apart, parents dead
Remembering all my life the enmity and hatred
Day and night thinking only of returning home . . .

Let four hundred million compatriots rise together:
The Great Wall of our hearts will be ten thousand miles long.

My mother and father learned these songs as children, just as I did. The songs told the story of their parents' generation, living far from home and cut off by war from parents they would never see again. In the Chinese tradition, poetry conformed to a tight schematic pattern—at its best, the self disappeared inside the experience of the poem. Compressed in the verses of these songs was an emotion that was never spoken.

AFTER YEARS OF FRAGMENTS, snatches of song, and pieces of memory, I finally sat down with my father and asked him to tell me everything he knew about our family history. He told me about our family's rise from humble origins in the waning years of the Qing Dynasty. He described how badly my grandfather had wanted to leave home and see the world. He remembered the chaotic retreat from the Japanese army and the air-raid sirens that meant there would be no school that day. But my father's story was full of gaps: His memories of China were the memories of childhood, couched in a child's apprehension of the world.

> We were playing hide-and-seek. My father was taking a nap.
> I hid in the bay window on the other side of the bed from
> where he was sleeping, and I was afraid to come out. But he
> discovered I was hiding there, and he said, "Come out," and
> he played with us. That was my only memory of him.

I spoke with my father's brother and sisters, all of whom had emigrated to America in their twenties. An incident from half a century ago would be recalled differently, with each person's version fixed and distinct—pieces of China they carried with them that had hardened over time, like precious pebbles worn smooth. I met the part of my family who had stayed behind in China, including my father's cousins and distant relatives who had never left our ancestral village.

A few were trying to make sense of the past, but most were not—whether you had left China or stayed, it hurt less to let it go.

My relatives did not like telling their own stories. They often began by insisting they had nothing to say. Their narratives frequently opened with ignorance, a denial, even a death, as if to end the story before it could properly begin. Not one of them, it seemed to me, had faith that their memories mattered. *In fact, my experience of China was very shallow* was the first thing my aunt Nellie told me. *We don't know much about family history,* said my uncle Luke, *because we never had a chance to talk about it.* My father's story began with absence: *My grandfather's father. Nobody knew his name.* They brushed over details and they downplayed drama. Sometimes when they were relating something particularly painful, they laughed. Perhaps in a world where so many people had suffered, one person's story did not matter. Suffering only made you more like everyone else.

The young women in the factory towns of the south did not think this way. In a city untroubled by the past, each one was living, telling, and writing her own story; amid these million solitary struggles, individualism was taking root. It was expressed in self-improvement classes and the talent market, in fights with parents and in the lessons that were painstakingly copied into notebooks: *Don't lose the opportunity. To die poor is a sin.* The details of their lives might be grim and mundane, yet these young women told me their stories as if they mattered.

*   *   *

Sometime during the reign of the Kangxi emperor, maybe around 1700, a farmer named Zhang Hualong left his home on the crowded North China Plain for the Manchurian prairie, where virgin land was so plentiful that anyone could make a fresh start. In those days, every village in north China seemed to have someone who had migrated; then as now, it was often the younger and more enterprising people who went out. Zhang Hualong had two sons, who traveled farther north to settle in a village called Liutai, in the Manchurian province of Jilin. The site they chose was known as Pauper's Valley because of its poor climate and swampy land. Fourteen generations of Zhangs have lived there. I am of the eleventh.

As with Chinese migrants of the 1980s, the journey of my earliest known ancestor was not legal. In 1644, the Manchus, an ethnic group living on China's northeastern frontier, conquered China and established the Qing Dynasty. Soon after, the Qing rulers declared Manchuria off-limits to the Han Chinese, the majority ethnic group of the rest of the country. Their aim was to monopolize the region's natural resources and to preserve their homeland: As long as the frontier remained intact, they believed, their people would retain their vitality and forestall the corruption and decadence by which dynasties inevitably fell. To seal off Manchuria, the emperors ordered the construction of a two-hundred-mile mud wall planted with willow trees. It stretched from the Great Wall northeast through most of present-day Liaoning and Jilin provinces, with fortified checkpoints along its length.

The border was called the Willow Palisade, and it was even more porous than the Great Wall. It was completed in 1681, and perhaps twenty years later my ancestor breached it to settle in Liutai, which means "sixth post"—one of the fortified towers along the border that was built expressly to keep out people like him. The Chinese who entered illegally to farm were called *liumin*, wanderers. Over the next two centuries, my pioneer ancestors farmed—planting sorghum and soybeans, and living in log cabins surrounded by primeval forest.

In the latter part of the nineteenth century, Manchuria's population began to swell as farmers from north China fled drought and famine. This migration, of twenty-five million people over the next half century, would be the largest in the country's history until the present wave. The region's economy boomed, new railroads linked the interior to coastal and foreign markets, and foreigners spouted prophecies as breathless as those heard today. In 1910, the British consul-general posted in Tianjin wrote:

> There is little doubt that Manchuria is to become, in the not far distant future, a competitor of America in supplying agricultural products for the markets of Europe. The flour mills of Harbin . . . are placing their products upon the local markets at prices with which it is impossible for American mills to compete . . . What the United States may lose through diminished sales of farm products must more than be made up through increased trade in manufactured goods.

My family rose to prominence in this economic boom. My great-grandfather, Zhang Ya'nan, bought an oil press and a flour mill and used the money from these ventures to become the biggest land-owner in Liutai. Around 1890, Zhang Ya'nan oversaw construction of a family compound with five central rooms and eight wings. The ancestral tablets and portraits occupied the central rooms, while the living ate, worked, and slept along the sides. That was how a Chinese family lived—the dead intruding on the living, and filial devotion built into the very architecture of the houses. The compound was named Xinfayuan, which means "New Origin." It was surrounded by high walls, with Mauser pistols mounted at each corner and an armed militia to protect against bandits. The measure of a family's prosperity was in the food they ate, and at Xinfayuan even the hired hands dined on steamed buns filled with sweet bean paste. Portions were so generous that they inspired a song whose lines my father would recall a century later.

Xinfayuan, a fine place
The dogs lead the way, the people bring the food,
Two and a half jin of bean-stuffed buns.

In the last years of the Qing Dynasty, my great-grandfather was awarded a degree in the imperial civil service and given three hundred taels of silver by the imperial court to build an ancestral temple. This was standard practice: Once someone became an official, he had to observe the proper Confucian respect for his ancestors. My great-grandfather took four wives—also standard practice—and set up a school inside the family compound for his nine children, both sons and daughters, to attend. Perhaps because of my great-grandfather's rise, the court awarded his own father an imperial military title, general of the third rank of the Qing Dynasty, and gave the family money to build a memorial arch praising his filial piety. Thus was created an illustrious family pedigree out of nothing at all. A farmer became a general, and a mill owner a government official: Here on the frontier, molding a new life did not take so long.

My great-grandfather fulfilled the other duties of a Confucian patriarch. He oversaw the writing of a family genealogy that stretched back to the ancestor who had migrated to Manchuria. And he laid out a sequence of names that his descendants would carry for the next twenty generations, which together formed a poem.

Feng Li Tong Xing Dian
Hong Lian Yu Bao Chao
Wan Chuan Jia Qing Yan
Jiu Yang Guo En Zhao

The phoenix stands in the palace of prospering together
The swan connects and nurtures the dynasty of treasures

*Ten thousand generations pass on the continuing family
    celebration
Nine ornaments display the favor of the nation.*

My family prospered late, coming into glory at the very moment
the Qing way of life was ending. The estate, the temple, the tablets
and portraits and relics would all be destroyed in the tumultuous
century to come; many lives would be cut short. But not everything
was laid waste. My Chinese name is Tonghe: The first character in
my name was decided a century ago by a great-grandfather I never
knew.

*   *   *

In the village where my grandfather Zhang Chun'en was born
in 1899, almost everyone shared his family name. As a child he
attended the family school, where he memorized long passages
from the Four Books and the Five Classics dating to the time of
Confucius. That he did not comprehend a word of these texts
was unimportant; education was intended to shape a child into
proper behavior, imprinting him early with the virtues of obedience,
respect, and restraint. The ultimate aim of learning was to pass
the civil-service examination and become an imperial official—
a system that had persisted, virtually unchanged, for a thousand
years.

But this world was already breaking apart by the time my grandfather was a boy. The nineteenth century had seen traumatic en-
counters with the West; following China's defeat in the Opium
Wars of the 1840s and 1850s, the monarchy was forced to sign a series of "unequal treaties" that opened ports to foreign trade and gave
legal and economic privileges to the Western powers and Japan. Re-

formers blamed traditional education for China's humiliating decline. Their efforts led to the abolition of the civil-service exam in 1905 and the spread of schools that taught modern subjects. In 1911, when my grandfather was just entering his teens, the Qing Dynasty collapsed and a republic took its place.

Even as a child, my grandfather was determined to leave home—then as now, all paths to success led away from the village. His older brother, whose name was Zhang Feng'en, would someday run the family estate. But as the second son of the first wife, my grandfather was in a privileged position: He could go away. In the spring of 1913, he enrolled in the Jilin Provincial Middle School. It was the first school in the province to teach what was called the New Learning, which dispensed with the classics in favor of mathematics, history, geography, and the natural sciences. He left home three years later to attend Peking University, the head of a national network of modern schools.

Most of the students there came from the wealthy merchant families of the coast; my grandfather was an outsider, like a scholarship boy from a Colorado mining town showing up at Harvard. But as a center of progressive learning, the university also attracted other ambitious young people from the provinces. One contemporary of my grandfather who worked in the school library was Mao Zedong. My grandfather likely struggled with the New Learning. In the Peking University archives, I found a book bound with string that listed, in spidery calligraphy, the exam results for pre-law students in 1917. Foreign subjects were not my grandfather's strong suit.

WESTERN HISTORY: 70

ENGLISH LITERATURE: 70

CHINESE LANGUAGE: 80

LOGIC: 90

BEHAVIOR: 100

If the traditional value system had been intact, my grandfather would have obtained the highest university degree and gotten a job in government. But the New Learning was taking him in unexpected directions: My grandfather won a provincial scholarship to study in America, so he quit school after his sophomore year. He married a young woman named Li Xiulan who had been chosen by his family—three days after the wedding, he boarded a ship for America.

My grandmother was then studying at Peking Women's Normal College, one of the first colleges in the country to accept female students. She majored in physical education and music; she marched in student protests and smoked cigarettes and chose a new name, Li Xiangheng, because it had more unusual characters than her old one. After graduation she taught high school in Jilin City, the provincial capital.

For seven years she wrote letters to America, the land that had consigned her to spending her twenties alone, and the land that would later claim her children, one by one. Her letters have not survived. All that remains of the young woman she was is contained in a few terse sentences in my grandfather's diary, like the bright flash of a forest animal glimpsed through the trees: her solicitude, loneliness, sparks of ill temper.

> Xiangheng plans to return home because my mother is sick.
> I bought a pair of shoes to send home for Xiangheng.
> In Xiangheng's letter she creates an uproar, saying she has suffered a great wrong.
> I got three letters from Xiangheng, all urging me to go home. Because my own plans are not finished, I cannot return yet.

My grandmother wished to go to America too, but my great-grandfather laid down the law. Foreign countries were not for women, he said. A woman should stay home.

*   *   *

January 1, 1926

China's internal chaos is a cause of much worry. China will surely have one day when it is prosperous. I will see this in my lifetime. Every person must work hard for the coming of this day.

My personal conduct must be honorable and in my dealings I must be more frugal.

I had lunch with my landlord, Harry Weart. His neighbors, an old couple, like to play with dogs and birds and they spoke of their pets. I am disgusted by this kind of talk.

My grandfather arrived in America in 1920. It was the era of bathtub gin, petting parties, and Al Capone, but he barely noticed. In the pages of his diary, he wrote about his search for a proper course of study and about the political situation in China. These two subjects were connected: By acquiring the right skills in America, he would learn what was necessary to help his homeland become a modern nation. He flirted with literature and economics before settling on mining engineering: Industrial development would be China's salvation.

During his seven years in America, the situation back home deteriorated. The national government basically ceased to exist, as warlords with personal armies fought one another across the country. In my grandfather's American diaries of the 1920s, the people who loomed largest were the Chinese warlords Wu Peifu and Zhang Zuolin.

January 26

Zhang Zuolin has already set free Ivanov [the Russian director of the Chinese Eastern Railway], so the Harbin question is temporarily resolved. The cause of the incident in Harbin was directly related to Feng Yuxiang's return to the Northeast. One man favors an alliance with the Russians and the other with the Japanese, but each is pursuing his own interest.

China still does not have a person who manufactures machinery. To have it begin with me in the future would be a most wonderful thing.

January 28

Today there was heavy snow and winds and the roads were almost impassable. My colleague Backland got married today at five o'clock . . .

Manchuria and Mongolia have become one of the world's big problems. If we don't handle this properly, it will be hard to prevent their becoming a second Korea. This is the homeland of my ancestors. How can I offer it up to someone else? I swear that I will take the defense of the territory and the welfare of the people there as my own responsibility.

March 4

My glasses were broken so I went to the eye doctor for a new pair. They cost twenty-four American dollars. So expensive!

Jilin's forests are naturally suited for manufacturing paper, and Jilin exports large quantities of leather products each year and even more of fur, while its railroads are very convenient. I will look into working in the paper industry.

June 4

I did surveying at Mount Franklin today. The trees were lush and fragrant and the air fresh. The early mornings are very cold and at night my throat itches . . .

If China wants to become prosperous and strong, it must develop its steel industry; otherwise it cannot resist the encroachments of foreign nations. Right now its machinery relies entirely on imports. If a war begins and resources from the outside world are cut off, then China will surely be defeated.

November 12
I cleaned a coal-cutting machine today and took it apart. It was most interesting.

To govern a nation and teach its people, or to occupy a place, one must have good propaganda. To rely solely on military power will lead to defeat.

Thousands of Chinese students went to America during the first two decades of the twentieth century, the first large wave of people to go abroad for study. They saw Western learning as the best way to help China, and they gravitated toward practical subjects like economics, the natural sciences, and especially engineering—the chosen major of more than a third of the Chinese students in America between 1905 and 1924. My grandfather attended the Michigan College of Mines, in an old copper-mining region near the Canadian border. He graduated in 1925, thirty-third in a class of forty-four; apparently the New Learning was still giving him trouble.

I CAME UPON my grandfather's diaries by accident. My father said that the family had abandoned everything they owned through the years of the Second World War, the civil war, the flight to Taiwan, and the trip to America. More than a year after I started researching our family history, I was talking on the phone with my father and I asked him if he owned anything that had belonged to his father. Unexpectedly, he said he had two diaries, one from my grandfather's time in America and the other from when the family lived in Chongqing during the war. They ran close to a thousand pages.

"It isn't very interesting," my father said. "He just writes things like, 'Today the Japanese army is closing in around the city.' Stuff like that."

"Actually," I said, "that's pretty interesting."

Through the pages of his diary, I came to know the grandfather I had never met in life. He was a young man searching for a purpose, dreaming of a wide range of careers. He found and quit jobs about as often as the migrants did, quickly growing bored and anxious that he wasn't learning enough. He was lonely and adrift.

> July 14
>
> In the factory when I have free time, I think of all kinds of troubles. I feel like a single boat floating on the great ocean. Even if the heart desires quiet, it cannot be.

> November 18
>
> I have worked almost two years. Sometimes I feel I am not interested in it. But you must handle work yourself even if it has no interest for you. Now with China's situation so bad, this is precisely the time for men to make a firm resolution to establish their own enterprises. I must try hard 120 percent.

Self-improvement was a constant theme in the diary. After he finished his schooling, my grandfather spent two years doing practical training at mines and factories in the Northeast and the Midwest. He enrolled in a Chicago night school to study electrical machinery. The diary entries bristle with alien English words he was trying to learn: *Goodman Standard Shortwall Machine. Ratio of cement sand and slag. Pyramid Pump Open Hearth Mixer Blast Furnace Cor-rugated Underframe Door.* He copied down inspirational advice from the titans of American industry.

> Marshall Field's Ten Things Worth Remembering
> 1. The Value of Time
> 2. The Success of Perseverance
> 3. The Pleasure of Working
> 4. The Worth of Character
> 5. The Dignity of Simplicity
> 6. The Improvement of Talent
> 7. The Joy of Originating
> 8. The Virtue of Patience
> 9. The Wisdom of Economy
> 10. The Power of Kindness

From afar, his family pressured him to come home. Reading my grandfather's response in his diary—*My desire to return home is strong, but my studies are not finished yet*—reminded me of Chunming, who had expressed an almost identical thought in hers. *Who knows why I am not going home for the new year? The main reason: I really do not want to waste time. Because I must study!*

But at heart these journeys were different enterprises. The factory girls go to the city to improve their lives; my grandfather left home so he could return one day and better serve his country. You could say that my grandfather left home *for* home, while the girls leave home only for themselves. Chunming in her diary never stopped circling her favorite subject, which was herself: how the city was changing her, how others might see her, and the minute details of her physical appearance: *My eyes do not have double eyelids,* she wrote, *but they are not too small. Their being single-lidded has not affected their vision. I don't have thin lips but my mouth can speak persuasively. I speak loudly and boldly, not gently, but this has been my nature from birth.* Through hundreds of pages of his diary, no such self-portrait of my grandfather ever emerges. The entries read like classical poems—terse and controlled, the individual implied but never visible.

During his time in America, my grandfather changed his Chinese name. The chosen characters of the new name, Shenfu, appear to come from an ancient phrase, *shenshenzhengfu,* which translates as "many diligent men drafted into service." That was what my grandfather aspired to be: an army of men, dedicated to service, the self disappearing inside the name.

*   *   *

My grandfather returned to China in the summer of 1927. On his first day home, his father organized a celebration in the village for his favorite son, who had brought honor to the family by going all the way to America. On the second day, the patriarch took out a wooden rod called a *jiafa*—used in traditional households to discipline children and servants—and beat him with it. In America, his son had switched from studying literature to mining engineering without parental approval, never mind that his father was seven thousand miles away and understood nothing of the American university system. In a Chinese family, a father's word was law. The beating was so severe that my grandfather could not sit down for several days.

His father wanted him to stay home and help run the estate, but the young man resisted: He hated the entanglements of life in the family compound and he was glad to escape. He took a job as head of mining affairs at the Muling Coal Mine near Harbin, in the far northeast of the country.

In 1931, the Japanese army marched into southern Manchuria. Within six months, the military had seized the entire region and established the nominally independent state of Manchukuo, which was essentially a Japanese colony. As the Japanese moved in, my grandparents fled "inside the pass," south of the border that divided Manchuria from the rest of China. In 1937, the Japanese army invaded China proper, advancing along roads and railways to capture cities in the north and the east. Unoccupied China moved inland, and my family with it. Home in Manchuria became a distant place that the children would know only in stories and songs.

> *I have fled my home village,*
> *Forsaken its inexhaustible treasures.*
> *Wandering, wandering,*
> *Wandering all my days inside the pass.*

THE WAR SET IN MOTION a million migrant journeys. During the eight years of the War of Resistance Against Japanese Aggression, as the Chinese call the Second World War, the nation's capital moved twice—from Nanjing to Wuhan, and in late 1938 to Chongqing, deep in the southwest, so far beyond the reach of modern communication and transport arteries that the Japanese army could not follow without endangering its supply lines. From its mountain stronghold, the Chinese government held fast and waited for the Allied armies to defeat Japan.

When the war broke out in 1937, my grandfather helped ship equipment from a coal mine in the province of Henan, where he was factory manager, more than five hundred miles inland to Sichuan Province. As an official with the National Resources Commission—a government agency charged with building up the country's industrial base for the war—he was sent to far-flung mining areas to oversee the production of strategic commodities. He usually went first and wrote to my grandmother when it was safe to follow.

Each of their five children was born in a remote mining town. Nellie, the oldest, was born at the Harbin coal mine where my grandfather worked after returning from America; my uncle Luke and my father came into the world in a coal-mining region in central Henan Province. Coal in Sichuan, my aunt Irene; mercury in Hunan, my uncle Leo. The isolation of these places traced my grandfather's idealism. Most students returning from abroad lived in the big cities, but my grandfather thought his work might matter more in the backward parts of the country.

Personal ties fell away—in the confusions of war, the easiest thing in the world was to lose touch with someone. The family might arrive in a new place, enroll the children in school, then leave a few weeks later. In his six years of elementary school, my uncle Luke told me, they moved seven times. Communication with family back in the village was difficult; letters home to Manchuria had to trace circuitous routes behind enemy lines. More astonishing was how people found each other again. One day toward the end of the war, a handsome college student named Zhao Hongzhi walked into a canteen for mining bureau employees in Chongqing and recognized my grandfather. His family and mine had been friends a decade before in the Henan coal mines. Zhao was invited home to dinner and began to court my aunt Nellie, whom he had known as a child.

Family also reconnected in the course of the war. While my grandfather's older brother had stayed home to manage the estate, his son, whose name was Zhang Lijiao, went to Beijing to attend school while my family was living there. In traditional Chinese families, brothers and paternal cousins are regarded as equally close. My grandparents gave Lijiao a home and paid for his schooling; from the time they were children, my uncle Luke and my father looked up to "Big Brother Lijiao." When the family moved to Chongqing to escape the Japanese advance, Lijiao went with them.

The war was a frustrating time for my grandfather. War caused death and ruin but also missed appointments, work stoppages, and broken-down buses. Occasionally he wondered whether his work was worth the effort.

> July 17, 1940
> These few years have passed quickly without much mean-
> ing. First, I have no friends, because I have lived so long in
> the mountains, separated from the outside world. Second, I
> have no ideals in life, knowing only about mines and min-
> ing work. What is the ultimate aim of life? I have not de-
> cided yet. Forty-two years have passed in this way. This is
> worthy of pity and regret.

In the summer of 1939, my great-grandfather Zhang Ya'nan fell ill and returned to the family homestead from Jilin City, the provincial capital. The patriarch of a prominent family could expect a grand funeral, but my great-grandfather left instructions to be buried in a white cloth robe, a white hat, and straw sandals—the austere garments of a monk. The hat was to be inscribed with the phrase *baohen zhongtian*: "holding regret until the end of time," expressing sorrow that his homeland was still under Japanese occupation. My grandfather did not learn of his father's passing until the next year. Ensuring the proper burial of one's parents was a chief duty of a filial son, but war had made a return home impossible.

> March 24, 1940
> I was surprised to learn that my elder had passed away on
> the fifth of the month. Last summer he developed a stom-
> ach tumor. During the three months of winter, he could eat
> only milk powder substitutes each day. In his illness, he
> longed for us. This year he is seventy-five years old. He was
> always in good health and could have lived to be eighty or
> ninety. Only because of our country's calamities, his spirits

were unhappy and hurried his end. We can live no longer under the same sky with this enemy . . .

After September 18, 1931, I left home. It has been nine years already. Both my grandfather and my father have passed away. My life has seen so much change. To be a son and a grandson, how can I repay my country, how can I repay my grandfather and father!

Already forty-five years old when the Qing Dynasty fell, Zhang Ya'nan had lived long enough to see the world he knew disappear and be replaced by one where daughters wished to travel and sons left their aging fathers to work in strange places. He had not agreed with these choices; perhaps when his son left home there had been anger or bitterness between them. But the traditional Chinese diary was not the place for personal revelation, and the son did not write about these things.

*   *   *

My family was living in Chongqing when the Japanese surrendered in August 1945. A top priority for the government was regaining control of Manchuria's well-developed industrial infrastructure; my grandfather and a friend and colleague named Sun Yueqi were appointed to oversee the return of the Northeast's mines into Chinese hands. The region's chief asset lay beneath a remote town called Fushun—the country's largest coal mine and the largest open-pit mine in the world at the time.

It was a dangerous assignment. The war was over, but another one was just beginning. The conflict between the KMT government and the Communists—barely kept in check during the war years—was coming into the open, and the Northeast was shaping up as a key battleground. The Communists had the upper hand: Aided by Soviet troops that had entered the Northeast in the final days of the war, Communist guerrillas moved quickly into Manchuria to seize territory and war matériel left by the departing occupiers. On the other side of the country, the KMT soldiers in their wartime base of Chongqing could not get back fast enough.

Sun Yueqi was initially named to handle the return of the Fushun mine, but he made excuses, claiming business elsewhere, and recommended that my grandfather go in his place. The assignment must have felt like destiny to my grandfather. Here at last was a task that would redeem the disparate roles he had played in life: overseas student, mining expert, Manchurian exile, Chinese patriot. My grandfather accepted the assignment, although he did not tell my grandmother where he was going. On his way out of Chongqing, he stopped to say goodbye to his daughter, my aunt Nellie, at the high school where she boarded. She was fifteen years old, and she didn't think much of it; all her life, her father had been leaving to go somewhere for work.

He arrived in Shenyang, the Northeast's largest city, on January 7, 1946—his first time back in his homeland in fifteen years. An old friend named Dong Wenqi, who was now the city's mayor, warned my grandfather to be careful. "You are coming from Chongqing," Dong Wenqi said. "You don't know what things are like here." My grandfather was also cautioned by a contact from the Soviet side. The Russian told him to wait until the security situation in Fushun improved, and for a week my grandfather lingered in Shenyang.

Then the rumors began: He was afraid to go out, people said; he had come all the way to Shenyang to do nothing. On the morning of January 14, his boss at the Northeast Economic Commission telephoned to inquire about the stalled mission. Angry at the implication of cowardice, my grandfather set out for the mine that day with about six mining engineers and some guards from the local railway.

At the mine, they became virtual prisoners, watched over by Soviet soldiers and Chinese Communist police. In two days they accomplished nothing, and then they were told to leave. On the evening of January 16, my grandfather and his team, still under guard, boarded a Soviet train back to Shenyang. At nine o'clock that night, armed soldiers boarded the train at a deserted station west of Fushun. They ordered my grandfather and his colleagues off the train and marched them to a nearby hillside. In the dark winter night, surrounded by Manchurian wilderness, the soldiers stabbed them to death with bayonets.

My grandfather said a few words as he was dying, according to a newspaper account of the time. "I am from the central government," he said. "To die for my duty, I have no complaints."

*   *   *

In Chongqing there was no news. One day, my grandmother went to the temple to inquire about the fate of her missing husband. A temple visitor would throw two pieces of wood until they fell in a certain combination, and then draw a bamboo stick printed with a number. That number corresponded to a fortune, expressed in a poem whose meaning was often ambiguous. The fortune came with a ranking, ranging from "very best" to "very worst."

On that day, my grandmother's fortune turned up "very worst." And the meaning of the poem was so clear that my father, who was ten years old, would remember and recite it to me sixty years later, word for word:

> In past days while sailing the rudder was lost,
> Today still searching in the middle of the sea.   ·
> Even if the original thing could be found once more,
> It would cost much effort and weary your heart.

In Shenyang, rumors spread that my grandfather and his six colleagues had been killed. Dong Wenqi, the mayor and my grandfather's friend, received a phone call from the Soviet military commander in the area. Dong Wenqi visited the headquarters, and forty years later in his memoirs, he recalled the scene:

> I saw a truck parked in the middle of the yard with a coffin inside, wrapped in black cloth. I jumped onto the truck and opened the coffin; without a doubt, it was Shenfu. He was still wearing the dark-blue Zhongshan suit he and I had had made together in Beiping [Beijing]. His body had been stabbed eighteen times.

My grandfather's body was washed and photographed; the pictures showed multiple bayonet wounds and rope marks where his arms had been bound. His coffin was brought to the Temple of the God of War in Shenyang, where it was put on display for three months. *The bloodstained clothes in which he had been stabbed eighteen times hung in the temple for people to view,* Dong Wenqi wrote, *in order to strengthen their feelings of bitter hatred for the enemy.* Photographs of his corpse were widely disseminated, also for propaganda purposes. When news of the assassination broke in February 1946, student demonstrations in major Chinese cities demanded the evacuation of Soviet troops from Manchuria. In Chongqing, an estimated twenty thousand students protested the killings and the Soviet presence in the Northeast. Half a world away in Fulton, Missouri, on March 5, Winston Churchill gave his famous Iron Curtain speech and cited Soviet actions in Manchuria as an example of its hostile intent.

The murders were never solved. The KMT maintained that the Communists had killed my grandfather and his team, as a warning to the government to stay out of Manchuria. The Communists, in turn, said the KMT had staged the assassination to turn public opinion against the Communists. The Soviet Union blamed the act on local "bandit gangs." No one claimed responsibility for killing a group of unarmed civilians—a cowardly deed that also seemed a distinctly Chinese political act. The purpose was unstated but the message was clear just the same: The old war was over, a new one had begun, and my grandfather's death was the first of many to come.

THE CHILDREN REMEMBER how they heard the news. On a winter afternoon, their mother was called away to the house of a friend. When she returned, she went into her bedroom and began to weep so loudly that the children could hear her. Then she came out of the room, gathered her children around her, and told them their father had been killed. "Don't worry," their mother said then. "I am here." She told the children they would never see her cry again.

After my grandfather's death, my grandmother entered public life—in some ways, the broader stage suited her strong-willed personality. She was selected to serve as a National Assembly representative and spent much of her time in the capital city of Nanjing. At one point, she set up a coal distribution business to supplement the family income. She had spoken the truth: The children never saw her cry again. But her hair turned gray and she started smoking heavily; overnight, it seemed to the children, she became old. The prophecy at the temple had been right in that too. *Even if the original thing could be found once more, it would cost much effort and weary your heart.*

My grandmother always believed that the Communists had killed her husband. She said that Sun Yueqi, my grandfather's friend who had not gone to Fushun, should have died in his place. But Sun Yueqi was a survivor. He ended up defecting to the Communists in 1949—a banner year for defections—and heading the Revolutionary Committee of the Chinese Kuomintang, a toothless party that existed to maintain the fiction that China was not a single-party state. Years later, my father told me, he heard from him again.

> After I was in America, working at IBM, Sun Yueqi sent me
> a Christmas card. He said he wanted to see me the next
> time I came to Beijing.
>   I never saw him. I refused to see him.

Sun enjoyed a long career in government, and he lived to be 102 years old.

* * *

The funeral was delayed for more than a year. After the civil war officially resumed in the summer of 1946, battles raged around the village of Liutai; the area changed hands three times in the first year of the war. Finally the government decided to bury my grandfather in a Shenyang park that housed the tomb of the first emperor of the Qing Dynasty. Only the three boys got to attend the funeral, a fact my aunt Irene would recall with indignation sixty years later. The journey to attend their father's memorial service marked the first time my father, Luke, and three-year-old Leo traveled "outside the pass" to Manchuria. The boys' cousin Lijiao, who had become a lecturer at Peking University, also accompanied my grandmother.

The funeral procession had an armed escort. It was rumored that the Communists wanted to extinguish the entire family, a punishment from imperial times known as *miemen*. More than ten thousand people lined the route, pressing close to pay their respects and look on the heavy sandalwood coffin. My father, who was ten, remembered being thrilled at the crowds. In the imperial park at Beiling—which meant "northern tomb"—my grandfather was laid to rest near the "spirit walk," a path lined with giant stone statues of human and animal courtiers that were to serve the emperor in the afterlife. A small piece of black marble inscribed with the words TOMB OF MR. ZHANG SHENFU was the only grave marker. To the right of the tomb was erected a tall slab of stone known as a stele, which traditionally would be carved with the story of a person's life, praising his talents and deeds.

The government had drafted an inscription for the stele that blamed the Communists for my grandfather's death. But my family rejected this official judgment. Lijiao, like most young intellectuals of the time, was a fervent Communist supporter who disagreed with the government version of his uncle's death. My grandmother also opposed the official history, though her reasons were pragmatic: She believed the Communists might win the war. A tablet accusing the Communist Party of political assassination would not fare well under the new regime. Better, she thought, to say nothing at all.

After the funeral, in late 1947, my family moved to Beijing. The next year, the Communists would capture Shenyang and with it the Northeast, but by then my family would be fleeing to Taiwan. After the Communist victory, Lijiao would be transferred to Harbin and the country would be swallowed by political movements that would rule out independent travel. There would be no family left in Shenyang to look after my grandfather's northern tomb. And the stele next to his grave would remain blank for close to half a century. Over the years, the people in Shenyang who knew its story moved away or passed on. City residents came to refer to the tomb as *wuming bei:* the stele with no name.

*   *   *

The Communist revolution swept into Liutai in the summer of 1946. Party organizers fanned out to villages across Manchuria, evaluating every family's "class status" and confiscating land and livestock from rich households to distribute to the poorest ones. A second wave of land reform, the "Dig Out the Cellars" movement in the fall of 1947, sought to root out additional property that families had hidden away. Party activists taught villagers to denounce landowners in public meetings that were known as "struggle sessions"; their chosen targets were cursed, humiliated, and beaten. The third wave, in the winter of 1948, was the most extreme and ended in the deaths of countless "enemies of the revolution." The escalating violence was seen as essential to breaking the old system. *In correcting wrongs*, Mao Zedong wrote in a 1927 essay on peasant revolt, *it is necessary to go to extremes or else the wrongs cannot be righted.*

In Liutai, Communist activists and villagers attacked our family estate of Xinfayuan. They tore down the wooden eaves of the buildings and set fire to the books in the library; they took my grandfather's collection of mineral samples from his student days and threw them in the river. The new village government commandeered the east wing of the estate's main hall for its office, while the west wing was turned into a storehouse and a place for grinding rice. Several poor families moved into the west wing and the back hall, where members of my family had formerly made offerings to their ancestors.

Zhang Feng'en, my grandfather's older brother, fled the village when the attacks began and went to live in Beijing with Lijiao and the rest of the family. Feng'en had been the firstborn son and the lord of the manor all his life, but in Beijing this status was meaningless. My grandmother criticized his backward ways and his idleness; she railed at his habit of spitting on the floor. He suffered these rebukes in silence. In the capital, he knew his place: He was just an old man from the countryside who had outlived his birthright.

The children liked him, though. When they were alone, he would tell them stories of a grand family estate they had never seen.

"Did you have many concubines?" the boys asked eagerly, but only out of their mother's hearing.

"No, only my father had many concubines," the old man answered with a touch of regret.

The coming of the revolution to rural villages like Liutai set the pattern for the mass movements of the Communist era. Political campaigns would come in waves, each one more extreme than the last; acts of violence were applauded as proof of revolutionary purity. History does not say much about the 1940s land reform and the lives it ruined, perhaps because later movements played out in the cities and claimed more prominent victims. And historians have not paid attention to people like my great-uncle, who was forced to flee his home and live out his days as a guest in someone else's house. His wife fared worse. When her husband escaped to Beijing, she stayed behind in the village. That was as it should be: A woman should not travel. A woman should stay home. My great-aunt was beaten to death, most likely by people she had known all her life, in one of the surges of revolutionary violence that engulfed my family village in the late 1940s. I don't even know her name.

*   *   *

My father's map of Beijing is different from mine. Several years ago, he and my mother visited me there and we drove into the countryside northeast of the city. In the car, my father smoothed out a road map and read aloud the names of towns: Gubeikou, Xifengkou. These had been famous passes on the Great Wall built by the Ming emperors; I knew them as tourist sites that were overrun on summer weekends. To my father, these were the places that surrendered without a fight, one by one, as the People's Liberation Army tightened its net around Beijing when he was twelve years old.

"There was no battle for Beijing," my father told me. "Do you know why? The generals stationed here had never been loyal to

Chiang Kai-shek. They went over to the Communists without a fight."

It was the autumn of 1948, and my grandmother was right: The Communists were winning the war. As the military defeats and the defections piled up, people looked to the peripheries of the country for escape. The island of Taiwan, one hundred miles off the coast of China, was one possible refuge; the Shanghai merchant families favored the British colony of Hong Kong. Some people talked about a retreat to the southwest, which had saved China during the war against the Japanese: From mountain bases in Chongqing and Guangxi Province, on China's border with Vietnam, those who fled there might one day fight their way back into the heart of the country.

Families splintered before the Communist advance. A father might depart with the older children while their mother and younger siblings stayed behind, or a family would leave its youngest child in the care of grandparents while the rest went on ahead. These separations were thought to be temporary—everyone expected the KMT to regain the military initiative before long. My grandmother agonized over where to go. Again she visited the temple, and the bamboo sticks told her: Go to Taiwan.

In the autumn of 1948, Chiang Kai-shek and his wife, Soong Mayling, went to Beijing. They toured the Summer Palace, a vast park on the city's northwestern outskirts that had been built by the Qing emperors as a refuge from the summer heat. Zhao Hongzhi, the boyfriend of my aunt Nellie, happened to be visiting the Summer Palace that day. He took a photograph of the president of China and his wife as they walked for the last time through the gardens and pavilions and beside the lake lined with willow trees. The next year, with much of the country already lost, Chiang Kai-shek moved the nation's capital back to its wartime base of Chongqing. Many families moved with him, and then the capital was shifted once more, to the nearby city of Chengdu. Finally in December of 1949, Chiang Kai-shek boarded a plane for Taiwan, where he would set up a new government, leaving behind many of the people who had followed him to the end.

NOT EVERYONE WANTED TO LEAVE. My grandmother invited Lijiao and Zhao Hongzhi to accompany the family to Taiwan, but they both turned her down. Zhao was a college student and Lijiao a professor; like many intellectuals of the time, they supported the Communists and looked forward to building a new nation. My father and my uncle Luke were too young to have political views. Zhao and Lijiao were old enough, and that maturity sealed their fates.

My aunt Nellie, according to family lore, wanted to stay behind too. A junior in high school, she was torn between the wishes of her family and her Communist sympathies. She was also in love—her boyfriend, Zhao, believed in the revolution and planned to stay. But he convinced Nellie that she must leave, to help her mother with the four younger children. The two of them agreed that wherever they ended up, each would place a "Seeking Person" advertisement in the biggest newspaper in the city so they could find each other again.

"That is nonsense!" said Nellie, when I related this version of the story to her recently. "He wanted me to go to Taiwan with the children and then come back to China."

As the oldest child in the family, Nellie had always been her father's favorite. She accepted that exalted status as her birthright, but she had learned to keep her own counsel. When I asked her if she had wanted to stay behind that autumn of 1948, she brushed me off. "I didn't care whether I left or not," she said, "but I had all this responsibility to take care of the younger children."

One summer afternoon in Beijing, I visited Zhao Hongzhi, her old boyfriend. He was eighty years old and he had just moved into an apartment complex down the block from my own. His wife was home and I met her for the first time. No emotion showed on her face as she greeted me: the niece of her husband's old girlfriend, arriving to talk about that long-ago love affair.

In the living room, Zhao spoke carefully about his childhood and his acquaintance with my family. His wife moved through the apartment and finally settled down at the adjoining dining room table to read the newspaper. Occasionally she rustled its pages to let us know she was still reading. The air conditioners in the new apartment had not been hooked up yet, and the place was sweltering.

"Was Nellie involved in Communist activities?" I asked Zhao.

"No," he said. "She was still in high school."

"But I had always heard she didn't want to leave China."

"She didn't want to leave China."

I ventured a look at him. Zhao sat perfectly straight on the couch—as stiff-backed as a young cadet, and arrogant in this knowledge. Silently he pointed to himself, his thumb aiming at his chest like a dagger that has found its target. In the next room, the newspaper was silent.

THAT AUTUMN OF 1948, the National Assembly was still in session. My grandmother was in Nanjing, trying frantically to spirit her children out of Beijing as the Communist troops moved on the city. Boat tickets to Shanghai were sold out, and the municipal airport had closed. My grandmother paid a visit to a general in the air force name Zhou Zhirou, where she played the only card she had. "My husband died for our country," she said, "and I need to get my children out." The children left Beijing for Nanjing on a DC-3 military transport plane, which took off from a city street that had been converted into a makeshift runway. That was one of the last flights out of Beijing in October 1948.

Zhao Hongzhi went with my family to see them off. He was riding home on his bike when the DC-3 roared overhead, carrying away his love like the last scene in *Casablanca*. Years later, he wrote in an essay:

> I saw off my childhood sweetheart, who was then attending Tianjin Nankai Girls' Middle School. When the plane took off and passed overhead, I was just returning from the airport, passing the Beijing Zoo on my bike. I had told her I would go to the liberated areas in one week. At the time, I thought this behavior was heroic and handsome.

Zhao received one letter from my aunt, from the island of Taiwan. Nellie had decided to major in foreign languages, a subject that Zhao had deemed suitable for women. He did not hear from her after that—there would be no contact between Taiwan and China for four decades. After Nellie left, Zhao quit college and traveled with fellow students to the "liberated areas" outside Beijing that were already under Communist control. He changed his given name to Lisheng, which meant "establish a life": It was common during the revolution to take a new name that symbolized a break with the past. The following winter, the students marched alongside Communist soldiers when they entered the capital. Zhao found a job in the city education bureau. During the Anti-Rightist movement of 1957, which targeted intellectuals critical of the regime, he lost his job as a college professor and was sent to the countryside to do manual labor. He stayed twenty years. He was already in his fifties when he regained his job and his Communist Party membership. By then he no longer wanted to be in the Party, but he didn't dare turn it down.

I never heard Zhao say that he regretted staying in China. It was not the Chinese way to speak of regrets—there would be too many, and there was no point. In an obscure way, he seemed proud of this choice that he had made, and its memory remained golden, unsullied by everything that happened afterward. "I wanted to stay, to help China," he told me. "We were very idealistic then. Who can say we were wrong?"

*   *   *

The ship that brought the civil war refugees to Taiwan was called the *Prosperity*. Nellie went first with the three boys and a family servant who had been my father's wet nurse, whom the children called Mama Wang. The voyage took two days and two nights, and almost everyone was seasick. When the ship arrived in the harbor of Keelung in Taiwan, Nellie could see her father's former colleagues and students who had come to meet them at the pier. But nobody was allowed off the ship without a proper identification card—even during the chaotic final moments of the civil war, the Chinese bureaucracy churned on—and none of the children had paperwork. Nellie was frantic. Then she noticed some of the ship's crew carrying luggage off the ship from a side exit, and she took the children that way. Mama Wang hung back; she had bound feet and was afraid of losing her balance on the narrow walkway. "You have to walk, or we will go back," Nellie commanded, and Mama Wang obeyed. The ship actually returned to China with many of its passengers still on board—they became residents of Communist China, having come within a few feet of Taiwan. My grandmother and my aunt Irene made it to Taiwan two weeks later.

The island was never home to them; from their perspective, it was only a way station until the day they recovered the mainland again. The refugees from China were called *waishengren*, people from the outside provinces. They lived apart from the native Taiwanese and never picked up the local dialect. In school, their children learned by heart the mountains and rivers of China and sang songs about a Great Wall they might never see. *The Great Wall of our hearts will be ten thousand miles long.* The country of their childhood and their ancestors became the province of memory, a place to be re-created in the imagination.

My father lived in Taiwan for eleven years, almost as long as he had spent in China. When he told me the story of our family, China took several hours; he dispensed with Taiwan in three sentences.

> We lived in Taipei for about six months, then moved to Taichung. We ate chicken only at the lunar new year and two or three watermelons in the summer. My mother was a legislator when she died.
>
> One by one, we came to America.

The government had set up a donation fund to support the family after my grandfather was killed. My grandmother had used the money to buy gold bars and Chinese government bonds; the bonds became worthless, but the gold sustained the family for years. *We carried the gold bars in our belts when we traveled,* my father would remember. Because they were children of a national martyr, the government covered their college tuition and even paid for school uniforms.

On the fourth anniversary of her father's death, Nellie, who was then a college freshman, wrote a poem that was published in the *Central Daily News,* the newspaper of the KMT:

> Four years now, Father,
> The grass on the grave is taller now,
> The plains of the north country are once again covered in
>   snow,
> Ah, your child wandering on the island in the sea
> Is sending her heartfelt longing to you.

The things that have been lost
Can be found again,
But what I have lost
Is my father's love,
Clothes that are torn can be mended,
But, ah, this is
A heart that is torn!

January 16, four years ago today,
That day when people sang the song of victory,
You became the first sacrifice of the handover,
Liaoning, the Fushun Coal Mine—
The place where no one dared to go,
But you . . .

Perhaps it is just as you often said,
"To live, you must live with strength,
To die, you must die with purpose."
"A road is made by the steps of man,
Success depends on your hard work" . . .

Yes,
The tears that will never stop flowing,
The telling of bitterness that will never end,
The blood debt that will never be washed clean,
The wound that will never be healed,
Turn suffering into strength for living then!

But I hate it!
Father.

Many people wrote her letters saying they were moved by her poem.
One young man who called himself "Wastrel" sent Nellie several

verses of his own. His poems passed over her own grief; her father's killing, he wrote, should inspire everyone to the task of building the nation. The young man didn't know Nellie's address, so on the envelope he wrote simply: Zhang Ailei, Taipei City, National Taiwan University.

To shout out is madness
Only silence is strength
To roar out grievance is to lose heart
Only the iron in the furnace can become steel.

On the eve of the storm
There are no waves on the sea
In deep places
Running water makes no sound

Gather up your suffering
Even a pen can become a gun

It is hatred
It is a blood debt
Oh, what a debt!

It is not only yours
It is not only his
It is not only mine

It belongs to everyone
Who has bones
Who has flesh and blood
Who has human shape, and a heart

Who has a soul
It belongs to all of us!

Nellie saved the poems; she thought they were better than her own. The next year, the young man came to National Taiwan University as a freshman and the two of them met. His name was Zhao Yanqi, and he eventually became her husband.

*   *   *

These were bad years for my family who stayed behind in China. In 1950, the year after the Communist victory, my father's cousin Lijiao married a nurse named Zhu Shulan and they moved to Harbin, where he worked as a professor at an agricultural college. They had two sons and a daughter. In 1957, Mao Zedong gave a speech inviting intellectuals to criticize the performance of the Communist Party. Lijiao, who was then the head of the college dean's office, publicly suggested that the Party should value intellectuals for their skills and knowledge. A person's level of education, he said, was not a measure of his revolutionary commitment.

It was a modest statement—but in the context of the times, it was poison. The country's leaders, surprised by mounting critiques of the Communist Party and even of Mao himself, turned against the very people they had encouraged to speak out. More than 500,000 people were labeled "Rightists" and fired from their jobs or sent to do manual labor in the countryside. Lijiao lost his dean's position and had his salary cut. His crime of candor was compounded by his origins: His father and grandfather had been landowners in Manchuria, and his uncle's family had gone to Taiwan. This family history would make Lijiao forever suspect in the eyes of the Party.

By the time Lijiao's children started elementary school, they already understood that their bloodlines were bad. On every form they filled out in school, there was a blank for "class status." The children would write "Landlord," conjuring a phantom family estate that had disappeared long before they were born. Teachers bullied the sons and daughters of landlords; children taunted one another in the vocabulary of class struggle: *Your father is a Rightist! Your family are landlords!* China under Mao was an aristocracy in reverse: Pedigree had always been a national obsession, but now the higher a family's standing had once been, the worse off it became.

The Cultural Revolution, which began in the summer of 1966, completed this overthrow of the established order. For more than a century, Chinese leaders and thinkers had wrestled with how to fit their traditions into the modern world. The Cultural Revolution proposed a simple answer: Throw everything out. Over the decade that followed, radical student groups known as Red Guards beat, and sometimes killed, their own teachers. Seventeen million students went to the countryside to labor on impoverished farms, a life that rural Chinese had been fleeing for centuries. Education, long the mark of achievement and the path to mobility, was deemed "counterrevolutionary." The Cultural Revolution took everything the Chinese people had long held sacred and smashed it to pieces, like an antique vase hurled against the wall. It finished off the world of moral certainty and Confucian values into which my grandfather, and countless generations before him, had been born.

And what took its place? For a while, radical fervor was enough. But when the Cultural Revolution finally ended and pragmatic leaders like Deng Xiaoping took over, the Chinese would find themselves living in a vacuum—stripped of all belief and blank as newborns, looking upon a ruined world they must somehow make anew.

In 1968, Red Guards came to my grandfather's tomb in Shenyang. They dug up the coffin and scattered his remains; they smashed the tomb and the grave marker. They beat the base of the stele until it cracked, but they left the stele itself intact. No one seemed to know what it was—its blank face revealed nothing.

* * *

One after another the children went to America, as their father had before them. But my grandfather had gone overseas in order to someday return and help China. His children left home to develop their careers—and there was no China to return to anymore. The money for emigration was partly borrowed from friends, partly paid for in slices of gold, the money that had been donated to the family after my grandfather was killed. His death was transmuted into the journey to America.

> In those days if you wanted to come to America [my father told me], you needed $2,400 to be in a bank until you graduated. My older sister went without much problem. We gathered together $2,400 through savings and borrowings. She spent some of it, but she made up the money and returned the $2,400 so Luke was able to go to America with the same money. They were four years apart. But Luke and I were only two years apart, so when it came time for me to go, the money had not been replenished yet . . .
>
> There was a yellow box where we kept the gold bars, and gradually everything was gone. We went to borrow money from friends, but no one wanted to help us. My father was already gone: Why should they help us?
>
> I was the one to go out and borrow the money. I remember going to one family friend's and sitting in their house. They ignored me. Finally, they said the father is not here, but I knew he was having lunch.

After the money was in hand, the next task was getting a visa. Anyone leaving Taiwan had to pledge to the officers at the American consulate to return as soon as his or her schooling was finished.

> I graduated from college in 1957 and did a year and a half
> of military service. I finished the military in January 1959.
> Every day I went to the American consulate in Taipei with
> a novel and waited for the officer to call my name. Then
> around five o'clock he would call my name and say it's too
> late. After six months, I got it at last.

My grandmother pushed her children to leave. She felt that Taiwan was too small; America was the only place for further education. But the journey by ship across the Pacific Ocean was too costly to be taken more than once. Every time she said goodbye to a child, she knew it was for the last time.

An ocean away, her children continued to do what was expected of them. The girls had more freedom to study what they wanted; Nellie majored in education and Irene in English. My father, who had the sharpest tongue in a family of fluent talkers, was drawn to politics and the law. But the boys were expected to study science and engineering, like their father, and like all the best students who went abroad. When Luke graduated from high school, his mother said to him, "What do you want to study? I hope you will follow in your father's footsteps." Luke agreed that he would. His mother gave him a book called *Field Geology*, a thirty-year-old textbook that his father had used when he was studying in America. And that ended the only conversation Luke ever had with his mother about his future.

My grandmother knew her children's strengths and weaknesses and she told them so. Nellie was smart but lacked persistence for the medical profession she wanted to pursue. Luke was stubborn and would be good in academia. My father was smart but talked too much for his own good. Irene was diligent but a crybaby. Leo was a poor student, but he would be good in business. All of these divinations turned out to be true. Nellie gave up medicine and became an elementary-school and special-education teacher; Luke grew up to be a geology professor and department head at the University of Maryland. My father studied electrical engineering and later switched to physics; he did scientific research at IBM and served as a dean and vice president at the Hong Kong University of Science and Technology. Irene, who cried often as a child from the teasing of her older brothers, toughened up and became an executive in the pharmaceutical industry and later headed a biotech company. And my youngest uncle, Leo, became a successful and wealthy entrepreneur in Taiwan. In this way, my grandmother decided the fates of all her children.

MY GRANDMOTHER DIED of emphysema in 1965. Irene was visiting her in Taiwan that summer; her brothers and sister had pooled their money to pay for the trip back. On her deathbed, my grandmother called Irene to her. She had saved all the money her children had sent from America, and she wanted it to go to her youngest son. Leo was the only child who had not gone abroad. Because his four older siblings had all broken their pledges to return to Taiwan, the American consulate had refused to grant him a visa. My grandmother told Irene where to find the clothes in which she wanted to be buried. "Dress me in them now," she said, "because it will be harder after I am dead." She had managed everything, all the way to the end.

*   *   *

My father returned to China for the first time in 1975. He was a member of a delegation of physicists selected by the U.S. Academy of Sciences—one of the first American delegations to China, at a time when the two countries did not have diplomatic relations. Science was seen as neutral ground, with no need for government involvement—it was science that had taken my father to America, and science that brought him back. My father was thirty-nine years old. He had left mainland China when he was twelve, and it was a new country he was looking at now. At a national athletics meet, he was thrilled when the announcer called out "Jilin Province!" He heard the cheers, and it seemed as if all the anti-China propaganda he had been taught in Taiwan fell away at that moment. "I felt like this at last was really China," he told me. "All those years they said that Taiwan was China, but this was really China."

He saw remnants of the radical era that was now ending. My father's delegation toured a commune—a fake one, he learned later, that had been set up to impress visitors. On visits to school campuses, my father was amazed to see students talk back to their teacher. This was a result of the Cultural Revolution but still, he felt, an improvement on the old ways. One day my father visited his old middle school, which was half a mile east of the Forbidden City. As he peered through the gate, a man wearing slippers and a T-shirt came out to talk. He was the head of the school's revolutionary committee, a position akin to principal in those days. The man had a question: "How many hours is the train to America?"

My father requested to meet with his cousin Lijiao. He told his delegation's handlers that his cousin had taught at Peking University in the late 1940s but he had no idea what had happened to him since. The answer came back that Lijiao had been sent to the remote northwest and couldn't see him. It was a lie, my father learned later—Lijiao and his wife were living in the Northeastern city of Harbin—but it would have been politically dangerous for them to meet a foreign visitor then.

The Cultural Revolution was in its final stages, but it could still do a lot of damage. The country's premier, Zhou Enlai, was hospitalized with cancer; the Gang of Four, a leftist faction identified with the worst excesses of the Cultural Revolution, was in charge. One day my father was surprised to hear his government handlers say that Deng Xiaoping, the Party official most committed to modernization and reform, would soon be deposed. His handlers were so worried about their own futures that they let this slip in front of my father. The following April, Deng was purged from the Party leadership for the third and last time. In our house in suburban New York, we listened over and over to the records my father had brought back from China.

> *The sun in the east is rising,*
> *The People's Republic is growing;*
> *Our supreme leader Mao Zedong*
> *Points our direction forward.*
> *Our lives are improving day by day,*
> *Our future shining in glorious splendor.*

My father returned to China for the second time in 1979. The United States and China had established diplomatic relations; Deng Xiaoping was firmly in charge, rehabilitating the millions of victims of the Cultural Revolution and launching economic reforms that would soon change the face of the country. My father again requested to meet with Lijiao, and this time Lijiao and his wife were brought to Shenyang to meet him. When my father's train pulled into the station, he could see Lijiao waiting on the platform, and he saw that he was crying.

Lijiao wanted to know everything that had happened in the intervening thirty years. My father told him how hard life had been in Taiwan, how his mother had raised five children alone and most of the family friends dropped off after their father died. Lijiao talked about how much better life was under the Communists. He did not tell my father that he had been paraded through the streets as a class enemy when the Cultural Revolution began, and later sent to work on a rice farm near the Soviet border. He did not mention that his two sons were just then returning to the city after ten years of rural labor, or that neither of them had gone past the eighth grade. He did not say how his mother and father had died.

At one point, Lijiao's wife asked my father, "Do you know what has been happening here in China?"

"Yes," my father answered. "More than you do."

My father returned to China often, as scientific exchanges between China and the West picked up. In 1982, he stayed with Lijiao's family in Harbin; Lijiao's younger son remembers my father standing up a few minutes into the evening news broadcast and saying, "I can't watch this fake news." In 1984, my father stood on the rostrum at Tiananmen Square during celebrations to mark the thirty-fifth anniversary of the Communist revolution.

After I moved to Beijing in 2000, my parents visited at least once a year. I sometimes felt that they had forgotten how to deal with Chinese people. They lacked patience for the endless small talk and petty courtesies that were the basis of social interaction, and they put off visits to relatives who I knew were waiting anxiously for them to call. Occasionally they embarrassed me: My father once referred to a friend's cleaning lady as a *yongren*, literally "a person who is used," an old word for servant that had not been heard since the Communist revolution. But they still knew everything about Chinese history, language, literature, and culture, and by some mysterious extrasensory ability they always knew which were the best restaurants in town.

When I tell my family story to American friends, they ask me how my father could go back to China and spend time with officials from the party that murdered his father. When I lived in Prague, I met the American-born children of Czech émigrés, who were so opposed to the Communist regime that they had refused to teach their children to speak Czech growing up. The Cuban exiles are so virulently anti-Castro that they will not return as long as he is in power. But Chinese immigrants are different: No matter what terrible things happened to their families in China, they go back, on whatever terms the government allows. This is in part the pragmatism that runs so deep that it excuses the past, but it is more than that. China to them is not a political system or a group of leaders, but something bigger that they carry inside themselves, the memory of a place that no longer exists in the world. China calls them home—with the weight of its tradition, the richness of its language, with its five thousand years of history that sometimes seems to be one repeating cycle of tragedy and suffering. The pull of China is strong, which is why I resisted it for so long.

*   *   *

The house was at no. 6 Fenzi Hutong. Face Powder Alley: During the Ming Dynasty, this had been one of Beijing's red-light districts, named after the heavily made-up prostitutes who lived here. The house was now the Flourishing Garden Home for the Aged, a nursing home run by the local Communist Party branch. It was a one-story red building with yellow ceramic roof tiles, on an alley of crumbling courtyard homes. I opened the front door, walked through a dim hallway, and came into what was once the central courtyard of a traditional Chinese house.

Sixty years ago, my father had lived here. This had been his family's last home before they left China in the autumn of 1948. And this was where, on a cold and clear afternoon in January 2004, I started my investigation into my family history in China. My guide was Zhao Hongzhi, the eighty-year-old man who had once dated my aunt Nellie. The courtyard was roofed over now, and the trees that once graced it were gone. A lattice of fake ivy and plastic flowers spread across the ceiling. Two old men sat under it reading newspapers; one was bent over with a humpback that gave him the shape of a question mark.

Zhao walked into the courtyard behind me. He pointed to a row of rooms on the left. "That's where the kitchen was." He pointed to the right. "Those were the bedrooms."

"Please speak quietly," a nurse urged us. "It's their rest time."

Zhao pointed again, as if tracing the ghostly imprints of people only he could see. "That's where your grandmother slept. Sometimes I slept in the living room right outside her bedroom. I was her godson, you know."

WE LEFT THE HOUSE at no. 6. A sharp wind was blowing, and Zhao walked fast with long strides. He was tall, with silver hair, a high nose, and well-defined cheekbones that had been drawn with a precise hand; at the age of eighty, with all the suffering he had endured, no one would begrudge him a long rest at the Flourishing Garden Home for the Aged. But he had other things on his mind.

"You know about my matters with your aunt?" Zhao asked.

I said yes, feeling embarrassed.

"She married Zhao Yanqi, your uncle. They have won many prizes for ballroom dancing. Me, I can't dance at all," he said, as if this single failing had thrown him off course.

We walked a few blocks to his apartment. His wife was out of town for a few days, and he was in an expansive mood. He took out a manila envelope of photographs. The first one was a black-and-white studio portrait of my father and his siblings on the eve of their departure from China. Zhao stood in the back row, handsome and serious in fine-rimmed glasses; beside him, Nellie looked very much a child with her round face and fuzzy sweater. My father, in front, had a skinny dark face and his head cocked to one side, wearing the quizzical look of children that seems to ask how they suddenly came to be in this world. Another photo: my aunt on the covered walkway of her house in Ottawa, already in her sixties, elegant in a form-fitting Chinese dress in ivory splashed with red flowers.

"Does your wife mind?" I asked.

"She is very open." As evidence, another photo: he and Nellie standing together. "She even allowed us to have our picture taken together."

Zhao Hongzhi had failed to marry into my family, but he had become the guardian of my family history. When my aunts or uncles came to Beijing, they always paid him a visit. When a distant relative in our family passed away, he was the first to know. And when I wanted to see the house at no. 6, my father told me that I should meet Zhao Hongzhi, because he still lived in Beijing and only he would remember the way.

I think my family was the link to a life he could have had, if only everything had been different. Zhao had carefully protected that tie through decades of political turmoil. When he chose the name Lisheng at the time of the revolution, it symbolized more than his newfound political commitment. The character *li* was used by all the males in my father's generation of our family. The political statement concealed a personal meaning: Zhao was reborn as a Communist and as a member of our family.

We acquired the house at no. 6 in a strange way. During the war, it had been used by the occupying Japanese army; later it was taken over by Sun Yueqi, my grandfather's friend who had not gone to Fushun. After my grandfather's death, Sun Yueqi sold the house to my grandmother at a low price. Perhaps this was his form of penitence, although he never said as much.

Twice my family lost this house. We lost it in October 1948 when we fled China, and we have lost it again to economic development. The old house was torn down and rebuilt as a restaurant, then a kindergarten, later a local Communist Party office, and now a nursing home. Residents pay one hundred dollars a month, and there is space for thirty beds where my family once lived. The current tenants will also have to go soon: The home is set to be demolished to make way for a subway line.

In the 1990s, my family applied to the city government to get the house back, under a law allowing for the return of homes seized during the Cultural Revolution. The city rejected the request but paid ninety thousand dollars in compensation. The family split the money seven ways: to my father and his four siblings living abroad, to Lijiao's family, and to a great-aunt in Beijing. The money did not mean so much to us. But my great-aunt's daughter was planning to go to America to study, and the money helped pay for her trip. For almost one hundred years, my family has been leaving China for America. My grandfather came back, and his death bought the house at no. 6; half a century later it was turned into yet another journey to America. And that was fitting, because the history of a family begins when a person leaves home.

No one in the factories of Dongguan had been properly educated for the task at hand. In the past, education in China had always been focused, and paths were clear. During the Qing Dynasty, a male heir read the Four Books and the Five Classics in order to qualify for the imperial civil service. In Taiwan, my father and his brothers had studied science so they could go to America. During the Cultural Revolution, students in mainland China memorized their Little Red Books in order to survive Mao's political campaigns. But there was no curriculum for Dongguan. The factory world was a place without tradition or pedigree, and people had to learn how to redefine themselves. Most young men and women had cut short their schooling to go out to work; the college graduates I knew had majored in subjects laughably remote from their current jobs. A schoolteacher who had studied political education trained factory managers, while a reporter at the local paper had studied accounting and worked in forestry management. Viewed from Dongguan, the needs of the Chinese economy were changing so fast that the education system was not even trying to keep up anymore.

But if the national curriculum was irrelevant, commercial schools thrived in the city. On nights and weekends, their dimly lit classrooms were crowded with teenagers in factory shirts, all of them cramming the skills they had never learned in school. English and computers were the most popular subjects, but there were also lessons peculiar to the city's manufacturing economy. Some lectures focused on how to make plastic parts; seminars were conducted on the topic of injection molding. Such classes did not impart a comprehensive body of knowledge—usually they taught students just enough to talk their way into jobs for which they had no real qualifications. That was the key to Dongguan education: Whatever else you needed could be picked up later.

You don't know everything you need to know, the teachers reminded their students over and over. *But through doing you will learn it.*

One young migrant woman told me she was studying at a school run by the Suren Enterprise Management Consulting Company. The name, Suren, stuck in my mind: It meant "molding people." Classes taught assembly-line workers how to behave in an office setting; graduates sought jobs as secretaries, clerks, and sales assistants. "In four months, we raise their quality," Huang Anguo, an executive at the school, told me when I met him for an interview. "We are the only school doing this kind of training." The 680-yuan tuition—about a month's salary for an ordinary worker—included four softcover textbooks that Huang handed to me with what seemed like reluctance:

ENTERPRISE MANAGEMENT
BUSINESS SECRETARIAL SKILLS
ETIQUETTE AND QUALITY
SOCIAL INTERACTION AND ELOQUENCE

The curriculum was so groundbreaking, Huang told me, that his teachers had not been able to find suitable textbooks, so they wrote these up themselves. He invited me to sit in on a class. I told him I was interested.

You must grab the opportunity or you will always be a step behind.

The next day I visited another school, run by the Dongguan Zhitong Talent Intelligence Development Company. Its White-Collar Secretarial Skills Special Training Class also targeted factory girls who wanted to move up into the office world. "We developed our own educational materials to teach this group of people," Liu Lijun, the manager of the training department, told me. Then he presented me with a set of textbooks:

ENTERPRISE MANAGEMENT

BUSINESS SECRETARIAL SKILLS

ETIQUETTE AND QUALITY

SOCIAL INTERACTION AND ELOQUENCE

I did not tell Liu Lijun that I had just visited a rival school with an identical business plan. I did not suggest that one school might have stolen the other's curriculum; in any case, it was more likely that both had copied it from somewhere else. I simply thanked Liu Lijun for the books and accepted his invitation to sit in on a semester of the White-Collar Secretarial Skills Special Training Class.

Respect the opinions of other people and do not casually point out their mistakes.

*　　*　　*

I went out when I was fifteen. First I worked in sales in a city near home. Then I came to Dongguan, where I was an ordinary worker and then an assistant at the Shijie Yaxin Television Factory.

In a factory with one thousand or ten thousand people, to have the boss discover you is very hard. You must discover yourself. You must develop yourself. To jump out of the factory, you must study.

You are here because you don't want to be an ordinary worker with a dull life. If you are waiting for your company to lift you up, you will grow old waiting.

The speaker's name was Tian Peiyan. She was seventeen years old, and she wore a blue blazer and a red-striped tie, as if she had just stepped out of a catalog for a New England boarding school. When she spoke, her thin cheeks flushed and she breathed audibly in cadence with her sentences, like someone running a race. If it seemed strange for a teenager to warn an audience about growing old, Tian Peiyan was persuasive: A former Zhitong student, she now worked as an educational consultant to the school.

Another speaker, Chen Ying, worked on the assembly line of a company called VTech, which made cordless telephones. She had a broad face and full lips; already twenty years old, she was in a great hurry to improve herself. People in the factory sometimes said to her: "You are so old and still an ordinary worker."

I am the same as you. I graduated from middle school. I worked on the assembly line until I became numb. I didn't even know what I was thinking about.

One day, I asked a friend: "What is life all about? Why are we working so hard?" My friend could not answer.

I went to look in books. They had no answers. I thought, "If you work on the assembly line, is there meaning in life? No."

So I started to take this class. In one month I learned a lot. I could not even say a single word in front of other people before. I was shy and afraid. What do you think of my eloquence now?

I think you all want to learn what I learned. Leave the assembly line. Don't let people look down on you any longer. Don't let people say, "You are the lowly workers." We must lift up our heads and say, "We can also be successful."

On warm spring evenings in 2005 after workers had returned to the city from the new year holiday, the Zhitong school recruited students for its White-Collar class. Teachers held free information sessions at sites around the city where the classes would be held. Sessions stretched over several nights; they were invariably packed. Some potential students attended again and again, agonizing over whether to enroll.

Recent graduates stood up and talked about how they had left the factory floor behind, relating their stories of transformation like born-again converts at a revival meeting. Time on the assembly line had left them ignorant and numb—*mamu*, a word that was chilling when spoken by a young woman still in her teens. They discovered the White-Collar class, and the class let them discover themselves. I once was lost but now am found. I now make 1,200 yuan a month as a clerk. *What do you think of my eloquence now?* But every triumphant testimonial had an undercurrent of warning: Change soon or it will be too late.

A lot of our students jump to new jobs even before the three-month course is up. Some of them are making 1,200 yuan a month. The investment return is one to five hundred.

If you do not work hard these two or three years, you will

spend your whole life at the lowest level of society. When you are twenty-four or twenty-five and are starting a family, your mate may also be an ordinary worker. Together you may make one thousand yuan a month. But if you move up, the person you marry may be a manager. Your whole world will be different.

The chief organizer of the class was named Deng Shunzhang. He was forty years old, and he had come to the Pearl River Delta after a zigzag career back home in Hunan Province that included teaching high school, working in local government, selling newspaper ads, and running a store that sold music cassettes. In Dongguan he had managed factories—toys, shoe soles, fake Christmas trees, and plastic Santa Claus figurines—but he did not look like a typical factory boss. He had dark kind eyes in a trim face the color of a walnut; he spoke deliberately, with the precise gestures of a Peking opera performer, and he never raised his voice. No matter what the weather, he always wore a suit, a sweater vest, and a tie.

Teacher Deng was the first kind adult many of the migrants had met in Dongguan, and during information sessions they asked him questions they had long harbored in secret. *How do you deal with sexual harassment from your boss? Is China a capitalist or a socialist country? If someone yells at you and you cry, does this mean you are a weak person?* Teacher Deng answered each one patiently. He left the hard sell to the former factory girls under his charge.

You will grow old waiting.

Leave the assembly line.

You must discover yourself.

I am the same as you.

More than two hundred young women signed up for the spring session of the White-Collar Secretarial Skills Special Training Class. Each student paid 780 yuan in tuition up front—more than a month's salary for many of them. They would attend class three nights a week over the next three months. That was plenty of time to become someone else.

*   *   *

Classes met on the sixth floor of an office building across from the VTech cordless-phone factory; the school's ground floor was a store selling mobile phones. VTech and a nearby Pioneer plant that made DVD players together employed sixteen thousand workers, a huge pool of potential students with stable working hours. Like everything else in Dongguan, education revolved around the demands of production. Classes ran from 8:30 to 10:30 at night so they would not interfere with overtime. If one factory's workday ran later, teachers would hold a makeup session for those who missed class.

In the evenings after ten-hour days on the line, the factory girls would head to school. The streets around the plant teemed with stalls selling fried snacks, fruit juice, hair accessories, and padded bras with cups the size of grapefruits. The stalls were strung with bare lightbulbs, and against the humid night they gave off a hard bright glitter like a carnival midway after the sun had gone down. The girls fought their way through the mobile-phone store, which was garishly lit and always crowded, and past a giant advertisement of three women in bikinis on a beach. Each woman wore a tiara and cradled a mobile phone, taunting the girls with pleasures deferred: sex, glamour, the newest Nokia.

The classroom had low metal stools and child-size desks that the students sat in two by two. An ad for the White-Collar class dominated the back wall, with a secretary in a revealing miniskirt under the slogan TRAINING RAISES COMPETITIVENESS. Even the bathroom, with its single squat toilet and a water spigot that emptied onto the floor, came with etiquette instruction: IN ORDER TO AVOID EMBARRASSMENT, PLEASE LOCK THE DOOR BEHIND YOU.

Each class began with a pep talk from Liu Jieyuan, the principal
of the school, who spoke with the forced cheer of a person selling
cookware in a late-night television infomercial. On the first day of
the semester, he surveyed the class of twenty-five young women and
said, "I would like to ask you not to wear your uniforms to class."

"But we come straight from the factory," one student objected.

"I want you to try your best and not make excuses. Okay?"

That day's lesson was "Raising Etiquette Attainments and Displaying the Charm of Character." Teacher Fu was an earnest-
looking young man in a white dress shirt, black pants, and a tie; all
the teachers were required to wear ties to class. There were many
other rules that the students would need to master over the next
three months, but Teacher Fu began class with a story.

"What is your dream? The middle person in the last row."

A girl stood up. "From the time I went out . . ." She slumped,
looking this way and that, frozen with fear at being singled out.

"Stand up properly," Teacher Fu told her. "Have confidence."

She stood straighter, slumped again, started, stopped, and finally
said in one breath, "From the time I went out, I wanted to be a sales
department assistant."

The class applauded. The girl sat down.

"Okay," the teacher said, "I'll tell you what my dream was."

> When I was a child, I liked history very much. I wanted to
> be in the history books. I wanted to make a great contribu-
> tion to the motherland.
>
> When I became older, I realized this was not practical.
> Then I decided I wanted to stand in Tiananmen and salute
> the three armies. But I decided maybe I will not achieve my
> dream. Being in Tiananmen saluting the soldiers is not real-
> istic for someone from the countryside. I will leave that to
> future generations.
>
> Later I decided I would bring my family from the coun-

tryside to the city: to raise my children in the city and to let them develop further. When you raise yourself up, you will lift up your family one level.

I believe that you have come to Dongguan for the same reason. We bear the same burden on our backs. We all want to move our families from the countryside to the city, to make this contribution to our families. Isn't this right?

If you walk out of the countryside, you will lift up your whole family. Your parents will be different because of your achievement.

Since I have come to Dongguan, I have experienced many setbacks. Many times I have felt like going home. But you must persevere. If you go back, it will be like you never came out at all.

He turned to the blackboard behind him and wrote: *How to mold a good etiquette image: Clothing.*

"The color of your clothing is very important. Now I will tell you what kind of character people will think you have when you wear different colors. Please write it down."

Red represents enthusiasm.
Orange represents excitement.
Yellow represents brightness.
Purple represents mystery.
Green represents freshness.
Black represents calm.
White represents purity.
Blue represents propriety.

Teacher Fu covered a lot of ground that first day. He gave tips on how to build confidence. *Practice boldly expressing yourself. Walk into a room like you own it.* For inspiration, he turned to history. *My idol* is Mao Zedong. *Chiang Kai-shek breached the dikes of the Yellow River to slow the Japanese army: That is daring to be decisive.* The flood that stopped the Japanese also killed several hundred thousand Chinese farmers, a fact that Teacher Fu did not mention. This was Etiquette, not History.

At 9:15, he interrupted his lecture to sing a few bars of a popular song. The lesson: *As long as you enjoy something, you must express yourself.* At 9:30, a student raised her hand to answer a question, the first time anyone had dared to volunteer. At 10:15, class ended a few minutes early, and Principal Liu returned for one last motivational harangue. "Tell yourself you are integrated with the White-Collar class," he told the students. "You are not like all those other people on the street."

It was the strangest jumble of ideas I had ever encountered, combining the primacy of the individual with rules that were at once New Age and rigid: *Purple represents mystery.* The message was modern—express yourself, be confident—but it came with traditional assumptions: *You will lift up your whole family.* And history was not so much missing from the Dongguan classroom as wildly irrelevant. How was a seventeen-year-old factory girl supposed to learn from Chiang Kai-shek, who flooded the Japanese army and drowned several hundred thousand of his own countrymen?

In the weeks to come, other rules would pile up fast. *When pouring tea, the cup should be 70 percent full. Purple eye shadow suits all Asian women. In pursuing success, knowledge contributes 30 percent and interpersonal relations 70 percent. Hold the receiver in your left hand and dial the number with your right. When smiling, the mouth should be opened so that teeth don't show, the lips flattened with the corners of the mouth slightly upturned. During the noon rest hour, do not lie horizontally on the chair or desk.* No action was so elementary that it didn't require instructions; the class sometimes felt like a crash course for Martians trying to pass as human beings. The heroes from history never varied. Chiang Kai-shek and Mao Zedong led the pack, with

Hitler a distant third. He was valued for his eloquence; the Nazi leader was a wonderful speaker. Etiquette, not History.

But I noticed something: The students did not fall asleep. They did not look bored. No one ever left to use the bathroom during the two-hour class; they were afraid they might miss something. All their lives, these young women had been taught by teachers and textbooks that struggled to make sense of the modern world. They knew by heart the incoherent mush of rules, self-help, and Confucian exhortation. They took only what they needed, grasping the principal lesson long before I did: If you look and act like someone of a higher class, you will become that person.

After the first day, I never saw any girl wear her factory shirt to school again.

ON MY INITIAL VISIT, I shared a taxi back to the city with Teacher Fu. This was only the second class he had ever taught—the first one had been that morning. Most of his teaching materials came from the Internet. Teacher Fu was the embodiment of the Dongguan education ethos: *Through doing something, you will learn it.* He was still a senior in college, but he had finished his classes early and come out to work; like almost everyone in the city, he was living life on fast-forward. His major was human resources management and his idol a Taiwanese management guru who charged 1,200 yuan per lecture. I wondered how all that squared with his other idol, Mao Zedong.

I asked Teacher Fu how long he had been in Dongguan.

"What day is today?"

"March 29."

"I've been here twenty-two days," he said.

As the taxi sped along the dark highway, he told me of something he had seen soon after he came to the city. At an intersection, a car ran a red light; down the road, Teacher Fu saw a motorcyclist lying in a pool of blood. He thought these two things must be connected and that he should report this information to someone, but he didn't know whom. "Maybe, like me, the person did not have any family here," he speculated of the dead motorcyclist. "It may take a long time before his family learns what happened to him."

We arrived at the building where Teacher Fu shared an apartment with four other teachers. People from the countryside rarely say hello or goodbye, and living in the city does not seem to have changed this habit. Instead he said what people in Dongguan often said to each other upon parting: "Be careful while you are outside."

*   *   *

Dongguan learning took place in humble settings. Classrooms were bare and dim and plagued by power cuts, and computers so grimy and ancient they looked like archaeological finds. The students were poor and spottily educated, and even their teachers apologized for their heavy rural accents. Almost none of the instructors had a proper degree; many, like Teacher Deng, trailed a string of failed businesses behind them. But for all that, they were revolutionary.

In the regular Chinese school system, students did not speak in class; often they did not even take notes until the teacher told them to. They studied a set curriculum determined by a government committee. Teachers pitted students against one another to make them study harder, and the entire system revolved around tests—a test to get into a good middle school, then a good high school, and finally a good college, or any college at all. Like the imperial civil service exam, the educational system was designed to reward the few: Every year, the equivalent of only 11 percent of the freshman-age population entered college. Students who fell off that track were channeled into vocational schools to learn employable skills like machine tool operation and auto repair, but the curriculum was generally so outdated that the schools functioned more like holding pens for the students until they went out to work.

China is trying to reform its education system. Some teachers have embraced "quality education," which emphasizes student creativity and initiative over rote learning. To that end, richer and more progressive schools have introduced electives such as art and music. Making higher education more accessible is another goal: In recent years, the government has sharply expanded college enrollment. But education remains one of the most conservative areas of Chinese society, burdened by hidebound teachers and administrators, political constraints, and a historical obsession with test scores.

The commercial schools in Dongguan belonged to another world. Unburdened by history, they were free to teach what they wanted. They focused unabashedly on practical skills; teachers used material from the Internet or from their own experiences working in factories or companies. They did not pit students against one another and they didn't give out grades. Since every student was there to improve her own job prospects, class rank was irrelevant. They ignored writing—the cornerstone of traditional scholarship—in favor of public speaking. Knowing how to speak would help the students win a better job, obtain a lower price quote, or sell more of whatever they ended up selling. "We are all in the sales business," the White-Collar teachers reminded their students again and again. "What are we selling? We are selling ourselves."

The teachers came from the middle and lower reaches of industry. Teacher Deng had worked for a decade in the Dongguan factories. Teacher Duan Mu, who taught eloquence, had been a salesman for an electronics company, while a young woman who had worked at a law firm now taught etiquette and makeup application. Most teachers were in their twenties, and like their students they had come to Dongguan from somewhere else to make their way; unlike most educated Chinese, the teachers did not look down on migrant workers. "These girls are a lot more able than I am," Teacher Duan Mu said to me after his first class. "To come out and work in the factory requires a lot of self-confidence."

The classrooms of Dongguan were heavily female; a survey of four thousand workers in nearby Shenzhen showed that one-third had enrolled in commercial classes, with a higher proportion of women attending than men. Young women had less formal education to begin with, reflecting a traditional parental bias against daughters. They felt more urgency to move up: Families pressured daughters to return home and marry, but a better job could silence parents and improve one's marriage prospects. The gender imbalance of Dongguan was probably also a factor—on a factory floor that was mostly women, studying was a way to keep from getting lost. *In a factory with one thousand or ten thousand people, to have the boss discover you is very hard. You must discover yourself.*

As I sat through a semester of White-Collar classes, I realized I was witnessing a secret revolution in Chinese education. The rejects of the traditional school system were given a second chance. The factory floor of the world was also in the business of molding people. These classes had no grades and no tests, and that was as it should be. The test was the world outside the classroom; the test was life.

*   *   *

From clothing colors, the girls in the White-Collar class proceeded to learn how to make hand gestures and how to stand, sit, cross their legs, walk, carry documents, and squat to pick something off the office floor. *A woman should sit on one-third to one-half of her chair. Use gestures in a natural, not forced, manner.* In early May, Teacher Fu devoted a class to the etiquette of eating, drinking, and going to banquets. On the blackboard, he wrote down the rules for attending a buffet dinner.

1. Line up to get food.
2. Get food in order.
3. Make multiple trips but take little each trip.
4. Get only a few foods so they don't all mix together.
5. Do not take home leftovers from a buffet.

Drinking was a big part of workplace socializing in China, though the relentless bullying turned pleasure into grim duty. Teacher Fu's instructions for alcohol consumption were detailed and unforgiving. As far as he was concerned, drinking was work.

> The order in which you touch glasses should be the same as the order in which you shake hands. You must start with the most important or the oldest person and go down from there.
>
> You must avoid getting drunk.
>
> In order to socialize in China, you must learn how to drink, as men must smoke cigarettes.
>
> Before you attend a party, you should eat or take medication if you are allergic to alcohol.

Teacher Fu then turned to the etiquette of Western meals. He wrote on the blackboard:

Appetizer→Bread→Soup→Main Course→Dessert→Fruit→Hot Drink

"I got this information on the Internet," he said, "but I've never had a Western meal myself. But today we are fortunate to have Reporter Zhang, who grew up in America." He motioned to me. I stood up and walked to the front of the room. *Walk into a room like you own it.*

I told the class at which point in the sequence you might order a glass of wine. I explained that sometimes you might not have both an appetizer and soup. I said that this might look like a lot of food, and it was, which is why many Americans are overweight. The students wrote everything down.

"Are there any questions?"

Teacher Fu raised his hand. "I have always wondered: What sorts of things are appetizers?"

I explained about different kinds of salad and seafood.

Teacher Fu raised his hand again and asked me to clarify the rules for using utensils. On the board, I drew a diagram of a place setting. I explained the soup spoon and the dessert spoon, the fork for salad and the fork for the main course. I described how to cut a steak, how you must hold the knife in your right hand and the fork in your left and then switch the fork to the other hand at the last moment. "Does it sound complicated?" I asked the class.

"Yes!"

"If you don't know what to do," I said, "just look at the people near you and copy what they are doing."

"And if you do something wrong," I was about to say, "it doesn't matter." But I caught myself in time. The key to success was correct behavior—that was the whole point of the class. Spontaneity was for Americans. Class that day ended with drinking-game drills. "If your manager is a little drunk, you may have to take over for him," Teacher Fu said, with the solemnity of someone talking about the need to land a 747 in case of emergency. He went over the rules for the finger-guessing game and the hand-slapping game—popular drinking pastimes in China—and then he divided the students into small groups to practice.

TWO WEEKS INTO THE SEMESTER, a young woman came up to where I sat in the back of the room. I hadn't seen her speak in class, and she blushed when she introduced herself. I had the feeling I had just become part of someone's self-improvement plan.

Her name was Jiang Haiyan. She had a wide pretty face with a dreamy expression, soft blurred features, and dyed auburn hair pulled into a ponytail. At sixteen, she was working on the VTech assembly line because her parents could not pay for both her and her older brother's education. "I figured between the two of us, it would be easier for me to survive in the working world, because his eyesight is very bad," she told me over dinner soon after we met. "So I lied to my parents and told them I didn't want to go to school anymore." Her brother was studying design in college now.

That act of Confucian self-sacrifice concealed a ferocious will to get ahead. Through a cousin working at VTech, Jiang Haiyan found a job assembling the tiny electronic parts that compose a cordless phone. On the third day of training, the boss asked for a volunteer to work in the production department. Jiang Haiyan had no idea what the production department was but she boldly raised her hand, figuring anything was better than the tedium of assembly. In the production department, she lied and told her new boss she had been a clerk at a factory elsewhere in Dongguan.

"How long were you a clerk?" the boss asked.

"One year," Jiang Haiyan said.

"So what are you doing joining this factory as an ordinary worker?" the boss demanded.

Under pressure, she found eloquence. "I wanted to develop myself in this area," Jiang Haiyan answered. Her boss assigned her to a job checking finished phones for flaws; after a month, she was transferred to the warehouse to keep computer records of factory materials. Her story was like all the migrant stories I had heard: Through speaking up and telling lies, she had risen.

Because she was only sixteen, Jiang Haiyan had borrowed a cousin's ID card to join the factory. "Everyone in the factory knows me as Chen Hua," she said. "Only my cousin and a couple of good friends know me as Jiang Haiyan."

"Isn't it strange to be called by someone else's name?" I asked her.

"No, it feels like my name now," she said. "In the factory, I am Chen Hua. When people call me Jiang Haiyan, I have to think for a second before I realize, 'That's me.'"

She was full of initiative. She had already taken a computer course, and she exercised in the hallway of her dorm to stay in shape. She carried a pocket-size book of English phrases to study in her spare time—*It's nice to meet you. It's been donkey's years.* When we parted after dinner, she returned to her dorm to read a book about sales promotion on loan from the factory library. Her dream was to be a secretary in an office.

ONE SUBJECT THAT NEVER CAME UP in class was ethics. Students learned how the office world functioned and they used that knowledge to lie their way into jobs for which they were unqualified. If this ruse worked—and it often did—what inevitably followed was a panicked phone call to a former teacher: What do I do now? One Sunday morning on the way to visit some schools, I was in a taxi with Teacher Deng when his mobile phone rang.

"How are you?" he said. "Production capability coordination? Okay. Let's say a factory has three production areas, with each one able to produce ten thousand TV sets a month. That is production capability. If one of the production areas is already at capacity, but it still needs to rush out an order, it may coordinate with another production area to borrow some of its capacity. What's your next question?"

After he hung up, he told me a former student had just landed a job and didn't understand the work but did not want to reveal her ignorance to her new colleagues. "I have students who are still calling me one or two years later for advice," he said. The teachers did not explicitly tell the students to be dishonest; that was an accepted fact of life. After I got to know Teacher Deng better, I asked him about it.

"In job interviews," I said, "the girls are often asked if they have experience. They say yes, but actually they don't."

I was trying to approach the topic carefully, but Teacher Deng pounced. "Yes, and the next question is: 'What did you do in your old job?' We teach them the details of the factory so they can answer in a convincing way."

"But they're telling lies," I said.

"Yes."

"What if they don't want to?"

"It's up to them," Teacher Deng said. "But people who are too honest in this society will lose out." I later learned, not from Teacher Deng but from his students, that the Zhitong school sold fake diplomas. Each one was a small book with a shrink-wrapped plastic cover, like the cheap photo albums some of the girls carried around with them. A counterfeit degree from a vocational college cost sixty yuan—around $7.50—while one from a vocational high school was half that. Formal education was not valued in Dongguan, but until then I had not realized how little it was worth.

*   *   *

One evening in early June, Chen Ying came to class wearing a long yellow skirt and matching top. She was the young woman who had spoken at the first information session; until now she had worn jeans and sneakers like the other girls. The outfit was an announcement that she was someone different now. She had quit her factory job and was visiting the talent market three days a week, hoping to be hired as a clerk or a sales department assistant. "It is like Teacher Deng says: There is no need to be nervous," she told me. "Actually, I quite enjoy doing interviews." Next class, Chen Ying was even more elaborately dressed: diaphanous lime-green skirt with lace trim, white stockings, heels. Before the lesson began, I watched as a visiting young woman from another class came up to Chen Ying and introduced herself. Chen Ying stood up and shook the young woman's hand and the two of them talked for a while.

I had never seen a migrant do that before, shake hands and speak with a stranger. Even urban Chinese did not perform that simple act comfortably. Chinese people are bad at dealing with strangers; if someone doesn't fit into their known universe of family, classmates, or colleagues, the usual response is to ignore him. My Chinese friends in Beijing were hopeless at parties—they stuck with whatever group they came with, locked into position like a squadron of fighter planes flying into combat in the one formation they knew.

The White-Collar class forced students to break free of the group. In the course of the semester, every student had to give a speech introducing herself. These always started the same way: *I am the same as you.* It was a funny way for a person to begin her own story, and it wasn't even true. But perhaps it was only by establishing that she was part of the group that a young woman gained the courage to stand apart from it. When Chen Ying stood up that day and shook hands with a stranger, she reminded me, more than anything else, of an American.

THE STUDENTS HAD LOST their fear of public speaking and now competed to answer questions. They took the initiative to greet their teachers; they greeted me. They were boisterous and chatty, and they were all friends now. But already the time was coming when they must leave this community behind. Now when the girls met each other, the first question was: "Have you been to the talent market?" The ones who had told stories of their experiences there, like travelers returned from a faraway land where the natives were ruthlessly inquisitive and cruel:

She asked me, "If you try to sell to a client and the person refuses, what do you do?"

I didn't know how to answer. I said, "It's normal to run into this."

In the interview they asked me, "What if three phones ring at the same time? What will you do?"

I said, "I will answer each one, figure out which is most important, and deal with it first."

A slim young woman with a boyish haircut described her interview at a telecommunications company called Huawei Technologies.

I always wanted to work at Huawei, so I went to their recruiting event. A bunch of people were sitting in a room, and the recruiting executive would point to one person and ask a question. Then she would say, "Okay, you can leave now."

Finally there were just three men and me. The executive looked at me and said, "You are not suitable. You can leave."

I thought: "What a loss of face this is for me! But this executive doesn't even know me. How can she know if I'm suitable or not?" So I kept sitting there and did not leave.

Then the executive asked one of the men, "Tell me about your proudest moment."

He was very nervous. He said he was still looking for work and did not have any achievements he was proud of yet.

I said to him quietly, "You can think about something you did in school that you were proud of." The executive heard me and looked at me.

Finally all three of the men had been eliminated. Only I was left. The executive looked at me and said, "Those three were all your competitive rivals, yet you tried to help them. Why?"

I said, "I don't think of them as my rivals. If we are chosen, in the future we will be colleagues and we will have to help each other."

The executive said, "I told you that you were not suitable, yet you didn't leave. Why?"

I said, "You don't know anything about me. You don't know if I'm suitable or not. I've always had a very good impression of Huawei, but I must say I am very dissatisfied with your attitude toward job-seekers today. Whether or not I will be a Huawei employee, as a Huawei customer I am very dissatisfied."

The woman smiled. She was very satisfied with my answer. So I was hired.

On June 2, class began with an electrifying announcement from Teacher Duan Mu, who taught eloquence. "I have heard good news. A student has already found work." The room buzzed. A young woman named Ma Xiaonan had found a job as a receptionist. She was the first person in the class to get a new job, and it reminded everyone that it was time to get moving. That day's class, and all the sessions from then on, focused on the job search. Teacher Duan Mu spoke about how to introduce oneself to a recruiter, and how to do as many interviews as possible, and how to spot and avoid pyramid schemes. At the end of class, each girl stood up and recited her personal motto:

The saddest person in the world is one without goals or dreams.
Because of youth, have confidence.
The most important person in the world: yourself.

Ma Xiaonan never came to class again. That was the only sign of her success: that she had disappeared.

JIANG HAIYAN WANTED to leave too. She started visiting the talent market for practice interviews, but her boss at VTech objected. He was short of people, he said, and he needed her help. Jiang Haiyan resorted automatically to another lie—her cousin in Shenzhen knew of a receptionist job at her factory—but her boss pleaded with her to stay.

"I want to quit," she told me. "But it's not so easy to say these things."

"Is your boss a bad person?" I asked. "He doesn't sound like a bad person."

"No, he's a good person," she said. "But several others have left, so he's really short of people."

"If you've made up your mind," I said, "you must tell him that you want to go, and he'll have to let you." Her dilemma seemed to me distinctly Chinese. She had lied her way into her job, and then lied herself up the work ladder; she had no qualms about the truth. But now her boss was making her feel guilty about abandoning the group, and she seemed powerless to cope with that. In traditional Chinese society, maintaining harmony with others was the key to living in the world. The moral compass was not necessarily right or wrong; it was your relationship with the people around you. And it took all your strength to break free from that.

One day after class Jiang Haiyan sought the advice of Wu Chen, who taught etiquette and makeup. Teacher Wu immediately took charge. "Where do you work?" she asked.

"In the warehouse."

"Have you been to the talent market?"

"Yes."

"To leave is your right," Teacher Wu said.

"But they've kept a month of my salary," Jiang Haiyan said.

"I know many people who are in this situation," Teacher Wu said briskly. "But if you've really made your decision, then you should go. If you have to, leave the month's pay behind. To pursue one's goals will involve hardship."

It was bold advice, exactly what the White-Collar class sought to instill in its students. But still Jiang Haiyan was unable to act. June turned into July; the semester would be ending soon, and the class was shrinking with every session as students jumped to new jobs. Jiang Haiyan bought a fake vocational high school degree but she was afraid to use it in interviews. Her talks with her boss dragged on without resolution; she considered enrolling in yet another class, this time to learn English. "It's so hard to know how to conduct my-self!" she said.

You could say Jiang Haiyan was afraid, and surely part of her was. But the situation seemed more complicated than that. She wanted to know how to treat other people—essentially, how the rules of tra-ditional Chinese behavior fit into the modern working world. But that went beyond the curriculum of the White-Collar class.

*   *   *

The Pearl River Delta attracted motivational speakers and manage-ment gurus of every stripe. At its high end, the market was domi-nated by corporate experts from Taiwan; some executive seminars were so exclusive they were by invitation only. The language of self-improvement suffused ordinary commercial life as well: Direct-sales companies, headhunters, and matchmakers all made their sales pitches in the vocabulary of aspiration. The bookstores of Dongguan were wall-to-wall self-improvement volumes. Some stores had no other sections. Dale Carnegïe was a perennial favorite, though some careless cutting and pasting was in evidence. *How to Win Friends and Influence Others* and *How to Stop Worrying and Start Living*. *The Quick and Easy to Effective Speaking*. The entrepreneurial secrets of the Chinese sold well—*Wenzhou People's Thirty-six Stratagems to Make Money*—and there was a mystical faith in the power of the numbered list. *Seven Secrets of a Self-Made Leader*. *Fifty-nine Details to Decide Success or Failure in Selling*. A few books offered relationship advice—*Why Men Love Bitches*—but business titles outnumbered personal themes ten to one. Self-help might be an American invention, but the Chinese had refined and renamed the genre to reflect their own narrower preoccupations: *chenggong xue*, success studies.

One humid evening in May of 2005, I walked past a bookstore in the pedestrian zone near my apartment. On a makeshift stage in front of the store, a man was speaking to a crowd of several hundred people, mostly migrant men in mismatched suit jackets and pants. "I wanted to write a book," the man said. "Did I wait until I learned everything before I wrote it? No. I learned as I wrote, and I wrote as I learned. The computer software can pick out all the words I wrote incorrectly. And that's what editors are for."

Laughter rippled through the audience. The man was of medium height, with a receding hairline and a face as plump, white, and shiny as a boiled dumpling. He was as unlikely a spokesman for success studies as you could imagine.

"So you want to be an entrepreneur," he continued. "You are waiting for the situation to be ideal. But will it ever be ideal? No. By acting now, you will make it ideal. Do you know all that you need to know? No. But through doing you will learn it, and this learning is very worthwhile."

Then the speech took a surprising turn. "Now I will talk about copying. I think copying is very important. Everyone always talks about how innovation is important. But you need to invest a lot of time to innovate and the risk is high. Why not take things that have already been proven to work in other places? That is copying."

The man's name was Ding Yuanzhi, and not long ago he had taught high school physics. His book, *Square and Round*, was said to have sold six million copies. Now Ding Yuanzhi toured the country teaching people how to manipulate their way to success as he had done.

———

> Every day you will feel an intangible pressure that does not let you stop your struggle. We are all people, but other people go to expensive restaurants and shows while you go only to low-quality ones . . . Why can other people enjoy luxuries while you enjoy only low-quality things? When you think of these things, do you not feel humiliated? . . .
>
> On the road every day pass countless Mercedes-Benzes. We don't have one now; that is not a tragedy. The tragedy is that we don't dare to long for one.

Square and Round was a perversion of an American self-help book. It did not urge people to discover themselves, to look beyond material success, or to be honest about their failings and in their relationships. It did not try to change its readers. Instead it taught them how to do better what they already knew so well: pettiness, materialism, envy, competition, flattery, and subterfuge. *Square and Round* was the literary equivalent of standing on a Dongguan street corner and preaching the merits of copyright violation. The crowd already belonged to you.

Square and Round painted a bleak world of complicated relationships, intense workplace politics, two-faced friendships, corrupt dealings, and status-conscious bosses with absolute power over one's fate. Colleagues undermined one another in front of their superiors. Bosses exploited their authority in order to belittle others and obtain bribes. Cynical men got the most attractive women. Money and status were the measure of happiness. Honesty was never the best policy. If the government had been paying attention, it would surely have banned this book—never had I seen such a dark vision of Chinese society so calmly acknowledged as fact. Ostensibly *Square and Round* was about how to get along in society while also being a good person. It advocated the traditional ideal of *neifang waiyuan*— internally square, outwardly round—a person who combined integrity with skillful interpersonal relations. But the book dispensed with integrity in seventy pages, while social skills took up almost two hundred, so anyone could see where its priorities lay.

I had always felt that social interactions among the Chinese were needlessly complicated. Confucian tradition, which emphasized not the individual but his role in a complex hierarchical order, placed great value on status, self-restraint, and the proper display of respect. The Chinese had been living in densely populated communities for several thousand years, and they had developed subtle skills of delivering and detecting slights, exerting power through indirect means, and manipulating situations to their own benefit, all beneath a surface of elaborate courtesy. Even Chinese themselves often complained that living in their society was *lei*, tiring. I had not appreciated just how tiring until I read this book, which devoted eight pages to how to smile and forty-five pages to lulling others into letting down their guard.

Shaking hands: *A handshake that releases immediately on contact shows your indifference to the other person.*

Paying bribes: *Try not to get into the habit of giving someone something every time he helps you.*

Seeking favors: *If you have a small request, first make some large re-*

quests and let the other person refuse. When he feels apologetic, wait for your opportunity to make your small request.

Toadying: *Remember the birthdays and important anniversaries of department heads and long-term clients and of their wives, parents, and children.*

More toadying: *If someone is wearing a two-hundred-yuan outfit, you say, "This outfit must have cost three hundred-something?"*

Bargaining: *Ask the price of expensive clothes first if you want to buy cheap ones. Ask the price of cheap clothes first if you want to buy expensive ones.*

Helping others: *Do not accept thank-you gifts and thank-you dinners . . . I would rather people remember my favors to them and the debt they owe me.*

Yet more toadying: *Letting people feel important is an effective way to arouse their enthusiasm.*

A good way to destroy a person's confidence was to look away when he spoke to you. Letting subordinates handle things while limiting your own appearance enhanced your importance. Staging fake customer phone calls during meetings could obtain better terms with suppliers. Sharing a company's financial secrets with underlings was a good way to win their loyalty. And visiting someone who was sick in the hospital was the best way to build relations. *If a man wants to make advances on a certain young lady, he should take advantage of when she is sick to ingratiate himself. That will surely be effective, because at this time she is weak and most in need of comfort.*

SQUARE AND ROUND was essentially a point-by-point rejection of the virtues Chinese tradition had preached for two thousand years.

Scholarship: *The ones with the best grades work for others; the ones with second-rate grades are the bosses.*

Modesty: *If other people don't understand you yet, your modesty would be seen not as a sign of virtue but of incompetence.*

Family: *[A friend] was temporarily hired by Shenzhen University, but his wife . . . urged him to go home, saying "If you don't come home, we will divorce." He thought his wife was more important than work, so he gave up his position and returned home. But she divorced him anyway.*

Loyalty: *If you and your best friend get along very well, then you are true friends for now. But if there is one million dollars' worth of business to be done, if you don't kick him aside or he doesn't kick you aside, then you have mental problems.*

Honesty: *A "white lie" is sometimes necessary. For example, for a patient with an incurable disease, honesty may destroy his spirits. A lie can help prolong his life and let him live his remaining days happily.*

The bleakest parts of the book concerned relationships. Invariably the rules of business combat could be applied to personal affairs. *First suggest goals your adversary can accept* was relevant to either a tough negotiation or a first date. A good way to break up with a girlfriend was "Being Courteous": *He suddenly becomes extremely polite to his girlfriend. If she helps him, he says thank you. If people leave, he says goodbye. This type of excessive courtesy makes a person cold and unapproachable.* This tactic was also useful in turning down friends seeking favors.

When all else failed, the author suggested his personal foolproof method to break down the defenses of others:

> To awaken and move the conscience of others and provoke
> their noble intentions, an important technique is to cry . . .
> Bite your lower lip with your teeth and let the tears glisten
> in the rims of your eyes while you look steadily forward.
> Next time you are wronged, assume this position, and I believe no one can remain unmoved.

THE AUTHOR of this manual of unscrupulous psychological manipulation answered the door of his Shenzhen apartment in a short-sleeve shirt, khaki pants, and bare feet. Up close, he looked older and sadder, with deep lines tracing his nose and mouth. He ushered me into a stylish bachelor pad—dark wood floors, white shag carpet, a curvy sectional couch in sage green—and poured me a Pepsi, setting it carefully on a glass coffee table.

Originally a high school physics teacher in Hubei Province, Ding Yuanzhi had come to Shenzhen in 1987 and landed a teaching job—through subterfuge, naturally. He had learned that the principal of the school where he wanted to work was a passionate lover of *The Dream of the Red Chamber*, an eighteenth-century novel. One evening, Ding Yuanzhi visited the principal at home. He did not state his purpose; instead, as he described in the pages of *Square and Round,* he drew the man into a lengthy discussion about the novel.

> The more we spoke, the better we got along, and without our realizing it several hours had passed. The principal suddenly looked up and realized it was already past ten o'clock. As if just waking up, he asked me, "*Ai,* what were you coming to see me about?"
>
> In our conversation of the past few hours, I had already fully won the principal's favor, so when I spoke of my own aspiration to come to Shenzhen to work, the principal naturally could not find a way to refuse me and agreed that I could teach . . .
>
> I vanquished many adversaries in getting transferred to Shenzhen. And I didn't have to spend a cent.

Soon afterward, Ding Yuanzhi and a friend decided to start a public relations company. That, too, was a calculated move. "We thought it would be easy to say, 'We are China's first public relations company,' " Ding Yuanzhi told me. "We figured the commercial bureau did not know what it was, so it would be easier to get approval." The problem was that Ding Yuanzhi and his friend didn't know much about public relations either. They held a single publicity event but couldn't drum up any new business. Then they started running public relations training for executives, and Ding Yuanzhi discovered he had a knack for it. He began reading the books of Dale Carnegie and making television appearances.

The publication of *Square and Round* in 1996 was similarly unorthodox. Ding Yuanzhi did not sign a legitimate publishing contract; he simply bought a serial number from a publisher and printed and marketed the book on his own. On weekends he traveled to bookstores around Shenzhen, set up a banner and a table outside the front door, and signed books. *Square and Round* was written at a middle-school level so even factory workers could understand it. "Migrant workers need consolation in their hearts," Ding Yuanzhi said. "They need to know that success is possible. These books are a solace to them."

I asked him what he thought about the other success studies books sold in China. He hadn't read a single one. "All the books in China just take their ideas from the outside," he said. "China really has no original ideas."

When I asked about his next project, Ding Yuanzhi left the room and returned with a Chinese edition of *Competitive Advantage* by Michael Porter. His next book, he said blandly, would recycle these ideas, again at a middle-school level. "My book will basically boil down Porter's concepts into comprehensible fashion," he said. "Shenzhen has a lot of bosses with only an elementary school education, but they are very hungry to learn." *That is copying.*

Meeting Ding Yuanzhi was a letdown. Nothing qualified him to be a teacher of success studies. He was not an impressive speaker and he did not have compelling ideas; his public relations business had never gone anywhere. And no one who had met him would ever take seriously his advice on seducing young ladies. But Ding

Yuanzhi had dared to do what others did not. He had set up a company. He gave talks. And he wrote the book on how to succeed. Action was the only thing that set successful people apart. *The difference between successful people and failures is not in the quality of their ideas or in the measure of their abilities*, he had written, *but in whether they trust their own judgment and dare to take action*. Chen Ying risked jumping to a new job, while Jiang Haiyan did not. In the end, that was the only difference between them that mattered.

*   *   *

On a Sunday night in July 2005, the students from the second session of the White-Collar Secretarial Skills Special Training Class graduated. For the ceremony, the classroom desks were pushed into a square formation with an open space in the middle for speeches and performances. At each setting was scattered a festive handful of peanuts, jelly candies, cookies, and disposable plastic cups of warm water. The teachers wore dress shirts, dark pants, and ties. Around fifty students attended, including new graduates, graduates from earlier classes, and students from the new semester that was about to begin. Principal Liu, the master of ceremonies, formally introduced the teachers one by one, to applause. Teacher Yang sang a song called "We'll Meet Again in Twenty Years."

> *Let us meet again in twenty years,*
> *How beautiful our great motherland will be then!*
> *The heavens will be new, the earth new, the sights of spring*
>   *more splendid,*
> *The cities and the villages all in greater glory.*

"I think if we meet again in twenty years," Principal Liu said, "you will all be millionaires and big bosses." He read out the names of all the graduates—about half the class—who had landed new jobs and could not attend tonight. Chen Ying was on the list; she had found work as a clerk in a hardware factory. "We hope that their work goes smoothly." Several of the graduates gave speeches.

> In ten years, this is my proudest moment, because I have never taken part in a graduation ceremony before. Now I'm doing sales at a company. It is very tiring and I'm outside all day. I am learning a lot.

> My name is Ye Fangfang. I hope you will remember me. You changed me from a timid person into a self-confident one. I have learned how to conduct myself. That is the integration of the square and the round. I will always remember you.

Halfway through the ceremony, the power went out, and a few students went around the room lighting candles. Jiang Haiyan, wearing a skirt, sheer stockings, and high heels, surprised me by performing a song and holding the whole room with her poise. During a song called "The Sound of Applause," the graduates circled the candlelit room and shook hands with their teachers, solemnly thanking each one in turn. Principal Liu announced that the third White-Collar session would begin in a week.

Only four of the graduates who had found work made it back for the ceremony. That was the true measure of the school's achievement: the absence of so many young women, scattered up and down the Pearl River Delta, who could not be here tonight because they had already moved on. The teachers were on the move too. Teacher Fu had graduated from college, quit the school, and moved to Shanghai to join his girlfriend. Teacher Duan Mu had been promoted and was taking on more management responsibilities.

In the coming year, everyone I knew at the Zhitong school would go through a major life change, or several. Chen Ying would jump to a sales job at an adhesive tape factory and then to a plant that made air conditioners, where she would be put in charge of purchasing and production with responsibility for twenty workers. When I met her for dinner a year later, she was transformed. She spoke in measured tones, carried a stylish baguette handbag, and confidently ordered dinner in a restaurant with antique-wood tables. She was making 1,600 yuan a month—two hundred dollars—and was being wooed by three men, all of them managers. She had a bet with a friend over who would buy a car first. "If you wanted me to go back to the way I used to be," she told me, "I don't think I would have the courage to go on living."

Jiang Haiyan would go home, come out again briefly to find a job, then return home again to help her family run a shop selling food and stationery. Her parents did not want her living in Dongguan because they felt it was unsafe. Caught in a net of family obligation, Jiang Haiyan was unwilling to challenge her parents directly. "I don't want to let my family feel I must do this, or it will be very hard on everyone," she told me when I called her at home.

Teacher Deng would cut his ties to the Zhitong school to pursue more lucrative work teaching management to executives, at five thousand yuan per session. "I'm forty-two years old," he told me. "I need to think about taking care of myself in my old age." One night after class, he would leave a suitcase with his mobile phone in the trunk of a taxi, and all of his former students would lose touch with him.

As the ceremony drew to a close, the lights in the room came back on, and the students sang one last song, "Friends." The music swelled and filled the room as Teacher Deng handed out his business card to the graduates and Principal Liu presented their diplomas, small books whose covers were wrapped in red silk. Inside was printed the name and logo of the Dongguan Zhitong Talent Intelligence Development Company in the blank where the name of the school would ordinarily be.

Friend, oh friend,
Have you been thinking of me,
If you are enjoying happiness,
Please forget me.

Friend, oh friend,
Have you been remembering me,
If you are enduring misfortune,
Please tell me.

Friend, oh friend,
Have you been remembering me,
If you have found your faraway shore,
Just leave me, leave me behind.

There were several ways to find a husband, and after a migrant woman landed a stable job that was the next order of business. Some girls consented to the services of a matchmaker back in the village, though that risked being paired with an unpromising young man who had never ventured far from home. Girls who had lived in Dongguan for a while sought introductions from friends, but when you met a man in the city there were things you didn't know about him, like whether he had a wife and children back home. Some girls signed up with dating services, but many people felt this method was too "direct." The boldest girls met men online. The hazards of that route had inspired a song called "QQ Love"; QQ was the name of the most popular chat service on the Chinese Internet.

> *This one claims to be so handsome*
> *With a good heart, and well-behaved*
> *Asking how old I am this year*

And how many one-night stands I've had
Scaring me speechless
What kind of E-era is this?
Hurry up and tell him "bye-bye"
Oh! QQ Love
Real or false, who can guess?

There was never any question of not looking. City life was lonely and sharing it with someone lightened the burden. And marriage was a filial duty; by the time a migrant worker was twenty years old, the parental pressure to wed was relentless and directed at both sexes. No one wanted to become the dreaded *daling qingnian*, a phrase that literally meant "aged youth" and was defined in the dictionary as "unmarried men or women between twenty-eight and thirty-five." The traditional timetable of the village matched the city's pragmatism: A young woman should lock in marriage early, when her value was at its peak.

The Dongguan Making Friends Club was the biggest dating agency in town. Originally set up to help women find mates in a city estimated to be 70 percent female, the club had grown to more than five thousand members. It was run by the All-China Women's Federation, a national organization staffed by well-meaning matrons who believed it their duty to "guide the masses," whether the masses wanted their guidance or not. Female club members outnumbered males two to one, which organizers pointed out was better than the city's female-to-male ratio of four to one, or five to one, or maybe three to two—like the population of Dongguan, its sex ratio was a highly variable statistic.

In America, dating agencies are set up so that a stranger can ask a fellow member on a date. But that seemed immodest to most Chinese people. Instead members met every Sunday afternoon at the club's headquarters, on the second floor of an aging office building, for what was delicately called "information exchange." The club also organized weekend outings for its members. In China, a date was a group activity.

THE MAN NEXT TO ME stood up. "Hello. My member number is 2740." He sat down.

Li Fengping, the middle-aged woman who ran the club's matchmaking arm, objected. "That's it? You must do a self-introduction."

The man stood up again. "I am from Hunan. Originally I only tested into vocational college, but later I studied on my own, so I could get a bachelor's degree." He sat down again.

Thirty people had assembled in the club's main meeting room on a Sunday afternoon in the fall of 2004. The space felt like a classroom with its fluorescent lighting and plastic chairs, and perhaps in response the members had segregated like schoolchildren, the men sitting in rows along the sides of the room, the women clustered in bunches for safety.

"I am from Guangdong. I am in sales, an ordinary worker."

"I am from Jiangxi. I am a very plain person."

A woman wearing a lime-green sweater and white jeans stood up. "Hello. I have been in Dongguan quite a while, doing sales. I'm from Hunan. My goal in coming here today is to give myself more opportunities."

Most of the introductions were brief and painfully shy. People gave their club membership numbers and native provinces but not their names; they described themselves as "ordinary." The men were electricians and lawyers and advertising executives and assembly-line workers; the women worked as nurses and clerks and teachers and salespeople and assembly-line workers. A fair percentage of both sexes were divorced. Occasionally a voice sounded from the school of self-help, and the mood in the room turned hushed, confessional.

I have gone through a lot. I have suffered many injuries. To-day, I have come through it.

I am a college graduate. I studied computers. I am an office manager. My goal is to find someone who loves me, whom I can love.

"Now," Li Fengping said, when the introductions were finished, "everyone can go and approach whomever you like."

No one moved.

After an excruciating silence, the woman in the lime-green sweater spoke up. "I have a suggestion. In the future, we should have more professional gatherings, so there are fewer of these awkward moments and we don't waste so much time."

"Yes, there should be more planning," a man sitting near her agreed. The matchmaking threatened to disintegrate into a finger-pointing free-for-all. Whenever I watched Chinese people interact in a group setting, I understood in my bones how the Cultural Revolution happened. People were terrified of being singled out, but from the safety of the group they could turn on someone with a speed and ferocity that took your breath away.

Suddenly a pretty elementary school teacher with fierce dark eyes stood up.

"What's your name?" she demanded of a man slumped in his chair against the wall.

He sat up straighter and answered her.

"Where are you from?" she asked.

"Guizhou."

"I like you very much."

She sat down. There was thunderous applause.

And then, silence again.

The man sitting next to me—member 2740—stood up and left. I turned to Li Fengping and suggested that people might be allowed to walk around. "Can't we turn on the music?" someone pleaded. In the end, the pressure to walk across a room and approach a stranger under the eyes of thirty others was too much to bear. Most members fled the Making Friends meeting as soon as they could. The man who had been singled out by the schoolteacher made no move to approach her, and she remained seated too, staring straight ahead with a determined look on her face.

AFTER THE GATHERING, I went up to the woman in the lime-green sweater. She was shorter than she appeared at a distance—barely five feet tall—with a curvy figure and restless dark eyes in a pretty heart-shaped face; she wore frosty pink lipstick and a glittering rhinestone barrette in her hair. She was twenty-nine years old and worked in sales. "In the past, I ignored my personal matters to focus on work," she told me. "But now I am thinking of it, which is why I've come here."

I asked what she was looking for in a man.

"It doesn't matter to me what a person's education is, or his job, or how much money he makes," she said. "To me, feeling is most important."

The woman was Wu Chunming. After I met her for the first time that day, it was what she had said to the gathered club members that I remembered—*My goal in coming here today is to give myself more opportunities*. That, and her voice: sharp as a scythe, and unashamed of its broad peasant accent that no number of years in the city could erase. Hers was a voice that won arguments and carried across construction sites and made men sit up and take notice.

Over time I learned the details of Chunming's story—how she had started out in a toy factory, was almost tricked into a brothel, talked her way into management, and struck it rich selling Tibetan medicine and funeral plots. After the government banned direct sales, Chunming got a job as a reporter at the *China Inspection and Quarantine Times*. The newspaper was run by the government agency in charge of import and export inspections, and the nature of her work would have been unrecognizable to any conventional practitioner of journalism. Chunming would decide to write an article about a company; her chosen subject, fearing trouble getting its goods through customs, would pay the paper for positive coverage. The price for good press was determined on a sliding scale, in the same way that advertising rates are set. Two thousand yuan bought a brief mention, while a full-length feature might cost fifty thousand yuan. This was journalism as extortion, and Chunming worked on commission and did well. Afterward she worked for two years in the sales department of a building-materials company, then in 2001 she and her first boyfriend set up a building-materials wholesale business. The venture lasted six months, during which Chunming lost her entire hundred-thousand-yuan investment—all her savings from her direct-sales days, minus money she had spent renovating her family's house. When I met her, she had landed as a salesperson at a Swedish-owned company that made paint and other coatings used on the surfaces of buildings.

The wild reversals of fortune in Chunming's life reflected the boom-and-bust ethos of south China. But perhaps the most unlikely part of her story was that in this most hardheaded of cities, she was still holding out for romance—as the man had said: *to find someone who loves me, whom I can love.*

*   *   *

Her first boyfriend was a driver at the building-materials company where she worked. Chunming did not particularly like him at first, but they spent a lot of time together and he knew how to charm women. Already twenty-five, she had never slept with a man before.

Soon after they started dating, Chunming sensed he wasn't right for her. He frequently borrowed money from his parents and lacked her gift for hard work. "He couldn't accomplish the big things and didn't want to bother with the small things" was how Chunming put it. Twice when they fought, he hit her.

"He used his hand like this, and slapped me hard on the face," Chunming told me, holding her hand out stiffly, palm up, to demonstrate. "The first time he hit me, I cried and cried. He promised he would never do it again. The second time he hit me, I didn't respond at all. I was just very calm. There is a traditional saying that the man who hits once will hit again. Now I know that it's true." That was in 2002, but Chunming stayed with her boyfriend for another year and a half. They shared a rented three-bedroom apartment across from the Wal-Mart in downtown Dongguan.

"Whenever I told him I wanted to break up with him, he wouldn't answer, or he would say I was just toying with his emotions. I didn't know how to get rid of him," Chunming said. "I would tell him we should break up, then I would come home from work and he would be there. I didn't know what to do." Resorting to indirectness, she wrote him letters in her diary: *This time I have really decided I must break up with you. We have no future.* The ink on the pages ran, because she was crying as she wrote. She left her diary on the kitchen table, but if he read it, he never let on.

It took another woman to resolve the matter. One day a woman from her boyfriend's hometown called Chunming and informed her they were having an affair. Chunming was relieved, and when she told her boyfriend that she knew about the other woman, he packed his things and left without argument. Since then she had not had a serious relationship, though she had many flings. Sometimes this was enough for her; in the future when she had made her money, she dreamed, she would have an apartment and a car and lovers whenever she wanted. At other times, these casual affairs made her more lonely. "If you just have lovers," she told me, "it's like you're always floating on the sea and can never come into harbor."

*   *   *

25-YEAR-OLD ACCOUNTANT SEEKS A GUANGDONG
MAN WITH A PROFESSIONAL SKILL, AN APARTMENT,
A LOVING HEART, AND A SENSE OF RESPONSIBILITY.

Women wanted a man with a good job and steady income. Men wanted a woman who was young and healthy. Women wanted a man who was over 1.7 meters tall—at least five feet seven inches—and had his own apartment. Men didn't care about height or real estate but they preferred a woman with a gentle temperament. Some women favored men from Guangdong Province, who would bring the benefits of local residency, while others felt a local man would have too much leverage over them. Men didn't care about residential status. Women had many more demands than men.

The members of the Making Friends Club filled out index cards with their personal information and what they wanted in a mate. The card listed a member's occupation and marital status and personal details like height, weight, and health. It also included characteristics that could appear only on a Chinese matchmaking application, such as political identity, apartment ownership, and the health and financial standing of one's family members. Political identity denoted whether a person belonged to the Communist Party; few club members were so exalted and most simply wrote "masses." The cards also mentioned whether a person had to support aged parents or younger siblings—those with no such burdens took pains to point out that their parents were healthy or their siblings already grown.

Taped to the back of every card was a photo. Women wearing lacy skirts and high heels posed in parks or perched on rocks set in the middle of artificial lakes, like damsels awaiting rescue; men in suits stood on hillsides. Both men and women were photographed in front of fancy apartment complexes where they almost certainly did not live. Many of the shots had been taken in street-side photo studios, where subjects strained to look natural while standing on a fake Great Wall or under a fake maple tree or beside a fake picket fence such as I had never seen in China. One man who listed dancing as his hobby struck a disco pose against a painted city landscape of McDonald's signs. The cards were filed in loose-leaf binders according to gender and year of birth: FEMALE 78, FEMALE 77. A fair portion of FEMALE 71 and FEMALE 72 were divorced with a child. The most aged female youths cohabited in the grimly titled FEMALES ABOVE FORTY.

Most of the members were not looking for love. They did not crave walks on the beach or hot-air balloon rides; their overriding concerns were pragmatic. HAVE AN ENTERPRISING HEART. HAVE GOOD ECONOMIC CIRCUMSTANCES. HAVE STABLE JOB AND INCOME. CAN EAT BITTERNESS. Women in particular were obsessed with height: As at the talent market, physical stature was a marker for quality—a promise that a man was healthy, stable, blessed. Although many women insisted on a man who was at least five feet seven inches, a handful would go as low as five feet five. No one wanted to date a man who was only five feet three inches tall.

The binders hinted at the reasons past relationships had gone sour. SEEKING A 28- TO 34-YEAR-OLD WITH AN OPEN PERSONALITY WHO DOESN'T GAMBLE. SEEKING A CULTIVATED PERSON NOT ADDICTED TO WINE AND WOMEN. An occasional brave woman threw caution to the winds: SEEKING A 35- TO 45-YEAR-OLD, THE REST IS UP TO DESTINY. Many women regarded apartment ownership as a prerequisite for a date. That was common in Chinese personals, which sometimes read like real estate listings, as in this ad in a magazine for rural women:

> A 27-YEAR-OLD MAN . . . DIVORCED WITH AN OPEN
> NATURE . . . POSSESSING A FIVE-BEDROOM TILE
> HOUSE WITH FURNITURE, MODERN APPLIANCES,
> AND A MOTORCYCLE, SEEKS A WOMAN TO BE A
> PARTNER FOR LIFE.

The preoccupation with property was not as mercenary as it appeared. Like height, apartment ownership was a marker, a sign that a man could be depended on. "The women aren't really asking for very wealthy people," a man named Tang Ao, who ran another matchmaking agency in the city, explained to me. "They just want some security."

Every member of the Making Friends Club I talked to was dissatisfied with the club in some way. Its male members were uneducated and low-class, I was told. Married men looking to have affairs sometimes sneaked in under an assumed identity. The club administration was "a bunch of grandmothers," Chunming said. Yet every time I stopped in at the club, some members were already there, poring over FEMALE 78 or MALE 71, still looking.

*   *   *

As Chunming moved up in the world, she left many people behind. Friends from her early days on the assembly line returned home to marry and have children. Most of the better factories did not employ women over the age of twenty-five as ordinary workers; older women were relegated to poorly run factories or menial jobs like housecleaning. For a migrant woman, social mobility was a survival tactic—the best way to remain in the city once her first bloom of youth was gone.

Chunming's friends, women in their late twenties or early thirties, had all survived this mass culling. Most, like her, came from rural villages, though a handful had grown up in a city and attended college. They usually ran factories that manufactured one microscopic piece of the vast supply chain stretching from Dongguan to the world. One woman and her husband made metal studs for decorating handbags; another couple manufactured the glue used to attach the heel of a shoe to the shoe upper. A twenty-six-year-old woman operated a shoe-sole factory, and another specialized in wooden flooring, and yet another sold building materials but was considering a move into the underwear wholesale business. For Chunming, this network of friends was family. On sales trips, she frequently showed up unannounced at a friend's apartment and stayed for days; her changes of clothes and spare toothbrushes were scattered up and down the Pearl River Delta. Once when I met up with Chunming in Shenzhen, she had been away from home for five days but was carrying only a clutch purse big enough for a lipstick and a mobile phone.

Spending time in Chunming's circle was like looking at one of those optical illusions that showed two things at once. Out in the city, they appeared plausibly middle-class. They owned apartments and cars, or planned to buy them soon. They took driving lessons and vacations; they got manicures and went on diets and learned Latin dance steps. They always knew about the newest Brazilian barbecue restaurant or the best place for frozen yogurt. At other times, the village seemed indelibly stamped on their DNA. Their apartments might be tastefully furnished, but the bathroom invariably had a squat toilet. Their medical knowledge was the folk wisdom of their grandmothers: To recover from illness they steamed chicken with ginseng, and when the weather cooled they ate pork lung soup to stave off respiratory infection. They still traveled long distances by bus and train, and almost none of them had been on an airplane. Tradition was most on their minds when they journeyed home for the new year, covering in one day a distance they had traveled over years.

CHUNMING SELDOM SPOKE of her early days in the factory. I don't think she was ashamed of it, exactly—it was more that the girl who had worked on the toy assembly line, who had kept a diary and struggled to learn Cantonese and memorized Benjamin Franklin's thirteen rules of morality, was so far from the person she had become. She still worked tirelessly to improve herself. The shelves of her apartment were almost entirely self-help books: *One Hundred Success Stories* and *Mary Kay's Nine Leadership Keys to Success* and an etiquette series with English titles like *Tone* and *Crass*. (Of all the ways to misspell *class*, that was the worst way.) On the living room wall was a giant glamour photograph of Chunming with shiny pink lip gloss and a jeweled barrette clipping back her hair. The apartment was a reflection of her character—carefully crafted, relentlessly self-examining.

Everything was an educational opportunity. From Korean soap operas, Chunming learned that you must hold a fork in your right hand and a spoon in your left, but a fork in your left hand and a knife in your right. It was also on Korean television that she saw Tupperware containers for the first time. Once I gave her a DVD of *Roman Holiday*—she had asked me for some American movies— and out of Hollywood entertainment she spun a Marxist morality lesson. "The poor journalist could have made a lot of money on the story of the princess," she summarized the plot for me. "When he gave up his chance to make a lot of money, he rose in morality." She did not know who Audrey Hepburn was but pronounced her "not as beautiful as Julia Roberts."

She was ruthlessly observant; in a sense she was taking notes on me the same way I took notes on her. The first time we met up, she picked the place—the European Style Coffee Western Restaurant—and then ordered the same thing I did, spaghetti Bolognese. She noticed that I often drank beer with dinner, and one night she announced that she had been practicing in private and could now have a glass with me. She asked how I liked my steak and which country had the most considerate men and how American mothers raised their babies. She was constantly trying on new versions of herself: coloring her hair, or perming it, or straightening it. Her clothes always matched, and I never saw her wear the same outfit twice.

Until I came to Dongguan, most Chinese people I knew belonged to the educated class, and they felt keenly the difference between us. They wanted to know whether I considered myself American or Chinese; they were invariably surprised, even offended, when they found out that I could not read Chinese well, or that I dated American men. They lectured me about democracy and the Iraq War and the inability of the foreign press to understand China. Their nation had experienced 150 years of submission to the West, and this troubled history rose up between us whenever we talked. This was the world of my grandfather, and all my relatives, the world that many Chinese still lived in.

Chunming and her friends didn't care about any of that. They didn't care that my Chinese was bad or that I didn't know the names of famous Chinese writers, and they never asked my views on democracy. They had been born without many advantages but also without the burden of the nation that weighed on the educated, particularly men. When I did meet one of Chunming's male friends, these preoccupations usually rose to the surface. One time, a surgeon friend of hers named Ah Qiang asked me what I did, and I told him I was writing a book about migrant women.

"*Nanfengchuang* had a lot of pieces about that," he said, referring to a Chinese newsmagazine. "You can just use their articles and save yourself a lot of time."

Chunming sighed loudly. "Different people have their own points of view," she said. "She might see things in a different way from other people, and that's what she wants to write about."

I felt like standing up and cheering.

She turned to me. "Isn't that right?"

"That's right."

Ah Qiang persisted. "You should write about the problems with the Chinese constitution," he told me. "We have such a beautiful constitution, but when it goes down to the lowest level of government, officials act against it."

"That is so far from what she's writing about!" Chunming said with exasperation. She took out her mobile phone and began checking her messages, a signal that the conversation was over.

Chunming understood me instinctively. In a sense, she was engaged in the same endeavor: seeing life from a different point of view and writing her own story. She had saved all the volumes of the diary she had written since coming out from home. "Someday if I have the means, I would like to write," she told me. "I would write only about the simplest, most ordinary things."

*   *   *

One Sunday evening in December 2004, Chunming invited me out to a Hunan restaurant with friends: a nurse named Ah Ning, who had very white skin and an appealingly raspy voice, and two young men who were supervisors in a factory. Chunming looked chic in a black sweater and plaid pants with wide cuffs; she carried a fake Fendi handbag. The men wore their factory shirts.

As soon as I sat down, one of the men turned to me. "In your opinion, what are the differences between Kerry and Bush?"

"He's trying to get you to say whom you voted for," Chunming said.

"I voted for Kerry," I said reluctantly. I did not particularly want the conversation to go in this direction.

"Do you think China is ready for democracy?" he asked. He didn't think so. "If we could vote," he continued, "I would vote for Chiang Kai-shek. I think he was a good leader." Then: "Do you feel more Chinese or American?"

Three bottles of Tsingtao beer appeared on the table. My interlocutor was visibly excited: The only thing better than bullying me with politics was bullying me with beer and politics. "Might as well get drunk tonight," he announced.

Chunming came to my rescue. "I think it's stupid when people force each other to drink," she said.

Ah Ning quickly changed the subject. She had recently enrolled in a modern dance class at a health club, she said.

"I want to learn how to dance, too!" Chunming said. "I want to learn the cha-cha."

"I want to learn yoga," Ah Ning said.

She turned to me. "Do you know how to mix drinks?"

"What kind of drinks?" I asked.

"Like cocktails," she said.

I said I knew a few basic ones.

"I really want to learn how to mix drinks," Ah Ning said. "I would even work at a bar for free just to learn."

"I was at a party with clients recently at a hotel," Chunming said. "There were many foreigners there, and we were drinking chilled wine in glasses. I was holding the wine glass by the bowl, but someone told me you must hold it by the stem." Her eyes widened, the way they did when she was surprised or excited about something. "There are so many rules! But it's good to learn these things, because there will be times in your life that you attend such parties."

The young man tried to edge back into the conversation by asking Chunming what kind of work she did. "My company is foreign-invested," she said coolly. I don't think either of the men said a word during the second half of the meal. After dinner, Chunming and Ah Ning rushed both of them into a taxi; they lived in a remote part of the city, which meant they had an hour's ride home.

We hailed another taxi to go check out a health club that was offering yoga classes. Chunming leaned back in her seat and let out a sigh. That man was a fellow Hunanese, she told me; he had been introduced by a friend who wanted to set them up. The man had called her that afternoon and said he was in town for just one day. "He's from the same part of Hunan as me; otherwise I would not have invited him to dinner," she said.

"He is so childish!" Ah Ning said.

"He is unacceptable," Chunming agreed. "He had nothing to say. And he is three years younger than me."

I didn't say anything—by then I felt a bit sorry for the young man. I also realized that I had just been on my first Chinese blind date.

AT THE HEALTH CLUB, dance class was over, yoga met only twice a week, and none of the instructors was around. Ah Ning suddenly realized that we were near the Making Friends Club. "I wonder if there are any activities tonight. Let's go see!" We ran down the street and up the stairs to the club. The main room was almost deserted: no making friends tonight. Chunming and Ah Ning sat down and began flipping through the binders of the club's male members. "There are so many beautiful women, and look at these men!" Chunming said.

She flipped rapidly. "I look at the pictures first," she said. "You can't tell from looking at the photo if someone is any good. But the photos are useful at ruling out the really bad ones." She pointed to a pudgy man with a hapless look on his face, standing behind a fake picket fence. "Only the most low-class people still get a photo done in a studio. That's the kind of thing I did ten years ago! It's much better to get a photo in a park or a natural setting."

Ah Ning seemed to have dated a significant portion of the club's male membership. She showed me a photo of a man leaning against a tree. "He looks tall, but in person he isn't. It's just that he is standing alongside that tree."

She flipped to another photo. "This man looks like he has a kind face, but he is really not a nice person."

Flip. "This man is forty-eight years old. I told him, 'Even if I could accept you, my parents never could.' "

Flip. "This person has mental problems."

Ah Ning had recently gotten divorced and she was aggressively seeking a boyfriend. She had dated more than twenty men from the club and once went on four blind dates in a single day. "I met one guy who said he was very happy living in his rented eight-square-meter room," Ah Ning told me. "I said, 'Oh, really? Are you so happy living in your eight-square-meter room?' " A blind date with a teacher also flopped. "When he finished chewing his gum, he played with it with his fingers. I couldn't stand it. This person is a teacher! He teaches children!

"Every time after I meet one of these men," Ah Ning said, "I feel like crying."

"After I meet one of these men," Chunming said, "I feel like throwing up." She picked up another binder—FEMALES 74—to show me her own photo. It was a black-and-white shot of a girlish-looking Chunming with cropped hair, in artful soft focus—perhaps too artful, because only two men had phoned her up after seeing her picture. Her stated requirements for a mate were: KIND, HONEST, HUMOROUS, HAS AN APARTMENT. Hers was the only listing I had seen that mentioned a sense of humor.

"The apartment is not an absolute requirement," she said. "We could buy an apartment together. I just meant I would prefer that he had one." But she absolutely would not date anyone under 1.7 meters, because a man that short gave her no sense of security.

AFTER WE LEFT THE CLUB, Ah Ning elaborated on the man with mental problems. "I went on one date with him and he told me he had been hospitalized for two weeks with suicidal tendencies," she said. "At first I felt like I should help him, since I'm a nurse. But then I decided I shouldn't get wrapped up in it."

The man continued to send text messages to her mobile phone at odd times. "I really don't understand how someone with mental problems could be the chief financial officer of a five-star hotel," Ah Ning said.

"He lied to you, that's all," Chunming said.

We went into the TCBY frozen-yogurt shop, where Chunming suffered agonies of indecision before finally ordering a blueberry-cheesecake frozen-yogurt sundae. She instructed Ah Ning, who was having her period, that she must not eat anything cold, so her friend ordered a hot strawberry milk instead. It had a chemical pink color, like industrial waste.

The visit to the Making Friends Club had not been in vain. There was a new activity this weekend called Eight-Minute Date, and Ah Ning explained what she had heard about speed-dating. Chunming was excited to attend. She loved to try new things and she was an optimist by nature. These qualities had helped her survive in Dongguan, even if they were a mixed blessing when it came to dating.

"The problem is," Ah Ning said, "sometimes eight minutes is too long."

*   *   *

Living in the city changes what young women from the countryside expect out of marriage. Surveys have shown that migration makes a rural woman more likely to meet her future husband on her own, marry later, want fewer children, give birth in a hospital, seek equality in marriage, and view divorce as an acceptable option. More than 60 percent of migrant women in one survey cited either "building a happy home" or "having a partner in the career struggle" as the purpose of marriage, while fewer than 10 percent chose "having someone to rely on for life."

In traditional society, a young woman would live with her husband's family after she married and submit to the rule of her mother-in-law. She would also give birth in the home of her in-laws, symbolizing the claim of her husband's family over the baby. But migration is freeing the younger generation of such obligations: Couples in the city often pay for a wedding themselves, and a migrant woman soon to give birth is more likely to return temporarily to her own family home rather than her husband's.

For a long time, scholars believed that the vast majority of migrant women eventually returned to their villages to marry, have children, and work on the farm. Many migrants in the 1980s and 1990s did follow this path, but the fate of newer migrants is changing. More young women are marrying fellow migrants and setting up house in their adopted cities. If they do return to their native provinces, they often move to a provincial city rather than to the villages where they were born. And marriage does not necessarily mark an end to migration: Young couples frequently return home to marry and then go out again together.

Spending time with Chunming and her friends convinced me that the conventional wisdom—that most migrant women eventually return to the farm—was flawed. Everyone in their circle had been away from home for years; it was clear that they would never go back. But because changing one's residential status was expensive and cumbersome, they did not count as official Dongguan residents either. The scholars who studied returned migrants always did their research in rural villages, where they could conclude only that a person like Chunming was temporarily away from home. They could not see that she had already resettled somewhere else.

* * *

Chunming had two dates from the Making Friends Club. The first time, a man came in a taxi from another part of Dongguan. She went downstairs to meet him on the sidewalk outside her apartment building. They took a good look at each other.

"Hello," he said.

"Hello," she said.

"I think you're pretty," he said.

"Let's just be friends, then," she said. The taxi had not left yet, so the man got back in and cruised off.

The second date took place at a soymilk restaurant near Chunming's apartment. The man got lost and was half an hour late, so she started eating by herself. It was nine in the morning. When her date finally showed up, he was upset that Chunming had started without him. He tried to take charge and order a soup for her but she refused it.

"He ordered hot soup and cold soymilk," Chunming told me. "Can you imagine? A hot liquid and a cold liquid: That was his breakfast."

After this liquid nourishment, the man suggested they go for a walk together. "It was nine in the morning and he wants to go for a walk!"

Chunming told the man she had some things to take care of, but he didn't take the hint. "Let's just be friends, then," Chunming said. Finally he understood. After that Chunming gave up on the Making Friends Club. She put more faith in meeting people through the Internet, which she believed drew a higher class of men.

One day when I was over at her apartment, Chunming showed me how the QQ chat service worked. When you went online, you could pull down a list of everyone who was online at the moment, selecting for traits like native province, city of residence, age, and gender. She warned me that people talked about sex a lot. "These are things we can't say in the real world," she explained, "so we say them online."

She had been online a few minutes when a man approached. He was a friend of a friend and had been introduced to her as potential boyfriend material.

Are you working?

Yes, are you?

No, I'm at home.

Where are you?

The man was an urban planner in Dongguan, originally from Shandong Province. He was twenty-seven years old, three years younger than Chunming, though she lied and told him she was twenty-five. The conversation quickly progressed to turning on their computer video cameras so they could see each other. The young man looked serious and heavyset, with glasses.

Sorry, I am ugly. Are you frightened?

Chunming turned to me. "He looks like an honest person."

Not at all, she wrote. *I think you look okay.*

Are you married? Do you have a boyfriend?

No.

Ah, so you are more conservative, then?

No, I am not conservative, but I am more traditional.

In what way?

She leaned back in her chair, looking at me, thinking aloud. "In what way?"

The young man was impatient. *Sex?* The conversation frequently jumped ahead of her; the young man typed much faster than Chunming did. Educated people knew how to type, but Chunming had little formal schooling.

No, not in sex, she wrote. *To be honest, I go online to meet a boyfriend.*

Why must marriage be the goal?

It doesn't have to be. To meet friends is good, too.

How much can you accept? He was asking whether she would have sex with a man who was just a friend, Chunming interpreted for me.

When can we meet? I am free after work.

"Oh no!" she squealed. "He wants to meet me!"

Chunming met up with the young man that night. He seemed like a good person and he had a good job, she told me afterward. But he was very ugly, with a potbelly and a zit at the base of his nostril. Over the next few months, she seesawed between these conflicting points of view. *He is very ugly. He went to a brand-name school. He is mature for his age. He is very ugly.* She accompanied him on a shopping trip to buy a sofa for his apartment. She slept with him once, but she could not bring herself to start a real relationship with him. "Most Chinese marriages are not built on love," she said. "Perhaps I will have such a marriage. But I am not ready to compromise just yet."

*   *   *

Dongguan was not just a place for young women to change their fates. Older women also saw the city as a place to redefine themselves. One day I visited a dating service called the Dongguan City

Metropolis Destiny Planning Company. The club was smaller than the Making Friends Club and claimed to be more exclusive. Members had to be vocational college graduates or earn at least two thousand yuan a month. I met with the company's managing director and his two female assistants, a grueling experience that involved all three of them speaking over one another while their mobile phones rang nonstop. One of the assistants was young and soft-spoken; the other, Xiang Yang, was a middle-aged woman of imposing bulk, with a red face and a fur hat with aggressive-looking bristles. Both women were single, and they appeared to be working at the company in part to advance their marriage prospects.

The managing director planned to set up matchmaking offices around the city using a franchise model. But from his business card I learned that he was also hedging his bets.

COMPREHENSIVE PLANNING

TOURISM BUSINESS

REAL ESTATE PLANNING

TUTORS AND HOUSEKEEPERS

LICENSE APPLICATION AGENCY

CREATIVE DESIGN

ARTS TRAINING

MARKETING AGENCY

PROPERTY AGENCY

ANNUAL ASSET INSPECTIONS

CIS INPUT

RITES AND CEREMONIES

HEADHUNTING

LEGAL CONSULTING

FINANCIAL ACCOUNTS

MANAGEMENT CONSULTING

WEDDING PLANNING

JOBS CENTER

CIVIL INVESTIGATIONS
TAX AUDITING

As we were talking, a middle-aged woman walked in off the street to inquire about the club's services. She had a handsome long face and wore a sober black blazer and matching pants. Xiang Yang offered to take both of us down the street to see the club's activities center. As we left the office, I noticed that its front window was plastered with real estate listings.

The woman's name was Sun Cuiping, and she was from Anhui Province. She had been laid off from her job at a department store, then divorced her husband when she found out he was having an affair. Friends in Dongguan had urged her to come take a look at the city—she had been in town twenty days.

"You're very brave," I told her. I was astonished that a woman whose life had been upended by a homewrecker had chosen to come to Dongguan, famous for its population of kept women and karaoke girls.

"You should write about the lives of middle-aged women," Xiang Yang urged me. "Things are very hard for us. I have just met Big Sister Sun, and I know only part of her story. Yet I know that she has suffered injury."

She was still talking when I noticed that Big Sister Sun was crying. She stood stock-still in the middle of the sidewalk and turned away so we couldn't see her face. Displays of emotion in the Chinese always caught me off guard: People were perfectly self-contained until the moment they started weeping on a city street in broad daylight. Big Sister Sun rummaged in her purse; I gave her a tissue. "Give yourself some time," I said, mumbling generic phrases of reassurance. "Take things slowly."

We continued walking. Xiang Yang had been unnaturally quiet, but now she started up again as if Big Sister Sun were not even present. "Big Sister Sun is of the sixties generation," she said. "She is nice-looking, she is tall, she is capable. Yet society has told her that it doesn't want her. She was a beautiful girl once, yet now she is of a certain age. She cannot avoid having white hair. She cannot hide her wrinkles."

She went on and on in this declamatory vein, sacrificing Big Sister Sun rhetorically before our eyes. I was appalled at her callousness, but when I ventured a look at Big Sister Sun I saw that she was nodding quietly in agreement. "Many of my friends at this age are getting divorced," Big Sister Sun said.

"Would that it had happened sooner!" Xiang Yang announced dramatically.

"This is the time when a man is economically more comfortable, and there are many activities for him," Big Sister Sun continued. "He goes to the hotel, and there are young women. He goes to the sauna, and there are young women. Then he goes to the hair salon, and there are young women, too."

"In society today, men's economic situation is improving but their morality is getting worse," agreed Xiang Yang. "We must guide society to support middle-aged women like Big Sister Sun."

We arrived at the activities center, which had exercise machines, mahjong tables, and a reading room. Xiang Yang was in full cry. "This is a very crucial time," she said. "If Big Sister Sun is not rescued now, she may, like the seaweed, just be washed into the sea forever."

I didn't answer her—I was beginning to have a pretty good idea of why she was still single. I would have liked to spend more time with Big Sister Sun, minus the interpretive commentary; it was unendurable to watch one woman cry while another compared her to seaweed. Big Sister Sun gave me her Dongguan mobile-phone number so we could meet up another day. When I returned to my apartment, I felt as if I had just been through a harrowing emotional experience—as if I had been the one who had burst into tears on the sidewalk.

In the months afterward, I called Big Sister Sun's number many times, but it had been disconnected. I never learned if she found what she was looking for in Dongguan, whatever it was.

* * *

Dongguan was China's capital of prostitution. Business and the sex trade went hand in hand; a night out with a partner or a client frequently concluded at one of the city's many karaoke bars, massage parlors, hair salons, or saunas that were all fronts for prostitution. The industry's steadiest customers appeared to be factory owners from Hong Kong and Taiwan—men with money to spend, living away from their wives. All of my male friends in Beijing knew of Dongguan's reputation; those who had passed through had been propositioned in hotel lobbies and phoned in their rooms at night: *Sir, do you want a massage?* I was curious to learn about this world, but I needed a man to get inside.

I knew an American in town named Ben Schwall. He had buzz-cut blond hair and a rugby player's build, and he had worked in the diamond trade in Taiwan. Now he ran a bunch of ventures in Dongguan that sold security systems and lighting fixtures and, inevitably, mobile phones. I called him up and asked if he could introduce me to karaoke girls who engaged in prostitution. Ben had been doing business in China for a while and he took this request in stride, organizing an evening out with a local businessman friend. "These guys are a little bit crude," he warned me.

Ben's friend picked us up in a brand-new Honda minivan that seated eight people. It had cost 280,000 yuan, he told us as we climbed in, and he had a second one just like it, as well as a BMW.

He asked Ben, "Is she your wife?"

"No, we're just friends."

"Then I have an opportunity." He laughed. His name was Gong

Yaopei, but everyone called him *Lao Gong,* Old Gong, which was also a familiar term for a husband. He was probably in his mid-fifties, with a handsome gaunt face and tired eyes, like most of the Chinese entrepreneurs I knew. He looked even more tired when he smiled.

I asked Lao Gong what he did. He responded in gibberish, something about scientific instruments used by hygiene inspectors to check for microbes in food.

"How did you get into such a specialized business?" I asked. He did not answer directly. Instead he said he had previously sold infrared devices used by surveyors to measure long distances. Chinese entrepreneurship was nothing if not opportunistic, and many businessmen were involved in a string of specialized and completely unrelated ventures. The classmate of one Chinese friend of mine ran restaurants, a chain of pharmacies, and an English school.

Lao Gong took us to an eight-thousand-square-meter Japanese restaurant whose chief selling point appeared to be that it was eight thousand square meters. The place was palatial: miles of plush red carpeting, stands of fake bamboo, giant tanks for lobster and abalone. Hostesses rushed up to Lao Gong and walked backward ahead of him, like courtiers afraid to turn their backs on the emperor. It turned out that Lao Gong owned yet another unrelated business—interior decoration—and this restaurant owed him money. "So I eat for free," Lao Gong said, "the more the better." He led us through a maze of hallways, grandly throwing open doors at random. I glimpsed private rooms the size of entire restaurants, an acre of table at which a squadron of sushi-eaters could sit down together. "He is the king of Dongguan," Ben marveled.

We were joined at dinner by another businessman with a lined face and gentle, even more tired eyes; he and Lao Gong had grown up together ("His family bullied my family during the Cultural Revolution," Lao Gong said). The other guests were a manager of a local bank and a teacher whom Lao Gong introduced as "the head of the middle school's music department, who is great at singing karaoke." Ben explained to me the nature of their friendship with Lao Gong: The bank manager approved his business loans, while the teacher made sure his son received good grades in school.

A young woman named Rong Rong sat next to Lao Gong. She was a senior at a university in Guangzhou, majoring in English. She wore a tailored brown wool suit with high heels and carried an expensive handbag. Rong Rong looked like a college student on a job interview, except that no college student in China dressed like that. She was Lao Gong's mistress, but I could not bring myself to believe it. A girl like that could get a job at a multinational company or go abroad for graduate school. "Why would a girl like her be with a man like that?" I said to Ben.

Ben had first met Rong Rong with Lao Gong three years ago, when she was just a freshman. He shrugged. "She likes gifts."

Over the fanciest meal I had ever eaten in Dongguan—fresh sashimi, Kobe beef, curry crab, sake—the men passed a stapled sheaf of papers back and forth. I asked to look at it: It was a list of point spreads on upcoming soccer matches in the English Premier League. The men were all big gamblers who visited the casinos of Macao several times a year.

Such men were known in China as *dakuan*—self-made businessmen whose wealth carried a strong whiff of corruption. They were widely despised for their flashiness and free spending; when one was arrested, usually along with the official who had profited from his bribes, it was cause for celebration. To many educated Chinese, the *dakuan* in their amoral greed stood for everything that was wrong with their country today. Perhaps it was perverse, but I liked them. When Lao Gong and his friends asked what my book was about, they listened to what I said and did not immediately tell me how I should write it; I was not pestered to prove my loyalty to China. They took things at face value, which went a long way toward explaining their success. They had nothing to prove.

The middle-school teacher was different: He insisted on categorizing and defining and pinning down everything, and he started with me. "So are you writing your book from the positive angle?" he asked.

I explained that there was no positive or negative, that I hoped the book would reflect how things really were. Later I overheard him say to someone else, "She is writing a book from the positive angle."

Then he went to work on Ben. "When you go back to America, are you no longer used to eating Western food?"

Ben said he liked both Chinese food and Western food.

"Do you like Chinese food or Western food more?" the teacher asked.

"Chinese food," Ben said dutifully. He said to me in English, "I can see where this is going."

"Chinese food is the best food in the world," the teacher declared. "And all Chinese people are good."

"Really?" I said. "*All* Chinese people are good?"

"No," answered Lao Gong, who had not taken part in our conversation until now. "Seventy percent of Chinese people are bad." He spoke with such authority that the teacher did not dare contradict him. And there the matter rested: *Seventy percent of Chinese people are bad.* You could see why one man was the king of Dongguan and the other just a middle-school teacher who was great at singing karaoke.

THE CLUB AT THE SILVERWORLD HOTEL had its own entrance, flanked by sixteen hostesses who bowed deeply at the waist as we entered. Its lobby was done in luxe nightclub style: black interiors, fluorescent purple lighting, an entire wall of glass shelves filled with bottles of Chivas Regal and Johnnie Walker and Great

Wall wine. The bottles were lit from behind, like rare works of art. We were ushered into a private room lined with couches that faced three television screens. The giant screen in the middle was for karaoke music videos; the one on the right was for selecting songs and ordering drinks. Lao Gong's businessman friend tuned the left-hand screen to the Liverpool–Manchester United match and proceeded to ignore everyone for the night. Money trumped sex: no surprise there.

Rong Rong and Lao Gong sat down on the couch. She plucked a grape from a plate of fruit on the table and popped it in his mouth; he swallowed it expertly, like a trained seal. Servers brought in fruit plates, glasses, ice cubes, lemon slices, soda, Chivas, vodka. This parade of petty commerce would continue through the night, as people moved in and out of the room offering cigarettes, bouquets of red roses, oversize stuffed animals, and ethnic-style dance performances. A woman called a *mami* came in to tally which customers wanted sex and which just wanted to sing.

Then the girls entered. There were seven of them, wearing shiny gold evening gowns with spaghetti straps that made them look like high school girls on prom night. They lined up near the door, bare shoulders hunched against the powerful air-conditioning. A couple of them jostled each other and giggled, but no one raised her head to look at a customer. Each girl had a plastic tag clipped at her waist with a four-digit number. It was the length of the number that impressed me—the Silverworld Hotel had a digital capacity for ten thousand girls. There were parts of Mongolia where phone numbers weren't even that long.

If a man liked a girl, he would tell the *mami* her number, and the girl would come and sit next to him on the couch and plant her hand on his thigh. Customers could be very picky, so the *mami* would send in wave after wave of girls, and a man could dismiss one after another like a sultan bored with his harem. But there was usually someone to satisfy even the most demanding customer. The

Silverworld Hotel was not large by Dongguan standards, and it employed three hundred girls.

A YOUNG WOMAN NAMED AH LIN, number 1802, sat down next to me. "Do any of these men want to go out?" she whispered. Ah Lin was seventeen years old, with creamy white skin and the small, perfectly round face of a child. She had attended two years of high school in Chongqing before going out to work; her father was a migrant and her mother farmed. Ah Lin had initially planned to join a factory, but friends said that working in a karaoke bar was more lucrative. She had been a virgin when she started, and back then she had cried when men groped her too hard. Now on average she had sex with a customer four nights a week.

The working day at the Silverworld ran from 7:30 P.M. to 11:30 P.M. A girl made two hundred yuan an evening—twenty-five dollars—for sitting with a customer, pouring his drinks, placing fruit directly in his mouth, applauding his singing, and enduring his hugging, kissing, and groping.

"If you're more popular, you earn more," Ah Lin said.

I asked her what being "more popular" meant.

"If you have bigger breasts," she said flatly, "or are more stylish."

If a girl went out with a customer for sex, the club charged eight hundred yuan for a single encounter; that was called *kuaican*, fast food. Spending the whole night cost one thousand yuan, though a satisfied customer might give double or triple that amount in tips. Some of the girls didn't like to go with men very often. The ones who did could make twenty thousand yuan a month—$2,500, an astronomical sum in the migrant world. The girls were not supposed to smoke on the job, to eat too much of the food that the customers ordered, or to have sex with anyone in the karaoke room. Other than that, they lived a casual and disorderly existence. In a city where most lives were ruled by the factory clock, they slept as late as they pleased and worked fewer hours than anyone I had met.

Ah Lin had seen enough of the world to draw some conclusions. Sichuanese men were the worst gropers, and stingy to boot. Foreign men were kinder than Chinese men. Some of the customers asked the girls to be their girlfriends, but Ah Lin would never fall for that. Yet she said she would like to have a boyfriend, and she wanted to get married someday. No one back home knew what Ah Lin did for a living. She told her parents she worked in a factory, and she sent home only a fraction of her earnings so they would not become suspicious. Some of the girls had worked in a factory when they first came out from home, but they would never go back to that life now. They had no illusions about that.

THE MAMI SITS AT THE APEX of the karaoke world. She matches up customers who want to have sex with girls willing to go out on a given night; a girl can request to stay in if she is having her period or not feeling well. The *mami* gets a cut from each girl's earnings, somewhere in the neighborhood of 15 percent. A good *mami* earns the loyalty of her girls, and when she moves to a different club the girls go too.

Two types of women work in the karaoke rooms. "DJs" manage the rooms, serving food and drink and helping customers select songs; the women who drink with customers are called *zuotai xiaojie*, young ladies sitting at tables. *Xiaojie* usually have sex with customers, and some DJs do as well. DJs don't give a cut to a *mami*, but they must bring in a certain number of customers each month or pay a fee to the club. Many clubs hire more DJs than they have rooms, pitting them against each other to please customers and earn more money for the club. The lowest people in the club hierarchy are the waiters, who come and go as invisible as eunuchs: Cut off from the sex trade, they have the least earning power.

The karaoke world is dreamy and unreal. Young women in evening gowns laugh at all your jokes, until their flattery feels as natural as breathing. "You have such well-preserved skin!" one *xiao-jie* said to me, then turned to Ben and exclaimed, "Your Chinese is so good!" They tease their customers and address them as *laogong*, husband; the men seem to like this, perhaps because they are unable to imagine, even in their wildest fantasies, a world without wives. Every once in a while someone stands up to sing and everyone else applauds. The room is dark and it has no windows, and your glass is always full.

The young women were disarmingly frank about what they did for a living. I met many of them on two successive nights at different clubs; when I said I was writing a book about Dongguan and asked about their work, not a single one played coy or denied that she had sex with customers. Occasionally I sensed small deceptions. They might overstate their earnings, or claim they had been tricked into this line of work; several told me, rather unconvincingly, that they planned to quit their jobs the following day. But they were not cynical and hard, as I had expected them to be. They were girlish and they giggled like teenagers, and sometimes as we were talking they started to cry.

I was torn about what to think of them. It would certainly be awful to have sex with the type of Chinese man who frequented karaoke lounges; in that respect, they had my sympathy. Yet much of their workday was spent in leisurely fashion—sipping cocktails, eating peanuts, watching music videos—and for that, they made more money in a month than someone like Min earned in a whole year. The initial decision to enter this world was surprisingly casual. Most of the young women I talked to had started working at a karaoke club because a friend or cousin was doing it, the same way a migrant would go to a certain city or factory because she knew someone there. After they arrived, they came up with reasons to stay: It was easy work, it paid well, and you could learn about the world.

The karaoke girls came from better circumstances than the factory girls I had met—that, too, was a surprise. Often they had grown up in a small city or a town rather than on the farm; a fair number were only children or the youngest in their families, which meant they had fewer financial burdens. Quite a few had attended high school, which placed them in the rural elite. Ah Lin, with two years of high school, was the most educated young person in her village. "At home they are expecting me to come out and make a success of myself," she said. "If they knew I was working in a place like this, they would never forgive me."

Compared to the factory girls, they were freer to do what they wanted. Maybe they were too free, and lacking a clear purpose had made them lose their bearings once they came to the city. No one had forced them into prostitution. In fact, they had chosen this line of work because they expected more out of life. Most of the girls wanted to return home eventually to set up a clothing shop or a hair salon—almost everybody knew someone who had done this. A motivated young woman could save enough money in a year or two to pull it off. But it was easy to lose your way.

The next night at another club in a five-star hotel, I met Ding Xia. She was twenty-three years old, tall, with sculpted cheekbones and a high nose—genuinely pretty, unlike most of the girls, who were just skinny and young. She had been out from home for six years and she claimed to have saved four hundred thousand yuan. Once she had made another hundred thousand, she said, she would move to a city where no one knew her, open a shop, and live a simple life. Her story did not hold together; for one thing, setting up a shop cost only a fraction of the money Ding Xia was talking about. Her lies seemed intended to justify, perhaps to herself, why she was still here.

It was also possible for a *xiaojie* to rise and become a *mami*. The *mami* in the club where Ding Xia worked was petite and businesslike; she wore a navy-blue pantsuit and carried a walkie-talkie, and the title on her business card read PROMOTIONS MANAGER. She told me she was in charge of sixty girls and had previously run a clothing business.

"Do a lot of girls rise from being a *xiaojie* to being a *mami*?" I asked.

"Very few," she said. "One percent."

"Why not?"

"You need to have skills to do this," she said. She politely toasted me with a glass of beer and excused herself. As soon as she had left, Ding Xia turned to me and said, "She used to be a *xiaojie* here." Then she put her finger to her lips. Ding Xia had worked at this club long enough to know. But most people moved in and out of jobs so quickly that to invent the past, along with the future, was easy enough.

AS THE NIGHT WINDS DOWN, the fantasy world dissolves: The food is gone, the bottles drunk, and everyone is tired of singing. Some of the *xiaojie* excuse themselves to change their clothes; they return wearing jeans and windbreakers that make them look alarmingly young. They yawn and rest their heads on the shoulders of the men. Sometimes this preserves for another moment the illusion that they are their sweethearts—but what they resemble most are sleepy and affectionate daughters, up past their bedtime.

Finally the bill for the evening arrives. There is a fee for the room, a bill for food and drink, and two hundred yuan, cash, paid to each *xiaojie*. The woman selling stuffed animals returns to the room to collect, but the colleague of Ben's who had showered a sulky young woman with attention all night long does not want to spend money on her now that the night is over. She relinquishes a stuffed bear reluctantly—another daughter, this one a little spoiled. The DJ punches her contact information into another customer's Palm Pilot for future room reservations, and everyone leaves the karaoke room together. The men, accompanied by the *mami*, head toward the elevator, and the girls disappear down a different hallway.

*   *   *

Occasionally a woman hit the jackpot. Ah Ning, Chunming's recently divorced friend, started dating a wealthy local Dongguan man. One evening she invited Chunming and me over for dinner. The block of apartments where she lived felt heavy with decay; wastewater from air-conditioning units dripped down the sides of buildings in rusty orange trickles, like tears. But inside the apartment was spacious and nicely decorated, with light colors and wood floors.

Ah Ning was wearing a long ivory skirt trimmed with eyelet lace and a matching cardigan. She looked pretty and happy, and she had cooked us a dinner of steamed fish, spicy spare ribs, and a soup of chicken feet, papaya, and tomatoes. Over dinner she told us about her boyfriend, who was away on a business trip. He was eight years older than she was. The two of them had recently returned from a vacation in Beijing, where he had spent most of his time gambling on soccer matches.

"What does he do for a living?" Chunming asked.

"He does everything," Ah Ning said.

Chunming's eyes widened. "Everything?"

"He grew up around here. All of the people from here are involved in gambling and smuggling," Ah Ning said. "It's just what they grew up with." At her boyfriend's urging, Ah Ning had started to play high-stakes mahjong and had recently lost six thousand yuan—about $750—in one game.

Each detail sounded worse than the last. "Is he good to you?" I asked.

"Oh, he is so good to me!" she said.

Chunming asked, more pointedly, "Has he been married before?"

Ah Ning lowered her voice. "Yes. He has a daughter, about seven."

That day Chunming had stumbled on a new method of meeting men. Someone had posted a photograph of a beautiful woman on a matchmaking Web site but listed Chunming's phone number next to it. She wasn't sure if it was a mistake or a prank, but all day long she had been bombarded with phone calls from suitors.

Are you the woman in the picture?

Do you have long hair?

Are you 1.66 meters tall?

After dinner, Chunming went into the living room to watch a television serial about doctors in ancient Korea struggling to aid the residents of a leper colony. Chunming found their humanitarian efforts very moving, but she was constantly interrupted by phone calls from strange men.

"Hello," she would say. "Who is this?"

Listening. Then: "Yes, someone posted that picture and that information but it isn't mine. Only the phone number is mine."

Pause. "Never mind, we can still make friends," she would say in honeyed tones. "Where are you from? What do you do?"

The men did industrial automation and worked as factory foremen; they were from Jiangsu and Gansu. After chatting some more, Chunming would say she was busy at the moment, but they should keep in touch. She was always the one to cut the conversation short. After she hung up, she scrolled through her phone messages. *Hello, I am a factory manager in Tangxia.* She beamed. "It doesn't matter. I can still make new friends. And maybe some of them will want to buy parts from our company." I had to admire her resourcefulness. She had turned a case of mistaken identity into her personal dating service, with the backup option of convincing these men to purchase parts for industrial molds.

"That woman must be really beautiful," Chunming said as she scrolled through her list of messages and missed calls.

"And yet when you tell them it's not you," I said, "they still go on talking to you."

"So many people in this city are so lonely," Ah Ning said.

THAT EVENING, we decided to check out the local nightlife, which centered on a newly opened shopping plaza of clubs and bars. Inside the places were dark and deserted, with purple neon lights and throbbing music and small groups of heavily made-up women whose air of unfathomable boredom marked them as prostitutes. Chunming fielded phone messages as we walked.

I am a government official. I have lived here six years.

What are you doing tonight?

Hello, can we make friends?

We ended up in a bar near Ah Ning's home. It was crowded with young office workers, and we stayed long enough to witness some strange scenes. After many drinking games, a young woman threw herself at a man who was probably a work colleague. She wrapped her arms around his neck and nestled into his chest. The man did not embrace so much as endure: He stood with his arms hanging stiffly at his sides, like a soldier consigned to guard duty during a rainstorm. When I looked again, the young woman had recovered and was chatting with her girlfriends; apparently the man had taken the opportunity to escape the bar. Nearby, a woman with fleshy thighs in a leopard-print miniskirt danced in a metal cage raised a few feet above the floor. After several songs, she crawled out of the cage through a low square opening in the back, like a door for a dog. She padded onto the floor, brushed off her knees, and then—in a small moment of glory appreciated only by me—resumed the upright posture of a primate. She walked over to the bar and ordered a drink.

A girlfriend of Ah Ning's joined us. Five bottles of Tsingtao beer materialized on our table, and the women played drinking games. Ah Ning and her friend drank fast; several men from another table wandered over for a dice game. Around midnight, Chunming suggested that she and I leave for Ah Ning's apartment, where we were spending the night. The men were still sending her messages.

Where are you now?

What are you doing?

I am a bundle of flaming fire.

AT ONE A.M., the phone rang. It was Ah Ning's girlfriend. Ah Ning was too drunk to walk, could we help? Chunming went out. The friend lived one unit over in the same apartment complex where we were staying, and Chunming returned to tell me that they had put Ah Ning to sleep on the friend's couch.

At two A.M., the phone rang again. Ah Ning was wandering around the hallway and refused to sleep, could we help? Chunming went out again. I struggled back into uneasy sleep.

At 2:30 A.M., Chunming returned. She walked into the guest room where I was sleeping, turned on the overhead light, and sat down cross-legged on the bed. "I have something to tell you," she said. When she had arrived at the friend's apartment, Ah Ning was rambling incoherently about having to go upstairs and explain things to a man. Chunming and the friend didn't know what she was talking about, but they finally agreed to take her upstairs. The man who answered the door was skinny and dark, wearing shorts and an undershirt. He and three other men in similar attire were playing mahjong. The man let Ah Ning and her friends in, led them to a spare bedroom, pointed to a bed where they should deposit her, and returned to his game.

It dawned on Chunming that this man was Ah Ning's boyfriend. He wasn't away on a trip, and he did not appear to be at all concerned about her. "She lied and said he was on a business trip, when he was home playing mahjong with his friends," Chunming told me. "And she always says that he's so good to her. And this guy was old! And really ugly!"

The next morning, we stopped by the man's apartment to leave Ah Ning's purse with her. The boyfriend answered the door. His face was narrow and tough and darkish red, like a cord of beef jerky; he looked to be in his forties. He did not say a word to either of us. Chunming was right: He didn't look like much. Ah Ning was still asleep in the spare bedroom. She could barely open her eyes, and she accepted her purse without saying anything. "Call me when you wake up," Chunming said.

The next time I saw Chunming, I asked her about Ah Ning. What had she said about that night? Was she still with the same boyfriend? Chunming said her friend had not been honest with her about it, and they did not speak of it again. Ah Ning had not, after all, hit the dating jackpot. She was just pretending to be happy. In the end her relationship seemed like just another case of mistaken identity.

9 *Assembly-Line English*

In Dongguan, I often went to restaurants alone. While I ate, I would write in my notebook or read an American magazine. Invariably a waitress or a restaurant patron would appear at my shoulder, looking on in reverence as I communed with my native tongue. "Your English must be amazing!" they would say at last.

I would explain that I was born in America.

"Your English is probably Grade Eight, then?"

I would answer that Americans did not get graded on our English ability, as the Chinese did. English was as ordinary to me as Chinese was to them, I would say, but this only compounded their sense of awe.

"Your English must be at least Grade Eight, then!"

People were always disappointed to learn I was a journalist. With my ability, I was told, I could be a highly paid translator at a trading company. English was the path to riches and satisfaction; to them I was like someone who had won the lottery but refused to cash in my ticket.

ALMOST EVERYONE IN CHINA had studied English in school, sometimes for years, but it was the rare person who could speak the language. Lessons emphasized grammar and the memorization of vocabulary lists; teachers were frequently as tongue-tied as their students. The group mentality was a factor—better to remain in anonymous silence than to risk embarrassment by opening your mouth. The ubiquity of English study seemed only to increase the respect for it: Despite many attempts and much effort, the language continued to defy mastery.

English also underlay the working life of Dongguan, where it was the language of business for the thousands of factories catering to foreign clients. This didn't mean people actually understood English; they learned just enough to function within their specific industry. Often they spoke in abbreviations and acronyms, a truncated language that would have confused any American. On an order form, FOB HK—short for "Free on Board Hong Kong"—indicated at what point a buyer would take ownership of a product he had ordered; L and W and H described its dimensions. Plastic packaging was PP or PE, though few people could have told you what those letters stood for. The machines of the assembly line also functioned in broken English, instructing workers to ROUTE FINDER and KEYBOARD TEST and PRESS ANY KEY TO SEND LOOPBACK Q TO QUIT.

Almost everyone I knew in Dongguan had gathered herself and made a determined assault on English at some point. For a while, Min spent her evenings studying a dog-eared textbook whose title was *Crazy English Crash Course*; the first third of the book was liberally marked up from her older sister's failed attempt on the language sometime earlier. Jiang Haiyan carried around a pocket-size phrasebook, and the last time I saw Chen Ying, the woman from the White-Collar class who had moved into management, she was planning to study English on her own and take the vocational college exam. Even the karaoke girls regarded English as a way out: It could impress a foreign customer into hiring a *xiaojie* as a clerk or a secretary.

Sometimes aspiring English speakers drew me into conversations as disjointed as the dialogue in a Beckett play.

How old are you?

Very good! How old are you?

Yes.

I was not surprised when Chunming decided to study English. She signed up at a language school that promised students would speak like American fifth-graders after a year of study. "I figure that's pretty good," she said. "A fifth-grader can express just about everything." The school's chief advertisement was the founder's nine-year-old son, who was said to speak English fluently. Chunming had her own reasons for learning the language. "If I learned English," she told me, "I could enter new circles." By then, I knew her well enough to translate that remark: English might be another way to find a husband.

*   *   *

The language school was in the Dongguan Science Museum, a haphazard pile of concrete shapes that might have looked futuristic in 1994 when it was built. Chunming took me there one evening after dinner. The museum was closed for renovation; in the darkness within, the scaffolding that clung to the walls looked like some skin disease that was eating away the building. We felt our way up five flights of stairs, as Chunming related the school's mythology in a whisper. Its founder had spent twenty years perfecting his teaching system; recently, he had patented it. The school had three hundred students. Its average monthly tuition was six hundred yuan, about seventy-five dollars.

On the top floor of the museum was a single office with the light still on. A sign at the entrance read:

ASSEMBLY-LINE LEARNING MACHINES

In a large fluorescent-lit room with low ceilings, half a dozen students sat apart from one another at long tables. On each table squatted an oval metal machine with rotating vertical panels that were fitted with cards; the cards were printed with columns of words that moved past the students in a steady stream. The machines filled the room with a muffled whirring sound, like a deck of cards being shuffled.

A column of words floated past me.

FUCK

CLEAN

RUDE

PIZZA

CREEP

At one end of the room, an older man sat in front of a computer. He handed me his business card without standing up. It said, in Chinese:

MR. WU'S DYNAMIC EDUCATION TECHNOLOGY LTD.

WU GUANXI, PRESIDENT

CHIEF DESIGNER OF MR. WU'S DYNAMIC LANGUAGE

PROCESSING FACTORY

INVENTOR OF MR. WU'S DYNAMIC EDUCATIONAL AID FACILITIES

FOUNDER OF MR. WU'S DYNAMIC EDUCATIONAL SCIENCE

ORIGINATOR OF MR. WU'S DYNAMIC WORLD LANGUAGE

HEAD COACH OF MR. WU'S DYNAMIC ENGLISH ADVANCED

SIMULTANEOUS INTERPRETATION TRAINING CLASS

Mr. Wu was forty-five years old, with a square face, baggy jowls, and rumpled hair that looked as if it had been slept on recently. He was somewhat overweight. He did not fit the image of a teacher or even a city person—he resembled the kind of government official you might meet in a small Chinese town. More precisely, he resembled the driver of the kind of government official you might meet in a small Chinese town. He did not look very dynamic.

The guiding principle of Mr. Wu's school was that treating people like machines was the key to mastering English. After learning the alphabet and the phonetic sounds of the language, a student sat at a machine while columns of English words rotated past. The student read aloud each word and wrote it down without knowing what it meant, week after week, until he attained the highest speed. He then proceeded to another machine that showed Chinese definitions of words; next he advanced to short sentences. At each stage, he wrote the word or sentence in English and said it aloud without comprehending its meaning. When a student achieved the top speed—able to write six hundred English sentences in one hour—he graduated to basic grammar. Only then did he learn the meaning of the words, phrases, and sentences he had been repeating for months.

Mr. Wu called this method "guidance-style teaching." As far as I could see, this meant there were no teachers—the machines imparted everything the students needed to know. His ideal student worked eleven hours a day: Study four hours, eat lunch, nap, study four more hours, eat dinner, study three more hours. That was the exact schedule of the Dongguan factory, down to the three hours' daily overtime limit mandated by the labor law. "On the assembly line, people can sit and work for eight or ten hours without rest," Mr. Wu said. "If only we could learn that way, how good it would be!"

His methods contradicted all received wisdom about learning a language—chiefly, that speaking, comprehension, and teachers were crucial to the process. Mr. Wu dismissed all of that. Chinese teaching methods focused too much on memorization, he said; the classroom turned students into passive receptacles. Assembly-Line English forced them into action.

"Your hand, brain, eyes, and mouth must learn to react quickly and automatically," Mr. Wu explained. "You don't have time to translate a word into Chinese or to memorize it. You must train yourself to respond instinctively." By pressing so many body parts into service, he said, Assembly-Line English stimulated different regions of the brain to work harder. Science had shown that human beings used only 5 percent of their cerebrums. Mr. Wu was full of such facts. The average person wrote two hundred sentences an hour. Women could recite ninety sentences a minute, but men could manage only seventy-five. If a person studied English for ten hours every day, he could work as a simultaneous interpreter in three years. In this respect, Mr. Wu resembled a man who had reduced the universe to a string of chemical formulas: No single fact was wrong, but the combination as a whole missed something. Yet he had a point—there *was* a problem with the way English was taught in Chinese classrooms, and student passivity was a big part of it. You might cram your way into a perfect score on the TOEFL exam—the most widely used test of English proficiency—but you could not memorize your way into fluency no matter how hard you tried.

After Mr. Wu's lecture, Chunming and I wandered around the classroom. She recognized a student she had met on a past visit to the school. Liu Yixia was twenty-one years old, with a round face, bright eyes, and a bowl haircut that gave her the look of a muppet. She had spent a year studying English here, doing clerical work in return for room and board and free classes. Under Chunming's watchful eye, Liu Yixia chatted with me in English. She didn't sound the least bit like an American fifth-grader. But she wasn't afraid to speak, and she didn't hide her mouth behind her hand or apologize continuously for her mistakes.

Now Liu Yixia had a job teaching English to factory executives—which surprised me, although it shouldn't have. In Dongguan, barely knowing something qualified you to teach it to others. I asked her what she planned to do next.

"How do you say 'international trade'?" she asked me in Chinese. I told her. Her aspirations seemed as wide as the world, and as easy as speaking a word aloud.

Chunming and I walked out of the building and crossed the broad green lawn in front of the science museum. Night had fallen, and floodlights cast giant shadows in our path. "I just have to set my resolve," Chunming said. "This year I will either learn English or start my own business."

*   *   *

In her first year out from home Liu Yixia lived, breathed, and slept Assembly-Line English. She worked in the office during the day, and in the evenings she studied on Mr. Wu's machines. She shared a small room behind the classroom with two other women; all three were studying English, but Liu Yixia worked the hardest. "I was a year older than the other two," she told me, "so I felt pressure to do better than them." She came from the poor, landlocked province of Jiangxi, where her parents farmed and raised ducks. She had always liked languages; at home, her parents spoke different dialects and she was used to switching between them, and when she started learning English in middle school she did well. But she did not test into college, and her family lacked the money to support her studies anyway, so Liu Yixia went out to Dongguan to work.

At Mr. Wu's school, she worked to improve her pronunciation—how she managed that when there was no one around to correct her mistakes, I don't know. She was Mr. Wu's star pupil, but they had a rocky relationship. "He was quite mean to me sometimes," she told me. "And he wouldn't let me memorize lists of vocabulary words."

"He wouldn't let you memorize vocabulary words?" I asked.

"He insisted I learn English his way. So I had to study my vocabulary lists in secret."

Liu Yixia had another fight with Mr. Wu when she left. "He wanted to take a picture of me," she said, "but I wouldn't let him." Mr. Wu used photos of his students in the school's promotional materials, but Liu Yixia was proud of what she had accomplished and she didn't want anyone else claiming credit. "Everything I've done," she told Mr. Wu, "I've done on my own, not because of you."

Even by Dongguan standards, Liu Yixia was in a fearful rush. In the nine months since she had left Mr. Wu's school she had held six teaching jobs, a whirlwind tour of the various incarnations of managerial incompetence. In one job, she took the initiative to visit other schools to observe different teaching methods; her boss accused her of moonlighting on the sly and fired her. At her next job, someone thought it would be a good idea to run a language school without scheduled classes. Whenever a student showed up, Liu Yixia would have to teach a lesson on the spot. "I taught five to six hours a day, all different levels," she said. "One minute I would be teaching elementary level, the next I would be teaching advanced." She was so exhausted that she quit after a month without getting paid.

In her current job, Liu Yixia taught two hours every evening and had the rest of the day to prepare lessons and study on her own. She earned 1,500 yuan a month—almost two hundred dollars, a respectable sum. But she was already clashing with the school's director. He wanted her to cover a lot of material quickly; she thought the students should gain confidence in speaking first. He overruled her teaching style, which featured games and student participation, in favor of lectures. The school director did not speak any foreign languages.

All of Liu Yixia's employers thought she was a college graduate with a degree in English, because that was what she told people in job interviews. The most impressive thing about her—that she had found a way to acquire a foreign language without formal study— was something she hid from almost everyone she knew.

SIX MONTHS AFTER WE FIRST MET, I visited Liu Yixia at her school in Shijie—yet another industrial district of Dongguan where I had never been. She had grown out her hair; she wore silver-rimmed glasses, a no-nonsense pinstripe dress, and black heels. She looked quite grown-up, although she wobbled a bit when she walked. Over spare ribs and rice at a fast-food restaurant, we talked, in Chinese, about English. Liu Yixia wanted to get a job as a translator at a factory so she could improve her English—*How do you say international trade?*—but without factory experience no one would hire her. She was obsessed with the language; our dinner conversation never strayed from this subject.

After we had finished eating, Liu Yixia looked at me and asked, "How do you think I should improve my English?"

"You should talk with native speakers as much as you can," I said. The moment I spoke, I realized this was basically useless advice, since I had rarely seen a Westerner in Dongguan outside the lobby of the Sheraton. In truth, the best way to learn English was to date a foreigner—untold numbers of *xiaojie* had attained fluency this way—but I could not say that to Liu Yixia.

"How about the travel industry?" I asked her.

She placed her palm flat against the top of her head. "Look at me. I don't meet the minimum height requirement. Tour guides must be at least 1.6 meters tall."

Right—that was another dumb suggestion. I had forgotten about all the ways in which height could affect the utility of English in a place like Dongguan. Meanwhile, Liu Yixia worried that her language skills were deteriorating; working as a teacher in the commercial schools of Dongguan felt like a dead end. In a city dominated by factories, private schools were just another low-level service. In the official school system, teachers enjoyed prestige and benefits, but Liu Yixia would never gain entry to their world. "They have their own system," she said. "They can't accept that I got my experience in society."

After lunch, Liu Yixia took me back to her school—a four-story office building that was almost deserted at this hour. A few teachers were shooting pool in one classroom; two young men sang karaoke in another, their reedy voices echoing down the hallway. The classrooms filled up only in the evenings when people got off work. Schools were usually dead at night, but in Dongguan the schedule for learning had been turned upside down, as if these institutions were tied to a time zone half a world away.

In her classroom, Liu Yixia showed me her English textbooks. She pointed out one that she liked because it encouraged students to practice what they had learned; she criticized another for covering too little material in each lesson. *From ABC to English Conversation* contained a sample conversation that bore no relation to Dongguan reality:

> Are those factories?
> No, they aren't. They are parks.

Liu Yixia picked up a piece of chalk and started scrawling words on the blackboard. What was the difference, she asked me, between the *s* sound in *television* and the *ge* sound in *change*? Where should the stress be in the word *consultant*? How was the *s* in *sea* different from the *ts* in *cats*? *Television. Change. Sea. Cats.* These were strange and unrelated questions, but that was what happened when your teacher was a machine.

She lived upstairs from the classrooms in a dorm with two other women. The room had two bunk beds, a small bathroom, and more textbooks: on Liu Yixia's desk, under her bed, in a backpack on the floor. She was an English-textbook junkie. "I probably have thirty books for learning English," she said. "No single book can have everything you need to know." One of her few possessions that was not a textbook was a photo album. It featured Liu Yixia in standard migrant poses: standing in front of a municipal building, visiting a park with girlfriends. She pointed to one of the pictures. "These two girls have now determined to 'soak themselves in English.' They want to spend the next year or two just learning it." Both of the young women were enrolled at Mr. Wu's school. They had shaved their heads to express their commitment, as Buddhist monks did when joining a monastery. To learn English, it was necessary to renounce the world.

*   *   *

Assembly-Line English was not the only dubious language enterprise in Dongguan. The English craze, pairing a feverish desire to learn the language with complete ignorance of how to go about it, was tailor-made for frauds. One company called Ladder English targeted ambitious parents. For a fee of 5,500 yuan—almost seven hundred dollars, a large sum for a Chinese family—the school supplied English teaching materials for children and regular home visits by "educational consultants" to track a child's progress. As a marketing tool, the school invited parents and children to free classes that had the energy of direct-sales meetings. Child-development experts lavished praise on the school's methods, while parents fought to sign up their children. A few teachers would take the children into another room and teach them a few English phrases; when the youngsters returned, babbling in a foreign language, their parents were usually moved to sign up on the spot.

In truth, Ladder English was riddled with deceptions. Its child-development experts and some of the most enthusiastic parents at the free classes were actually company employees, according to articles in the local press. Its "educational consultants" did not visit families more than once or twice, and they were not teachers but salespeople, who earned a commission of one thousand yuan per customer. The salespeople had to put up considerable money when they joined the company to buy educational magazines, pay transport fees, and rent rooms for the free classes. Ladder English was essentially a pyramid scheme, fueled by the desperation to learn English.

No one at the company, which operated on a franchise model, would agree to speak with me. As part of her tour of managerial incompetence, Liu Yixia had worked briefly for Ladder English and described its tactics. Salespeople were instructed to wait outside elementary schools as they let out for the day, to approach the parents who drove their own cars and feign affection for their children. "When the child came out, you would play with the child," Liu Yixia told me. "Then the parents and child together would be invited to attend the Ladder English lecture." Liu Yixia left the company after ten days. "I thought in some way it was cheating people," she said.

A different deception involved foreign teachers. Young black men who said they were from Canada or England showed up at schools around Dongguan, offering their services as English instructors. It could have been a watershed moment in China's march toward racial diversity, except that it wasn't. One parent told me her daughter's kindergarten class cried at the sight of their new teacher, because they had never seen a black person before. The school fired him.

One day I was visiting Liu Yixia when Joseph, her fellow teacher ostensibly from Canada, came into the room. He was black, about thirty years old, with a handsome face and an easygoing manner. He greeted me in heavily accented English.

"Are you married?" was his first question.

"What is your cell-phone number?" was his second.

After Joseph breezed out of the room, I asked Liu Yixia, "Where is he from?"

"He said he's from Canada."

"He's not originally from Canada," I said. "I can tell by the way he speaks."

She thought for a moment. "He also mentioned another country. Gan Da . . ."

"Uganda?"

"Yes. Uganda."

I finally understood the mystery of the black teachers. They were Africans, coming to backwaters and passing themselves off as native English speakers to school administrators who didn't know the difference. Over the years, more than thirty thousand African students had attended university in China, as part of Beijing's policy to support its allies in the developing world. It made sense for them to stay on as foreign teachers. At Liu Yixia's school, Joseph earned more money than she did and taught fewer hours.

Liu Yixia admonished me for giving Joseph my phone number. "You should be careful," she said. "He will be calling you all the time." She said that Joseph frequently hit on his female students; when he asked one for her number, she usually responded by never attending class again. Occasionally one of Joseph's students would ask Liu Yixia how to say a sentence in English: *I can be your friend but not your girlfriend.*

* * *

On Thursday evenings Liu Yixia taught English at a Japanese-owned electronics factory, and one evening I went with her. The four men and two women in the class worked in sales or management, and all were older than she was.

She handed back their test papers. "Don't worry too much about your scores today," she said, immediately breaking with a thousand-year tradition of grade worship. "The test of your English is not in that. It is in how much you can use."

The students started to review a lesson from the week before. Liu Yixia turned to a student in the front row and asked, in English, "What did you learn?"

"You want me to speak in English?" he asked, in Chinese—not a promising start. He struggled, then finally said in English, "I learned some stories. It is very interesting."

"Can you tell some English stories to me?" she asked.

A long silence. Then, in Chinese: "I have forgotten."

The next student said, "I learned some new words and expressions."

"What else?"

A long silence. Then, in Chinese: "I don't know how to say it."

"Okay, your turn," Liu Yixia said to a woman in the second row.

In Chinese: "It's hard to say."

Liu Yixia switched to Chinese. "Learning English is speaking English. If you are not speaking English, you are not learning English. You must not be afraid to make a mistake. I make many mistakes. I have never been afraid of this."

It was true. Liu Yixia could not distinguish between the *l* and *r* sounds. She couldn't even say the word *pronunciation*—she called it "pronuntion." She sometimes didn't understand what her students said; occasionally she corrected them when they were in the right. Often she answered their questions incorrectly. But she had the right instinct when it came to teaching, and somewhere along the way she had figured out the secret of learning a foreign language, which started with being unafraid.

THE STUDENTS CLUSTERED AROUND ME during a break. I had given a short speech in English at the start of class, introducing myself and speaking slowly enough that they could understand me. They were, after all, college-educated, and they had been taking this class for months. But after watching them struggle through the lesson, I realized they had probably not understood a word I said.

The men took the lead. "Which is better, China or America?"

"American cities are much safer, right? And the quality of the people is much higher."

"Do you miss China very much?"

"She has lived in China six years," the woman who had the best English in the class answered impatiently. "You still haven't figured that out?" The students asked me many questions about America. But not a single one ventured to speak to me in English.

After the break, they moved on to a lesson about a camping trip. Liu Yixia asked them to either read a passage aloud or tell the story in their own words. Every student chose to read the passage—they read well, much better than they spoke. Then she asked the students to retell the story to her. The woman with the best English in the class had memorized the entire text, word for word. The next student tried to pull off the same stunt. But when he forgot a single word in the text he stopped, a record thrown off by one faulty groove, until Liu Yixia prompted him.

It felt strange to me to sit in a Dongguan factory and watch young people so constrained by their own timidity. The city was built on making do and getting by; the secret of success was learning just enough to talk your way into a clerk's job or a teaching position or whatever else you wanted. But in Liu Yixia's classroom I saw the limits of that way of thinking. Learning a foreign language properly took time, and there were no shortcuts. You could not fake your way into English.

*   *   *

Misfortune dogged Mr. Wu. His school was evicted from the science museum after he fought with his landlord, and most of his students dropped out. His wife abandoned him and their nine-year-old son. He moved the operations of Assembly-Line English into his own home. Classes were crowded into the top floor of a four-story tenement building; his workroom was on the third floor and his apartment on the second. On the day that I visited, the stair landing was piled high with garbage, mostly cardboard boxes and old newspapers. Mr. Wu greeted me cheerfully and ushered me into his workshop, where we sat on metal stools and talked in the summer heat, surrounded by large pieces of scrap lumber.

His physical world had been compressed to humble dimensions, but Mr. Wu's ambitions were as expansive as ever. His latest breakthrough sat on a table: an English-language teaching machine wrought entirely of orange and turquoise plastic, from a mold he had designed himself. Assembly-Line English had entered the industrial age. The machine could now be mass-produced, and I learned that Mr. Wu had already manufactured five hundred of them; they were wrapped in newspaper and stored all over his apartment. He planned to lease them out to students so they could learn English at home. Mr. Wu's innovations had rendered teachers obsolete, and now classrooms were no longer necessary either.

I told him I wanted to learn more about his theory of teaching English.

"This is no longer just to learn English," he interrupted. "It is to develop the cerebrum. You can learn mathematics, history, anything from this. That is the wonder of the thing," he said, patting his invention fondly.

Suppose, Mr. Wu said, a history student wanted to learn about Japan's 1937 invasion of China. First he would read a text about the event that had been printed on cards and placed on the machine's moving panels. Another set of cards would move by with questions testing his mastery of the material: When did the invasion happen? What was the meaning behind it? Other prompts would appear, pushing the student to come up with new ideas, which he would write down in the form of a composition.

I asked Mr. Wu why this was better than reading the same information on a printed page.

"When your right hand is writing, your left brain is working," he answered. "When your left brain is working, your right eyeball is working. When you read a book, your eyeballs just stare at the page. But when you read on this machine, your eyeballs move quickly." He explained that he was developing a comprehensive curriculum for the machine and planned to look for investors.

"Is anyone interested?" I asked.

Yes, he said. An American had expressed interest.

"Who?"

"He was from Seattle. Michael." Mr. Wu looked vague suddenly. "I have his business card somewhere."

He took me upstairs to see his school. Ten Assembly-Line English machines were now squeezed into a single cramped room, set up on tables with only a few feet between them. Half a dozen students read aloud words and sentences, like a roomful of telephone operators murmuring in a language that almost resembled English if you listened hard enough. These were the diehards, all young women who had followed Mr. Wu from the science museum into the confines of his home. They leaned forward into the machines, pushed by their impatience to learn. In front of each student sat her evening's sustenance: bottled water, three plums. The place was stifling.

I trailed Mr. Wu around the room. I thought he was going to introduce me to some students, but he walked me over to one of the machines instead. "These are much more unwieldy than my new machines," he said. "It takes two people to carry one."

By now it was early evening, and I commented that it was getting a little dark to read without light.

"That's not bad for the eyes," he said. "Bright sunshine is bad for the eyes."

"I'm not saying bright sunshine is good for the eyes," I said. "I'm just saying it's not good to read in the dark."

"That's not true," he said heatedly. "That's only if your eyeballs are not moving. If your eyeballs are moving, it doesn't matter how dark it is."

I learned a few things about Mr. Wu that day. He had no background at all in education; before he set up the school, he had worked in a factory that made heating appliances. His English was poor, possibly nonexistent—several times when I used English terms during our conversation, he nodded and hurriedly changed the subject. The only English word I ever heard him use was "okay," as in: "什么事连上大脑，那就 okay." The word sounded strangely isolated at the end of a sentence like that. It meant, "Once you connect to your cerebrum, everything will be okay."

Mr. Wu was not good at dealing with people. He had angered his landlords at the science museum, and he had angered Liu Yixia, his star pupil. It was a good bet that he had driven away his wife, though it was hard to know if that was before or after he had mass-produced five hundred Assembly-Line English machines and stored them in their apartment. In the short time I had known him, he had angered me too; it was infuriating to interact with somebody so dogmatic. Mostly I could tell that human beings frustrated him. He preferred to talk about them in parts: their eyeballs, their hands, their brains. But people as a whole did not make sense to him. They were inefficient; they used only 5 percent of their cerebrums; they had a maddening aversion to sitting in front of a machine eleven hours a day to learn a language. People basically didn't work—it was as if their creator had used first-rate parts but then botched the assembly.

Machines were another matter. Someday with enough tinkering, Mr. Wu would construct a perfect assembly-line learning machine that would allow people to acquire the whole of human knowledge without ever leaving home. His faith in technology was absolute; he knew that machines were the answer. It was especially poignant that this man had been expelled from the science museum.

*   *   *

Self-improvement took Liu Yixia in new directions. At the Dongguan public library—which I hadn't even known existed—she checked out books like *Whole Brain Learning* and *The Bible of Jewish Home-Schooling*. She wanted to improve her memory and learn how to do business based on the teachings of the Talmud. She started taking pills to strengthen her cerebrum, because overwork caused dandruff and made your hair fall out. She was thinking of studying Japanese.

"I've heard it takes a Chinese person one year to learn English but only three months to learn Japanese," she told me. "I've heard that Beijing college graduates can earn one thousand yuan more a month for each language they speak. Is that true?"

I told her she should probably focus on improving her English first.

"I'm killing myself trying to increase my vocabulary," she said. "I am memorizing fifty words a day."

"Fifty words a day?" I repeated, amazed.

"Is that a lot or a little?"

The last time I saw Liu Yixia, she had engineered yet another makeover. She had dyed and permed her hair so it was long and crinkly, like caramel taffy. She had decided that an English teacher with ordinary black hair was *tu*, unsophisticated. "I did this to look more Western," she said. She had memorized an entire book of Grade Six vocabulary, five thousand words. The young women at Mr. Wu's school had shaved their heads again to express their dedication to learning English. And Mr. Wu had offered Liu Yixia a partnership in his new venture and promised her a third of the profits, but she didn't trust him. His people skills had not improved.

"With your level of English," he had told her recently, "you can muddle along for at most a year or so as a teacher. After that, there will be no more room for you here because I will have cornered the entire market. You can still go teach elsewhere, though."

"Why would he say something like that?" I asked.

"I think he was trying to force me to go back to work for him."

"That's awful."

"Yes," she said, "but I feel sympathy for him. He is all on his own."

She rejected Mr. Wu's offer. Instead she jumped to an Internet company to run its English-language Web site aimed at foreign clients. A month after she arrived, the company collapsed and the owner disappeared, owing more than one hundred thousand yuan in staff salaries. Liu Yixia had joined a lawsuit with the other employees to get their back pay, though they were not hopeful about it.

Some months later, in the spring of 2007, Liu Yixia landed a job in the international trade department of a factory that made microphone parts. She dealt with foreign customers, accompanied them on factory visits, and attended trade fairs. The job required Grade Six English and a college diploma. "I don't have those things with me," she had said when she interviewed for the position. In the evenings now, Liu Yixia taught English to her colleagues or to private students at home. Counting all three jobs, she made five thousand yuan a month—$625, an excellent salary for Dongguan. She planned to save money and set up an English-language kindergarten. That was her five-year plan.

After she got the job in international trade, Liu Yixia sent me her new contact information by e-mail. It was the sixth mobile-phone number she had given me since we met. *Sometime I feel very tried, but sometime I feel very enrich,* she wrote. Her English was still full of mistakes; she was moving too fast to correct herself. But who was I to criticize her? In the two years I had known her, she had gotten exactly what she wanted.

PART TWO *The Village*

After Min's mobile phone was stolen in the summer of 2004, she built a new life from scratch. She called up her cousin—the only phone number she knew by heart—and he put her back in touch with her older sister, and also with me. Min returned to the talent market and got a job in the human resources department of a Hong Kong–owned handbag factory. The position paid eight hundred yuan a month, with no overtime and every Sunday off. She was eighteen years old, and this was the fourth factory she had worked at in a year.

I visited Min in her new dorm, which was neat and newly white-washed, with photos of Chinese movie stars taped to the wall. Over noodles at a nearby stall, I asked her how her friend was.

"Do you mean my boyfriend?" she asked, rejecting the common Chinese euphemism. "Since he went home, I haven't heard from him."

"Don't you send messages by phone?" I asked.

"I forgot his number."

"So you can't find him, and he can't find you?"

She nodded. "Maybe I'll see him at home during the new year."

I asked Min about her two friends from the old factory, the ones we had visited together. "One of them got a job at a factory in Changping, but I don't know which factory," she said. "The other one went home to get engaged, but I don't know where her home is." In the village, everyone knew everyone else and people were connected in multiple ways. But Min's friends in the city were linked only through her; at one stroke, she had lost ties to almost everyone she knew. "I have no more friends now," she said.

So she started over. In her new factory, she met Ah Jie. He was three years older than Min and as skinny as a hastily drawn cartoon character, with long limbs and a narrow handsome face and a bashful smile; when he spoke to strangers, he blushed to the rims of his ears. He worked as an assistant on the factory floor and he met most of Min's demands for a mate: He had a good heart, he didn't smoke, drink, or gamble, and he was over 1.7 meters tall. Almost right away, Ah Jie began pressuring Min to marry him. She told him to put away some money first; in truth, she did not want to think about marriage yet. "I want to save some money and maybe start a small business. If I marry so early, I'd have to stay home," she told me. "To stay outside and work your entire life is better than staying home."

She told her parents about her new boyfriend. "Where is he from?" they asked.

"He's from the factory," Min said, stalling.

"Where is he from?" they asked again.

He was not from Hubei Province, which was all Min's parents cared about. In traditional China, a young woman married into her husband's village, but usually it was close enough that she could go home to see her own family on occasion. Migration now made it possible for two people from towns a thousand miles apart to meet and marry. To a young woman's parents, that was a catastrophe: Unaccustomed to long-distance travel, they worried that a daughter who married a man from far away would virtually disappear from their lives.

When Min met a boy she liked, she made it a point to learn as little as possible about his origins. "Is your family poor?" she asked Ah Jie once. "Very poor," he answered. That was all she knew, and it was fine with her. "I don't want to know their family situation, and I don't want them to know mine," she told me. "In the end we must rely on ourselves."

THAT AUTUMN, Min seemed more settled than I had ever seen her. She spent most of her free time with Ah Jie. Her older sister, Guimin, moved to Dongguan and got a job in the shipping department of Min's factory. The sisters shared a dorm room and ate lunch together every day. As winter approached, both of them made plans to go home. Ah Jie lobbied Min to bring him home to meet her family, but she decided against it; with her parents so opposed to the match, she felt it would be awkward. Guimin's negotiations with her boyfriend, who lived in Hunan Province, were more fractious. For a long time she insisted she wouldn't go home at all, then suddenly she changed her mind, planning to bring her boyfriend with her. Their parents did not approve of him either, but Guimin was three years older than Min and willing to challenge them.

On a Sunday afternoon in January, Min and I walked to a park near her factory and sat on a low wall next to a basketball court. She was wearing new clothes she had purchased for the trip—her first pair of jeans, a denim jacket, and boots with chunky heels. In the pale sunshine, we ate oranges and made plans; she had invited me home to her village for the new year. That day, Min talked of nothing but home. The vegetables in the countryside tasted better than the ones in the city, she said. If a wild mushroom crumbled in your hand it was poisonous, but a firm one was safe to eat. When a pig was hungry, it would stand on its hind legs and squeal. People stole chickens around the new year, so you had to keep a close watch then. The best recipe for a facial was crushed pearl powder mixed with the white of a freshly laid egg. The life in the countryside was pleasant, but you could go from one end of the year to the other and almost never see money.

"Have you ever thought about going to the countryside to live?" Min asked me.

"The Chinese countryside?" I said. "No."

"I guess it's too lonely there," she said.

*   *   *

In lives blurred by journeys to strange places, there was one fixed point in the migrant universe: a farming village that was home. Agriculture brings little economic benefit now; family plots, of just under one acre on average, are too small to be profitable. But across China, the family farm is still being tended, because that is what people have always done. The land is less an income source than an insurance policy—a guarantee that a person can live and will not starve.

The continuing link to a family farm has stabilized China in an age of mass migration. Its cities have not spawned the shantytown slums of so much of the developing world, because the migrant who fails in the city can always return home and find someone there. A teenager may go out for work, leaving his parents on the farm. A husband who migrates may have a wife at home tilling the fields, or sometimes the other way around. A married couple might go out together, leaving young children in the care of their aged parents. In the city, a migrant may look desperate, but almost every migrant has a farm to fall back on.

The return to the village to celebrate the lunar new year in late winter is the central event of the migrant calendar—in the six weeks around the holiday, almost 200 million people travel on China's trains. As the new year approaches, the impending journey becomes the main preoccupation of the factory world. Job-hopping stops as workers focus on saving money to return in style. Couples enter delicate negotiations: Whose family will they visit and what is the status of their relationship? This reckoning can be painful, and migrants unhappy with their lot may decide not to go home at all. The holiday is the hinge on which the whole year turns—it is the time to quit a job, take a rest, get engaged, start again.

The passage home is often as traumatic as the initial journey out to the city. The Chinese railway is the last part of the transport network to operate much as it did in the days of central planning. Today in China, the better off travel by plane and car, and both forms of transportation have responded to the market. Airlines have improved service and cut prices; highways are constantly expanded and upgraded to serve industry and the growing ranks of car owners. But the railway remains the dominion of the poor—set up, it sometimes seems, only to deliver misery more efficiently.

During holidays, it is virtually impossible for an ordinary person to buy a ticket at a fair price. Railway offices reserve tickets for the well connected or sell them to scalpers, who charge exorbitant rates. Because ticketing is not computerized, ticket sellers don't know which seats will free up in the course of the journey; unless a passenger departs from the first station, getting an assigned seat is impossible. Tickets go on sale only a few days before a trip, feeding panicky crowds that camp out overnight in stations. On train rides lasting hours or days, toilets become blocked and faucets stop running and people squat in the aisles holding their heads in their hands. The passengers rarely complain, and they remain good-humored in the most dreadful conditions. They spend much of their energy monitoring everything they have brought with them. This is another reason that the new year trains are always crowded: No migrant can return without gifts.

At home, the travelers fall back into the slower rhythms of the farm. Hierarchy governs village life: The older men, the chief decision makers in their families, choose what is best for the community too. A family eats and farms together, and at night the children often sleep with their parents in one large bed. The older children discipline the younger ones, and the younger ones obey. Guests show up unannounced and stay for days; communal routines of eating and sleeping and, these days, television viewing absorb them easily. There are no secrets in the village.

In the city, this way of life is already dead. Small families live in high-rise apartments alongside neighbors who are not their kin. People forge relationships with those they do not know. Young migrants in the city have lived freely among strangers; they have competed for jobs; they have dated whom they pleased. No matter how fondly they recall their rural childhoods, in truth the village cannot take them back.

It is not a new story. The ache of the traveler returning home is a classic theme in Chinese literature. One of the first poems a school-child learns, from the eighth century, is about a man who goes back to his village after a lifetime away, to find that he no longer belongs.

> *I left home as a youth, and as an old man returned,*
> *My accent unchanged but my temples turned gray.*
> *The children see me but don't know who I am,*
> *Laughing, they ask where the stranger is from.*

*   *   *

For the journey Min carried a down jacket, a box of traditional medicine whose chief ingredient was donkey hide, a pink Dooney & Bourke purse made by her factory, Nestlé milk powder, a gift box of cookies, two men's dress shirts, a plastic heart-shaped box of candy, and one thousand yuan—about $120, a month's pay folded into a tight square. Of her own things she brought only a mobile phone, an MP3 music player, and a makeup mirror; everything else she carried was a present for someone. It was February 2005, one week before the lunar new year.

Our bus to Guangzhou filled up in minutes. A sign taped to a window warned: WELCOME PASSENGERS TO THIS LUXURIOUS BUS. BECAUSE LATELY PASSENGERS HAVE LOST VALUABLES, PLEASE DON'T SLEEP WHILE RIDING AND HEIGHTEN YOUR VIGILANCE. Most of the passengers took their chances and fell asleep immediately. Factories flew past on both sides of the highway, but Min's mind was far away. "When I was a kid, we walked half an hour to elementary school," she told me. "Some kids came from villages several mountains over. There were wild boars and wolves then. You wouldn't see the wolves but you would hear them. You don't hear them anymore."

The train station in Guangzhou was mobbed; every year at this time, four and a half million people passed through on their way home and back out again. The vast concrete plaza in front of the station had been cordoned off into zones, and police were everywhere, shouting orders through bullhorns that turned their every word into deafening garble. As people entered the main concourse, they instinctively broke into a run: Being Chinese has conditioned them to know that there will never be enough of anything. Min and I had assigned seats, thanks to a cousin of hers who was traveling partway with us, but we started to run too. In the mad crush of people, we squeezed onto the 7:32 hard-seat overnight express to Wuchang.

The life on the train was communal, and the moment we pulled out of the station the passengers behaved as if they were already home. They removed their shoes and stripped down to their undershirts; they peeled tangerines and cracked *guazi*, salted melon seeds. Mobile phones went off constantly, their ring tones merry and intrusive: "Happy Birthday," "Dixie." A man across the aisle spread a newspaper on the floor beneath a seat and folded himself into the tiny crawl space until only his lower legs were visible. Passengers crowded the aisles and perched on the metal sinks next to the bathrooms and crammed into the spaces between the cars, squatting in rows in their dark suits like crows strung along a telephone wire.

Metal carts barreled through, forcing the human pile to rearrange itself every few minutes. The carts sold chicken legs and warm beer and hot dogs skewered on sticks. The vendors called out: *Hot milk, hot milk, good for you.* Only the well-off bought food on the train. Most people had carried their own—hard-boiled eggs and wafer cookies and mason jars filled with green tea so cloudy that algae could grow in it. At 10:45, a sweeper came through. We had been on board only three hours, but she pushed before her a mountain of peanut shells, orange peels, and empty plastic bottles. Nobody on earth generates trash faster than the traveling Chinese.

Time passed slowly for Min. This was only the second long journey of her life. She peered out the window; she checked her watch; she fiddled with her mobile phone. She gave me regular reports—*We still have nine hours to go*—until I told her to stop. She broke open her gift box of cookies and ate a few—"It's okay," she assured me, "there's a lot more"—then disappeared to visit her cousin. She returned with a salted chicken wing wrapped in cellophane, and some information: A favorite tactic of thieves was to distract a passenger with a "found" wallet while simultaneously picking his pocket.

Just past midnight, a message on my mobile phone welcomed me to Hubei, Min's home province. We slept fitfully. At three in the morning, the family across the aisle came suddenly awake, like a coiled spring releasing, and their laughter and talk filled the car as if it were the middle of the afternoon. At 6:57, we arrived at the station, said goodbye to Min's cousin, and boarded a bus for home.

AT 10:12, the bus crossed the Yangtze River, and Min jerked awake. She said aloud the name of every town we passed on the highway: Huangshi, Meichuan, Huangmei. "We're almost there," she said, her voice tight with excitement.

Min's mother, Chen Meirong, was waiting by the side of the road outside a town called Dajin. She was forty-two years old, with deep-set brown eyes and high cheekbones—a big-boned beauty rare among country people. She had a wide smile with lots of teeth, and I don't think she stopped smiling the whole first day Min was home. The two of them did not hug when they met—that is not the Chinese custom—but Min touched her mother's arm and stroked the edge of her ear as they talked. She had not been home in two years.

Dajin was a one-street farming town, where purveyors of animal feed and pesticide still outnumbered stores selling motorcycles and mobile phones. The roadside businesses reflected the rural ethos of never throwing anything away: In Dajin you could pay someone to repair a clock, a watch, a stove, a phone, or a television set. In the city, it was rare to see such businesses anymore; urban people had greater faith in the quality of new products. At the outdoor stalls, the most prominently displayed items were hard-shell suitcases, a reminder that the best option in town might be to get out.

Min was full of home-improvement plans. She wanted to buy a DVD player for the house. "Let's buy a hot-water dispenser too," she said. "It's much more convenient that way."

Periodically Min's mother would look over her daughter's head at me. "This place is terrible!" she would say, with a big smile. "And we are so poor!"

At the turnoff to their village, Min's mother hailed the local version of a taxi: a motorcycle pulling a metal box mounted on two wheels with narrow planks for seats. Five young women already sat inside, wearing tight jeans and puffy jackets—migrants, like Min, returning for the holiday. As the taxi rattled down the dirt road,

Min looked backward at the sight of people coming home. A young woman wearing black leather pants and stiletto-heel boots walked past rice paddies; a man in a pinstripe suit dragged two ragged toddlers, one by each hand. A man riding a bike smiled and waved. "That's the father of my elementary school classmate," Min said. "He's gotten old."

We climbed out of the taxi at a cluster of two-story brick houses. Min's father walked up the path to meet us—a thin, drawn face, a tired smile—and Min saw that he had gotten old too. The house was quiet. Min's younger sister and brother were visiting relatives; another younger sister was home, watching television. She looked up briefly when Min entered and then returned her attention to the screen.

Over bowls of noodles with liver and boiled eggs—Min's mother put three eggs in her bowl in honor of her homecoming—Min caught up on the news. Her father said he wanted to buy a motorcycle.

"How much does that cost?" I asked him.

"Seven or eight thousand," Min answered for her father.

"So much!" I said.

Min's father ventured that he could get one for less than three thousand yuan.

"That's no good," Min said. "Do you want to spend all your time repairing it?"

The phone rang. It was a friend of Min's, calling from Dongguan to see if she had arrived safely. "My mother is thrilled to death to see me," Min reported. "My mother and father have aged a lot, and the house is all messy and cold. You don't feel like doing anything but sleeping."

The phone rang again. It was Ah Jie, who was staying in Dongguan for the new year. "I can't talk now," she said in a low voice. "There are a lot of people here." Because Min's mother disapproved of the match, Min had taken the path of least resistance: She had lied and told her mother she had broken off the relationship. Now she had brought her secret home. Every time the phone rang, it threatened to expose her.

In a few days, Guimin would be arriving home with her boyfriend. *I am bringing my boyfriend home,* Guimin wrote me in a phone text message, *even though at home they don't approve of my dating someone so far away.* Another day, she wrote: *I am already grown-up and know how to handle things. They really don't have to worry about anything.* It sounded to me like she was readying for battle.

*   *   *

As soon as Min got home, she started a campaign to civilize her family. On foggy mornings, she went through the house closing windows; dampness, she informed her mother, was bad for one's health. When her father lit up a cigarette after breakfast, he got a lecture: He shouldn't smoke, and he must rinse out his mouth with tea, or else his teeth would turn black. Min walked through the house pointing out improvements she wanted: a hot-water dispenser, a washing machine, a walk of poured concrete across the muddy yard. In village homes, it is common to throw trash, put out cigarettes, and spit on the floor; every so often, someone sweeps up the mess and dumps it in the yard. Min put a plastic bag in the corner of the children's bedroom and ordered her siblings to dispose of garbage there instead. I watched as she repeated the instructions to her mother.

Guimin's impending arrival troubled her. Min was afraid her parents would be impolite to her sister's boyfriend. People from the countryside were not used to strangers, she said, and they might insult him without meaning to. Guimin was the talk of the village: No other young woman had brought home a boyfriend from so far away before. "My sister is coming home with her boyfriend," Min told every neighbor she met.

"Where is he from?" was always the first question.

"Hunan," she said—and there the conversation died, because there was no good answer to that.

The Lus' house had been built in 1986, the year Min was born. Downstairs there was a main room, with a bedroom on each side; the children's room had two double beds and a television set that was always on at full volume. The main room contained a wooden dinner table and behind it a shrine, with the spirit tablets of the deceased ancestors, a photograph of Min's grandmother, and a wall hanging that spelled out in iridescent gold characters the hierarchy of the universe: HEAVEN, EARTH, NATION, PARENTS, TEACHERS. On the wall next to the shrine were taped academic prizes won by the two youngest children. LU XIU IS FIFTH IN HER CLASS. LU XUANQING IS A "THREE GOOD" STUDENT. Everything surrounding these living quarters was functional. Upstairs was a deep pit in the floor for storing grain, sides of raw pork and cured fish hanging on hooks, and a room knee-deep in clouds of cotton—this year's crop, as yet unsold. To one side of the house was the kitchen, its walls black from cooking fires, and to the other a shed for the ox and the black sow and her piglets. Chickens wandered underfoot and laid their eggs beneath the kitchen cabinet where dishes were stored.

Electricity was used sparingly to save money, and most dinners were eaten in near-darkness. There was no plumbing and no heating. In the wet chill of a Hubei winter, the whole family wore their coats and gloves indoors, and the cement walls and floors soaked up the cold like a sponge. If you sat too long, your toes went numb, and your fingers too; the best remedy was to drink a cup of hot water, holding it with your hands while the steam warmed your face. The children often watched television standing up, jumping up and down to restore feeling in their toes.

Min enjoyed status at home now. At mealtimes, the younger children ate quickly and left the table; Min lingered to chat with her parents and with me. Her mother and younger sisters cooked and cleaned and washed clothes, while her father fed the pigs and did odd jobs around the house. Min did not help out with housework. She spent a lot of time on the phone, planning visits with friends who had returned home. Ah Jie continued to call with bits of news: He had helped Guimin buy a train ticket home. He missed Min. He dreamed she had gone off with another boy.

Min's three younger siblings still lived at home. Sar, the third sister, was sixteen years old; she had long black hair that reached to her waist and her mother's all-enveloping smile. She went to the same vocational high school Min had attended and planned to go out to work after she graduated in a few months. Xiu, the fourth sister, and Xuanqing, the youngest and the only boy, attended middle school. The children boarded at schools in town and came home on weekends; they knew little about the workings of the farm. When Min's parents slaughtered several chickens one morning and plucked out the feathers, Xiu stood in the kitchen doorway watching. "The children refuse to do this work," Min's mother said.

On another morning, Sar walked into the yard with a bowl of grain to call the chickens to breakfast. "*Turool . . . turool,*" she trilled. The chickens were nowhere in sight.

I pointed to a flock in a terraced field below the house. "Are those your chickens?"

She squinted. "They look like ours. *Turool . . . turool . . .*" The chickens ignored her.

Her mother came out of the house. "What are you doing? Those are not our chickens!" Sar's mother went up the path to hunt down the fugitives. Sar giggled and went back into the house.

ON HER SECOND DAY HOME, Min took her three younger siblings and two cousins to the nearest city, Wuxue, which was an hour away by bus. Home improvement was still on her mind: She wanted to buy a hot-water dispenser and a hair dryer. "The children never get to go anywhere," she said to me. "Let's take them to the city to have some fun." Their first stop was an Internet café where Min met up with a high school classmate named Hu Tao. He had a narrow face that came to a point at his chin and a tiny square mustache that hung on his upper lip, like a stray postage stamp. He wore a gray denim jacket and pointy black shoes and a tense scowl on his face; he looked like he was in tryouts to be a gangster. Hu Tao worked at an uncle's restaurant in the city, but he was hoping to go out to find work.

"He likes me," Min said, out of Hu Tao's hearing, "but we've never had any feeling between us. Plus I already have a boyfriend. And he doesn't look very respectable, does he?"

The markets were crowded with shoppers ahead of the new year holiday. Stalls sold strips of red paper inscribed with auspicious couplets, along with posters featuring a heroic Chairman Mao and quasi-religious slogans: *He is the people's great liberator.* Min led the children through the stores buying things for the house: socks for her father, face towels for guests, shampoo. She bargained hard and got a hot-water dispenser for eleven dollars, and a hair dryer for $3.30. She bought disposable plastic cups, which were more sanitary than the porcelain cups the family shared and seldom washed. In the supermarket, the younger children filled her cart with sweet rice cakes and cookies.

Wuxue had things you no longer saw in the modern cities of the coast, like a grain storage warehouse and a military grain supply station—both relics of a time when people relied on the government for their grain ration. A store advertised Old Fogey–brand men's suits. Min had last been to Wuxue two years ago. This return trip left her sorely disappointed. "This city is no good," she said. "It's not as developed as the places outside."

Hu Tao disappeared for a while but reappeared after lunch to take the children to a roller-skating rink. He had acquired another gangster accessory—a cigarette tucked behind his ear, which made him look even less respectable than before. At a fruit stand, he stopped to talk to a young woman with bold black eyes and bleached hair that had grown out in an orange fringe. She walked ahead with Hu Tao, while Min and the children trailed behind. No one bothered with introductions.

The rink was packed and dark inside, lit only by a flashing disco ball. It was three in the afternoon. Min edged along the wall, feeling her way and trying to keep track of the children. In a dim bar area at one end of the rink, Hu Tao sat down on a stool and the girl sat next to him. "I think we should leave," Min said to me. We gathered the children and headed out, walking back the way we had come. At the bottom of a small hill, Hu Tao reappeared ahead of us, alone. He had made a choice, and it didn't involve the girl with the orange hair.

He asked Min about her place of work. Her factory made handbags and employed five thousand people, she said. Assembly-line workers were paid eight hundred yuan a month.

"I'd like to go out again," he said. "Things at home are not good."

"How was it at your other factory?" she asked. He had worked briefly in Dongguan.

"Not good. When are you going back?"

"The fifth day of the new year," Min said—then she made her bid. "You help us get tickets, and you can leave with us. Our factory is still hiring workers."

After they parted ways, Min was triumphant. "He'll get us train tickets back to Dongguan," she said. Hu Tao would use his local contacts to obtain tickets, and Min would take him out to the city and get him a job at her factory. On her second day home, she had already figured out the most important thing: how to get out again.

*   *   *

Seven generations of Lus have lived in Liemahuitou Village. Its ninety families, almost all surnamed Lu, live in brick houses beside low-lying rice paddies, the paths between dotted with temples where villagers burn incense for their ancestors. Terraced fields rise from the valley bottom, stacked into the blue-gray hills like an open jewelry box with many drawers. About the only unusual thing about the village is the extravagance of its name—Liemahuitou, "fierce horse turning its head." The name was derived from the shape of a nearby mountain. Generations have lived and died here without traveling twenty miles from home. A popular old saying celebrated the isolation: *To live an entire life without making a long journey is good fortune.*

In the early 1990s, though, young married couples began heading to the city to work, against the wishes of their elders. When Min's bachelor uncle moved to Wuxue to open a store, the family objected. "We felt unmarried people should not go out to work because they would learn bad habits," Min's father told me. In the past decade, migration has become the norm. Village children leave during middle school or even elementary school; both boys and girls go out, although some families prefer that sons stay closer to home. Each of Min's parents did a stint at a shoe factory in Wenzhou on the east coast, but returned without any savings. A few migrants a generation older than Min had come back to the village and set up small businesses. None of the younger generation had returned: Some had married and continued to work far from home, and a few had bought apartments in the nearby city of Wuxue.

Migration has become the chief source of village income. Together, Min and her older sister had sent home six hundred dollars the previous year, compared with the $240 their parents made selling pigs and cotton. The money paid for the schooling of the younger children, and it gave the sisters a voice in family affairs. When Guimin first went out to work, it was her arguments that convinced her parents to let Min continue her education past middle school. The sisters' level of education was unusual in the village. "We treat our daughters as sons," Min's mother told me one morning as she sat beside her bedroom window sewing an old-fashioned velvet slipper. Both she and her husband were middle-school graduates, which is rare for country people of their generation.

"A lot of people in the village disagree with me," she continued. "They say daughters don't need to have much schooling, since they will marry out anyway. But I believe to have knowledge is better than to have no knowledge."

Birth order was a major determinant of fate. Guimin, the first-born, had left home after middle school to find work. Min, next in line, went through most of two-year vocational high school, and Sar will graduate before going out to join her sisters. The two youngest, their mother hopes, will attend high school and college now that there is the money for it. "That's my ideal," Min's mother said, "but it's up to them and how hard they work."

Some of Min's cousins had gone out to work when they were only twelve years old. Of the twenty-seven kids in her sixth-grade class, ten went straight to work rather than entering middle school. Some parents seemed to regard their children as little more than cash machines: One neighboring family required each of its four daughters to send home ten thousand yuan a year. Another villager set up a bank account so the wages of his three daughters, working in a sweater factory, would come straight to him.

Married migrant couples faced their own dilemmas. One of Min's uncles worked as a bricklayer in Dongguan with his wife but kept their two teenage sons in the village school, hoping they might attend college one day. But the boys ran wild with no one to discipline them. "Since my son was fourteen, he has spent all his time with girls," Min's uncle complained one night over dinner at the Lus' home. "But how can I control him? I am in Dongguan, and so is my wife." His son stood at the far end of the room listening. "When I was his age," his father continued, "boys and girls didn't even speak to each other. But young people now live in a different world."

Only one person in the village around Min's age aspired to college: Lu Zejuan, who was one of Min's childhood friends. While Min was out working in Dongguan, Lu Zejuan had suffered a nervous breakdown from the pressure of studying for the college entrance exam. Min visited her on her third day home; Lu Zejuan was sitting in front of the TV wearing a nylon jacket with *450 Fifth Avenue, New York* stitched over the front pocket. She rarely left home now, to avoid hearing gossip about herself. When Min convinced her friend to go for a walk, some of the neighbors peered at Lu Zejuan and said her name uncertainly, because they had not seen her in such a long time.

Migration was so established that education looked like the riskier bet. Wu Jianhan, a classmate of Min's from another village, came to visit and stayed for several days. He wore black suit pants, a white dress shirt, and a striped tie—the same aspirational outfit every day, even when he was helping Min's father tile the roof of the outhouse. He had tested into college, but his older brother refused to pay the tuition. "He says that now even college graduates have a hard time finding jobs. He thinks I should just go to work instead," said Wu Jianhan one morning as he swept chicken droppings and spent firecracker papers from the dirt walk in front of the Lus' house. "That's his view. I have a different opinion." Wu Jianhan was working as a migrant in Beijing, but he refused to talk about what kind of work he did there.

Min and her older sister commanded respect in the village because they had risen to office jobs. No one else had gone to Dongguan, though they favored places that were equally far away: the shoe factories of Wenzhou, twenty-two hours by bus; the hair salons of Harbin, twenty-eight hours by train. "That's our belief here," Min said. "The farther away from home you go, the more splendid it is."

* * *

Two days before the new year, Min angered her mother. One of Min's uncles had invited the family over for a reunion meal, a key event of the holiday—but then the phone rang with a better offer. A glamorous young aunt who ran a hair salon in Wuxue had just come home and invited Min to go shopping in the city.

"Why go out when it's raining?" was all her mother said. She was clearly displeased at Min's rudeness.

Min stood her ground. "It's me that's offending my uncle, not my mother, so it should have nothing to do with her," she reasoned.

Her aunt, Huang Caixia, came by the house to pick us up. She was twenty-five years old, in a chic belted jacket, shiny satin pants, and running shoes. The first thing she did was to take out a crimson mobile phone which opened like a makeup compact and pass it around to general admiration. In the bus to the city, she and Min discussed hair-coloring tips and sang along to the pop songs on Min's MP3 player. Min's aunt knew all the words.

> *The thirty-six strategies of love*
> *Are like a game*
> *I want the remote control for myself.*
> *The thirty-six strategies of love*
> *You must maintain your charm*
> *In order to score and not be called out.*

Min told her aunt she wanted her father to build an indoor bathroom for the house. "He could put the washing machine in there, and there would be a place to bathe," Min said. "They could even add some tile so it would be like a real shower."

"And an electric hot-water heater," Min's aunt added.

"And an electric hot-water heater," Min echoed, "so we could bathe in the winter without being cold."

Her aunt figured the project would cost five thousand yuan, about six hundred dollars. "When you've lived in the city for a while, your thinking changes," Min's aunt said to me. "You're constantly thinking about how to improve life in the countryside." She and her husband worked in Wuxue and rented an apartment there, but their four-year-old daughter lived in the village with her grandmother. They planned to bring the child to the city as soon as they had saved money to buy an apartment. The couple had not requested a farm plot from the village when they married; her husband's parents still farmed a third of an acre, and that was enough. "The village is home," Min's aunt said. "But I don't feel comfortable there anymore."

THAT AFTERNOON, Guimin arrived home with her boyfriend. She was half a head taller than Min, with a pretty, fine-boned face and the natural poise of a firstborn child in a large family. As the boyfriend entered the house, he ran into Guimin's father coming out. He ducked his head, said "Uncle" in greeting, and handed him a cigarette. That was all: no introductions, no conversation, just cigarettes—the calling cards and currency of the Chinese male universe.

Over dinner, Min's parents did not say much to their daughter's boyfriend. Maybe it was shyness, or a tacit protest. But it was just as Min had feared: They were not showing the proper respect to a guest from far away. The boyfriend, who did not understand the local dialect any better than I did, sat politely without speaking. When the homemade liquor was poured, Min took charge. She turned to the man she already addressed in private as "Brother-in-Law." "Welcome to our home," she said, raising her glass.

*   *   *

Most days in the village began with a predawn phone call that shattered the quiet: Someone else had just come home. Min's parents rose early and moved through the house, slamming doors and speaking in normal voices while everyone else slept. Being considerate of others was not the village way: People spent all their time in groups, so they were good at ignoring one another.

Almost everything was done communally. The children got up together and stood in a line at the edge of the yard, brushing their teeth and spitting into the neighbor's yard below. Every meal was eaten together—vegetables, rice, and always pork, since a family typically slaughtered a pig in the autumn and dined on it all winter long. Bath time was also a group activity: In the evening, the women of the family would heat a basin of water. One after another, they washed their private parts and feet, without changing the water in between. Then the men would refill the basin and do the same. Every so often, the family members took a sponge bath, but that was usually different from the once in many days they washed their hair. Eventually every part of the body would be clean, although rarely at the same time.

Visitors dropped by all day long, and some stayed for days. A nine-year-old cousin of Min's slept between us in bed for several nights, then two of Min's cousins from her mother's side showed up, then two cousins from her father's side. Wu Jianhan, the boy who wore the dress shirt and striped tie, stayed longest; he was interested in Min, but she ignored him. Min's mother moved into her daughters' bedroom, leaving her own room to her husband and the boys.

At night Min, her mother, and I slept head-to-foot in a double bed under one comforter, lying immobile as dolls.

The focus of village life was television. The children sat in front of the set all day; if you visited a neighbor, you were usually given a front-row seat where you could pick up the same episode you had been watching somewhere else. Everyone's favorite genre was the historical costume drama about imperial court life. These soap operas appeared to be the villagers' primary contact with history, though it was a selective telling of the past. Wizards, fairies, magic, cults, miracles, murder, and adultery: The children were mesmerized by it all. While the Communist Party preached morality, rationalism, and scientific development, most of the entertainment on TV went counter to that.

The children straddled two worlds, the village and the fantasy universe inside their electronic gadgets. They might help their mother wash clothes in the river and then turn their attention to a handheld game of Tetris. Sometimes they seemed like they had just crash-landed on earth from the planet Television. When I took out my camera to change the film, Min's nine-year-old cousin came over to watch. "What does film look like?" he asked. "Does it look the same way it does on TV?"

Everyone was related, in ways so convoluted that even the Chinese language did not have names for them. One man who visited was Min's grandfather's younger brother's son-in-law; another day, we went to see her grandfather's brother's daughter-in-law's sisters and their father. I thought the children sitting perpetually in front of the television in Min's house were neighbors, but one day we visited her great-aunt in another village and I saw the same children sitting before the television: Of course, they were relatives. A young man who lived next door and worked in a shoe factory in Wenzhou came by so often I was sure he had a crush on Min. I was about to share this with her when I made another discovery: He was her father's cousin.

The villagers reacted to me in different ways. The ones who were working in the city struck up conversations and asked me about Beijing and America; they peered at my notebooks and tried to decipher my handwriting. Those who had stayed in the village, including Min's parents, were polite but shy—while they answered my questions readily, they never had any of their own. None of the older men spoke to me. As a young woman and an outsider, I was doubly irrelevant to them.

I never saw anyone read a newspaper or watch the evening news, and there was little sign of government. In the two weeks I lived in Min's home I did not meet a single official, and the law did not seem to cut very deep. Nationwide, the policy limiting most families to one or two children had been in force for more than two decades, yet here in the village the average family had more than two, Min's father said. The Lus had five children, but one family in the village had six, and another had seven. The man who had fathered seven children had been the village chief, one of the highest local positions.

MIN SLIPPED EASILY back into this world, but she kept her secrets. She didn't talk about her boyfriend or the factory, and I noticed that she opted out whenever it didn't suit her. She made her own plans to see friends, sometimes going against her mother's wishes; she spoke sharply to older relatives she didn't like. I never saw her do anything she didn't want to do. An aunt asked Min to bring her fourteen-year-old daughter out to the factory, but Min turned her down flatly. Another morning, an elderly uncle appeared at the house after breakfast and zeroed in, like a heat-seeking missile, on the new down jacket her father was wearing. It had been a gift from Min.

"How much does that cost?" the old man inquired. "Twenty yuan?"

"Even if you had three hundred and twenty yuan," Min snapped, "you couldn't buy that. That is a down jacket."

She was disdainful toward many of the older people in the village. "They always want to know how much money I make or how much money I brought home," she told me later. "I think these are private matters."

The young migrants dominated the holiday life of the village, enjoying the authority their money gave them. They went around showing off their mobile phones and new clothes; they compared job situations. They were the most active matchmakers, for themselves and for one another, and they gave cash to needy older relatives. In the past, such tasks had belonged to their elders, but now the older generation was too poor and powerless to fulfill these duties. Parents were left with little to do but gossip about their children's earnings and marriage prospects.

"I want her work to go smoothly. That is all," Min's mother said, when I asked about her hopes for Min. "What happens in the future is her own thing." She hoped that Min and Guimin would find boyfriends from near home. But in most ways, she seemed to have accepted that her daughters had moved beyond her ability to help or understand them.

FOR ME, the hardest thing about staying in Min's village was the collective way of life. No one was ever alone. When someone sat down in front of the TV, he called everyone around to come watch; if Min prepared hot water to wash her face, I must wash then too. A couple of times when I tried to read a book—ignoring the blaring television set nearby—the children came by one after another to talk to me with concerned looks on their faces.

Staying in Min's village made me think about my own family. Long ago when my parents were children in China, they had grown up in a similar way. In America, they had raised my brother and me very differently, encouraging our independence and freeing us from family obligation. My parents had not expected us to visit relatives; they never told us what we should study in school. And in all the years I lived abroad, my parents never once pressured me to come home. In Min's village, I realized this for the first time, and I was grateful.

One morning after a large family meal, I walked out alone on the muddy road toward town. I saw things I had not noticed before: a blackboard listing school fees and livestock vaccination rates, a store whose entire merchandise consisted of cigarettes and fireworks, children no more than four years old playing with lighters. In the next village, I saw a four-story house of white tile. On wealthier stretches of the coast were whole villages of white-tiled houses like these. Here there was only one, a beacon of things to come.

I had been gone an hour when my mobile phone rang. "Where are you?" Min demanded. "We're all waiting for you so we can eat lunch."

I hurried back, to amazed accusations. "You didn't eat lunch! Where did you go?" "What were you doing walking on the road all by yourself?"

The Chinese countryside is not relaxing. It is a place of constant socializing and negotiation, a conversation that has been going on for a long time and will continue after you are gone. Spending time in Min's village, I understood why migrants felt so alone when they first went to the city. But I also saw how they came to value the freedom they found there, until at last they were unable to live without it.

* * *

On the last day of the old year, Min's family and the families of all her uncles went to pay respects at the graves of their ancestors.

They threaded between the rice paddies—muddy ponds filled with dead stalks now that the harvest was in—crossed a stream where villagers were washing their clothes, and climbed a path up the mountain past orchards of cotton and tea bushes. In a clearing surrounded by pine trees were the grave of Min's paternal grandmother, who had died two years ago, and a stone tablet marking the graves of her great-grandparents. The mountain was called Lu Graves Mountain. "All of our old people are buried here," Min said.

Her mother set down bowls of dates and peanut candy, which were offerings for the deceased in the afterlife. Min's father burned paper money—labeled "Currency for General Use in Heaven and Earth"—and poured liquor on the ground in front of the graves. The young men threaded fireworks through the tea bushes, like Christmas lights lacing the shrubbery of a suburban house. Then all the members of the family went down on their knees in the wet earth and kowtowed three times. The burial, the fireworks, the burning of paper—all ran counter to official policy. To stamp out such "feudal" traditions, the government promoted cremation and charged each family a fine of several thousand yuan for a burial. All the families in Min's village, no matter how poor, paid the fine and buried their dead.

At home, Min's father carefully wrote a blessing for the kitchen god on a square of red paper. On the front door of the house, he pasted matching strips of red paper inscribed with a couplet to celebrate the new year. Min had picked up the paper strips in town without bothering to read them, but the words were perfectly apt:

The dragon travels the four seas to bring wealth home
The phoenix flies ten thousand miles to bring treasures here

That evening, the family set off fireworks and watched the annual new year's special on television. All through the night the firecrackers sounded—a piercing whistle, a silence, then a muffled explosion.

The light in the bedroom stayed on all night, as it must for the first three nights of the year. Nobody could remember the meaning of this tradition, but it was followed just the same. The village houses glowed in the night, scattered across the valley, their cold blue lights a reminder of the factory ships of Dongguan.

ON THE FIRST DAY of the new year, the children woke up early and took turns checking themselves in the mirror. Min tied her hair into pigtails and clipped a lime-green Barbie barrette through her bangs; the three older girls applied pink Maybelline lip gloss. The first of the year, by tradition, was the day for visits around the village. The younger children ran from house to house collecting sweets, while the older ones stayed to drink hot water mixed with sugar and chat with the adults. Before entering a neighbor's house, Min would consult with Sar on how to address the elders who lived there. She had already forgotten how she was related to many of the villagers.

At the house of an aunt of Min's mother, the three older girls conferred briefly, then Guimin took out one hundred yuan and gave it to the old woman; they also gave at the house of a great-uncle who had a lame leg. Traditionally during the new year, older people would give the younger generation *hongbao*—red envelopes of cash— but the money flowed in the opposite direction now.

The migrants of the village had developed a new tradition of their own. On the first day of the year, the only time they were all home together, the young people gathered at a Buddhist temple in the mountains. I joined Min, Guimin, and Sar as they set out that morning in a light drizzle. At a branch in the road, a small crowd waited for them. These were the young bucks of the village: some married, some not, wearing black leather jackets and jeans and smoking coolly as they watched the three sisters and me come up the path. The men carried armloads of firecrackers. One young man had pinned four cigarettes to the side of his head with the earpiece of his glasses—an embarrassment of riches.

The temple was a cream-colored building whose black slate roof curved gracefully upward at the corners. Before entering, the young men set off several deafening rounds of firecrackers. In the first room, a wooden plaque listed the names of everyone who had donated money for the temple's renovation. Min found the names of her father and all her uncles in a thicket of Lus under the heading GAVE FIFTY.

Alone among the young people, Min walked up to the altar in the temple's innermost room. She put money in a collection box and asked a middle-aged nun if she could pray for good fortune in marriage. The nun nodded. Min knelt and prayed that she would meet the person who was destined for her. The nun came up to Min and put a hand on her shoulder. "Earn some more money," she said. "Find a good mate."

It was the first time Min had ever prayed for her marriage fortune. She wasn't sure how much she believed, but that didn't seem to matter to her. "Even if you don't believe it," she said, "you must respect it." The nun gave Min a piece of red cloth—she must keep it safe and it would protect her. If Min enjoyed good fortune, she should return to the temple in one year and give thanks to Guanyin, the Buddhist goddess of mercy, who is the protector of sailors at sea, childless women, and people everywhere who are in distress.

*   *   *

After the new year passed, Min dropped her home-improvement projects. The water dispenser ran dry; everybody began reusing the porcelain cups. The plastic trash bag sat forgotten in the corner, until one day it was gone. Min's focus shifted to her impending journey out again.

On a snowy day, she traveled an hour by motorcycle-taxi and minibus to visit two sisters who were friends from middle school. Both girls were home from their migrant jobs on the coast; their parents farmed and cared for a mentally handicapped teenage son. When Min arrived at the house, she was surprised to find a daughter just over a year old, barely walking. She scooped up the baby in her arms and read the situation to me, like a veteran detective happening on the scene of a crime. "Their son is retarded, so they wanted to have another son. But they had a daughter instead. Of course, they love her just as much," Min said a bit defensively as she bounced the child up and down.

"Where are you working?" her friends' mother asked Min.

"Dongguan, in an office," Min said.

"Doing what?" the younger sister asked.

"Clerk," Min said.

"Very good!" the mother said.

Min turned to the older sister, Cheng Meilin, who was twenty years old, with a pretty delicate face. "What about you?"

"It's not good," Meilin said. "I'm in a restaurant."

"Waitress?" Min asked. Meilin looked away without answering. Her younger sister, Cheng Li, worked in the housewares department of a Henan supermarket. That put both sisters at the bottom of the migrant class system as far as Min was concerned: Service work was exhausting and brought the shame of having to wait on wealthy people.

Over lunch, Cheng Li told Min about her job. She worked thirteen hours a day and had only two days off a month, and that was docked from her pay.

"Come out with me to my factory," Min said suddenly. "We make handbags. The pay is seven or eight hundred a month for ordinary workers, and we get Sundays off."

Cheng Li looked at her mother, who said, "Let's see what your father says."

In the same village Min visited the house of another classmate, who was not home; Min learned from a neighbor that her friend had married a man twice her age and now stayed home caring for their infant daughter. The neighbor broadcast the details from her front door at top volume. "The husband is short. He is old and ugly. The parents did not approve of the marriage."

Min was troubled at the news. "She seemed to have such promise," she told me as we walked back through the village. "I thought she would do migrant work for a long time. I really thought she would go places."

ON THE NIGHT BEFORE Min and her older sister were to leave, the family sat watching television together. Guimin's boyfriend left to use the outhouse, and suddenly the mood in the room changed. Guimin and her mother began speaking in low harsh voices, the words coming fast—as if some unspoken argument had been building for days in silence.

Min's mother criticized Guimin for getting involved with a man who was not from their part of Hubei. "If you marry him," she said, her voice rising, "I might never see you again."

Guimin turned on her mother in a fury. "Every person has her own piece of sky," she said. "If you want me to break up with him, I'll break up with him right away. And I will never marry anyone." Her mother started to cry.

The boyfriend returned, and it was as if he brought the silence back with him. All at once the angry words disappeared, and nobody spoke at all. Guimin stared hard at the TV screen. Their mother got up and left the room. "Go help your mother," their father told Min. She stood up, her eyes big and gleaming with excitement, and went out. Guimin began to pack her belongings. Their father continued to watch television as if nothing had happened.

Min tried to reason with her mother. "Everyone must find her own way," she said. "If Guimin is not happy with him, she'll come back to us. If she is happy with him, then you will have stood in the way of this great happiness."

Guimin and her mother did not speak to each other the rest of the night. But they still slept in the same bed, head-to-foot, as they had the entire time she was home. Early the next morning, her mother helped her get ready to leave. The two of them talked normally, as if the previous night's scene had not taken place. The boyfriend behaved normally, too: No one had told him what had happened. Guimin and her boyfriend walked up the muddy path to the road, and Guimin said goodbye without meeting her mother's eyes. "Then we will come visit at the October holiday," the boyfriend said to the parents in parting. They nodded and smiled, as if he were still welcome.

*   *   *

ON THE FIFTH DAY of the new year, Min left home. Her classmate Hu Tao, as promised, had bought us tickets on the 3:20 to Dongguan. It was the slow train, sixteen hours, without assigned seats, but he had been lucky to get them in the post-holiday crush. We said goodbye to Min's parents and climbed on the back of the motorcycle of an uncle who would take us into town. "Hold on tight" was all her mother said in parting.

Min arrived at the station an hour early with two friends who had come to see her off. The train would arrive already packed and there would be a struggle to get on; the waiting room felt tense and expectant, like the last moments before the start of a race. There was no sign of Hu Tao. Every time Min called him, she heard a message saying that his mobile phone was off.

At 2:45, the platform number was announced and the waiting

room emptied with a rush. Min went outside to look for Hu Tao. She returned alone and conferred with her friend, Liu Liya. Perhaps the two of us should get on the train first and talk our way into tickets later. Liu Liya was doubtful. "They'll kick you right off," she said.

A little after three o'clock, Hu Tao appeared, with his clenched vacant expression and the little mustache still hovering on his lip. Min and her friends pounced on him.

"Where have you been?"

"Do you know it's three o'clock?"

He didn't know. His phone was off and he didn't wear a watch.

"Why is your phone off? We called so many times and couldn't reach you."

He said it had run out of power.

"I could just slap you twice across the face!" Min said. Hu Tao looked dazed as he handed the tickets to Min.

We joined the crowd waiting to pass through a metal gate to the platform. Policemen marched up and down yelling at passengers not to push. Min and I were among the first people through the gate, but Hu Tao fell behind. "Don't worry about him anymore," Min said. As the train approached, people swarmed up to it but almost every door stayed shut. One entrance opened; the crowd surged. Arms and legs reached out from the train, trying to hold off the crush of people. The passengers were trying to keep more people from boarding, perhaps because the car was crowded or they wanted to save room for their friends. Somebody got a kick in the stomach; voices rose in anger. The standoff lasted ten minutes, and the police were nowhere to be seen. At this crucial moment, they had disappeared.

Finally we spotted an open door a few cars back, ran over, and pushed our way on. The car was packed, but within an hour both Min and I had squeezed onto the edges of seats. Hu Tao had joined us, and Min gave him her seat and sat on his lap while they listened to her MP3 player together. This seemed a rare intimacy, and finally

Min came over to me. "That boy is the one who was my boyfriend before," she said.

"What? Hu Tao?"

She had dated Hu Tao the year before, when he lived in Dong-guan—he was the one she couldn't find after she lost her mobile phone. Hu Tao had called on her first day home, thinking to pick up where they had left off. These secrets had been held so deeply that I had no idea, and now I struggled to put the pieces together.

"Does he know you have a boyfriend?" I asked.

"No."

"Do you plan to tell him?"

"I want him to find work in the factory first," Min said. "Then I'll tell him and he'll be on his own. We can just be friends." She laughed at her own nerve. "He's not as good as my boyfriend now, right? My boyfriend is more reliable."

There were more secrets. Guimin was not returning to Dong-guan, as her parents imagined. That morning she had boarded the train for Changsha, the city where her boyfriend lived; they would move in together and he would help her find work there. "I'm the only one who knows," Min said. "You must not tell my mother. She'll be even angrier than she is already." She walked back down the aisle. Later I saw her sitting in Hu Tao's lap as he untangled her hair with his fingers. She looked at me through the blur of hair and hands, her smile full of delight and shame.

Later that evening, I got a message on my phone from Guimin. I told her we were on the train and hoped things worked out with her parents. *Thank you, I never worry*, she wrote back. *I am only walking my own path.*

At eight the next morning, the train arrived in Dongguan. It was warm in the south; Min took off her sweater and complained about the heat, forgetting already the misery of being cold the whole time she was home. She and Hu Tao walked out from the station to catch a bus to her factory. She would take a shower and wash her hair, things she had put off for days because there was no running water at home. Then she would take a long nap. She did not have a plan for resolving her dual-boyfriend dilemma, but in the end it would be decided for her. Later that morning, Min would introduce her boyfriend and Hu Tao, and each would be furious to learn of the other's existence. Min would try, and fail, to find Hu Tao a job in her factory. Her boyfriend would tell her, "If he isn't gone in three days, I will find people and come after him." Min would lend Hu Tao three hundred yuan. And he would disappear from her life, probably for good.

But now on the bus packed with returning migrants, Min's thoughts were elsewhere. There was nothing to do at home but watch television, she said; she reminded me how little the nearby city of Wuxue had to offer. She seemed to be running through everything she had seen at home, trying to figure out where she stood. As the factories of Dongguan came into view through the bus window, she looked at one after another without saying anything. "Home is good," she said at last, "but you can only stay a few days."

The Historian in My Family

In the spring of 2005 I went to my ancestral hometown. The Chinese call this *huijia*, returning home, even if you are going to a place where you have never been. My father was sixty years old before he returned to Liutai for the first time. I had already lived in China for seven years, and all that time I had resisted the pull of the village. But something about accompanying Min on her journey home made me want to see where my own family came from. It had been ninety years since my grandfather had left Liutai, and I wasn't sure how his death had settled on this place. I didn't even know what to think of *huijia*: whether returning home was a duty or a right, whether it would have any meaning after all this time.

The road to Liutai was lined with silvery birch trees, as in the setting of a Tolstoy novel, and fields of fertile black earth stretched to the horizon on either side. It was twenty days until the spring sowing. From the car window I saw farmers out with their oxen, turning the earth; others burned corn husks in the fields, the fires glowing across the plains. This was the Manchurian prairie that had drawn my pioneer ancestors, but I couldn't envision their Qing Dynasty world. Instead I thought of the *Little House on the Prairie* books I had loved as a child—that was the image that came to mind, and it was false to the core. The rural Chinese of the Qing had never written such books. Even today, most Chinese would have no faith that the history of a pioneer family was worth telling.

The road narrowed, crossed a mud puddle, and appeared to stop abruptly at a broomstick stretched across the backs of two chairs. An old woman demanded payment. It was a common sight in rural areas—a makeshift tollbooth, operating under no greater authority than poverty and stubbornness.

"Let us pass," my taxi driver pleaded. "We've suffered hardship today."

The old woman was implacable. "I have a lame leg," she said. "I've suffered hardship." I gave her one yuan, twelve cents, and the broomstick lifted.

The first scattered houses of Liutai appeared. I knew only one name, Zhang Lige. When my parents visited in 1995, they had met this distant relative by chance and had been invited into his home. "Is Zhang Lige still here?" I asked a young man on the side of the road. That meant: Is he still alive?

"He's not here anymore," the young man said, "but his wife is." He pointed the way. Two young women in their twenties answered the door; they were pretty in the northern Chinese way, broad-shouldered and big-boned, with their cheeks reddened by the wind. They brought me up the hill to the house of a great-aunt.

Shen Jingzhi was eighty-three years old, and she had lived next door to our family compound when she was young. As soon as she understood who I was, she began talking fiercely at me in a thick country dialect, her gums working silently in the spaces between the words. The woman's face was thin and puckered, like parchment, with bright rheumy eyes. I didn't understand anything she said. A younger relative, a man in his fifties with a handsome square face, translated from the dialect into Mandarin.

"The wall was here. I lived on the other side of the wall," the old lady said, conjuring with her bony hands a compound that had disappeared sixty years before. "Even though your family were big officials, they would always greet us when they saw us, no matter how low the person or how ragged his clothes."

I asked her if she remembered my grandfather, or his brother, or their father. Every time I said a name, she would listen and shake her head. "They were always in Beijing," she said.

But the younger man, whose name was Shen Zhenfa, knew everything. He knew that my father lived in America and had worked at a university in Hong Kong, and that I had cousins in Harbin. He knew of a relative named Zhang Hong and said he would get his number for me. He knew about my grandfather. "He was a remarkable man," Shen Zhenfa said. "He wanted to do something for China, and for this he died in the Fushun mine."

I asked Shen Zhenfa how he knew so much about my family.

"When my father was alive, he spoke a lot about this history," he said. "He did work for your family. He tended the pigs and the sheep."

Shen Zhenfa also remembered my father's visit. A decade on, the event seemed to have expanded in dimension. "He came with another person, I think from the government. He had big broad shoulders. Isn't that right?"

"Not really," I said. My father is a slight man; he has the shoulders of a Chinese physicist.

"Broad shoulders," Shen Zhenfa insisted, "and large eyes. Right?"

That was true—my father had large eyes.

"After your father came, the ancestral temple burned down."

The old woman said that government officials had come and

taken away the genealogy, the book that traced our family back three hundred years. She was haunted by this loss. "Without the genealogy," she said, "it is dangerous because relatives who are of different generations may marry by mistake."

After my parents' visit, the officials who had accompanied them had returned to the village, taken the genealogy, and mailed it to my father in America. I told the old woman I could get a copy back for her.

"There's no need," one of the younger women answered for her. "There are no more Zhangs here now."

I HAD IMAGINED there would be a village of people with my nose and my eyes, and I thought that everybody would share my name. But all of them had gone out long ago. My great-grandfather's grave, on a hillside overlooking the village, had been dug up and destroyed during the Cultural Revolution. The ancestral temple had been ruined by the fire, but Shen offered to take me to the site of the temple on his motorcycle. As we prepared to leave, the old lady stood up and clutched my arm, seeming agitated. She was still thinking about the proper relations between the generations. "But what will I call you?" she asked. "And what will you call me?" I took her hands in mine and said goodbye.

We sped through the village on Shen's motorcycle. The houses of Liutai sat amid rolling hills, each one set apart from the next and facing a different direction, like a fistful of dice flung across the valley. Along with the mud-and-brick cottages were newer houses faced in white tile; many younger villagers worked outside or had moved to the city. "The village has changed a lot in recent years," Shen said.

The houses thinned out. We climbed a slope to a field that was still ankle-deep in corn husks from last year's harvest. The walls that had surrounded the family temple were visible on three sides of the field—the lower section built of stones, the higher part of mud. What remained of the walls was perhaps four feet high. Beyond the wall, stretching into the distance, were cornfields.

The site felt like an ancient ruin—Karakorum, the Mongol capital of the thirteenth century—and not something that had been built only a century before. This place had been no older than the turn-of-the-century house in San Francisco where my brother lived. Maybe it was because so much ground had been covered, and so many people gone so far away, that it felt so old.

I pointed to the husks. "Who planted this corn?"

"We let a neighbor farm this land," Shen said warily, as if I might suddenly assert my hereditary claim to it. We looked at the windswept land in silence. "There used to be three courtyards," Shen said. "The old people told me when it rained you could walk from the front all the way to the back without getting wet." That was his way of saying how grand the place had been.

Maybe it's impossible to write the history of a small place in China, because everyone with talent or ambition goes out. History happens elsewhere. When I returned to my family home at last, no one was there for me—only an old woman with a few threads of memory and a man whose father had once tended the pigs and the sheep. My family had been scattered all over Manchuria, all over the world. For the ones who had stayed behind, only fragments of the past remained. There was not enough to tell a story. Shen had told me nothing I didn't know, only that he possessed the same pieces of history I already had.

I didn't feel sad. I had waited a long time to come here, and now I understood something. *Xinfayuan, a fine place:* I was the embodiment of it now. A family is not a piece of land. It is the people who belong to it, and it is the events that shape their lives. Occasionally these events are collected—this was my role now. My family was a story, not a place, and here in Liutai I could see the purpose of writing it.

I had been in the village only an hour, but it was time to go. Shen Zhenfa drove me back to where the taxi waited for me. "In the future when you come back," he said, "you just come straight to my house." Left unspoken in his invitation were the words: *Because you don't have a home here anymore.*

*   *   *

There are no more Zhangs here now, the young woman in my ancestral village had said. My closest kin in China were the family of Lijiao, the cousin my father had grown up with. That summer, three months after my journey to Liutai, I went to see them for the first time in Harbin, a Manchurian city two hundred miles from the Russian border.

They had stayed behind and suffered, and it was partly because of us. Our family's landowning past made Lijiao a class enemy and condemned him, his wife, and their two sons to a decade of labor in the countryside. The departure of my father's family for Taiwan had made things worse—during the Cultural Revolution, such connections made Lijiao's family suspect as spies.

When I visited, the family gathered in the three-bedroom apartment of Lijiao's daughter. Lijiao's three children were of my generation but already in their fifties. The older brother was tall and stocky, with heavy black glasses that made me think of Jiang Zemin; the second brother was slighter, with well-shaped cheekbones that narrowed to a point at the jaw. I recognized those features—that was my father's face. Both brothers met me in their undershirts and talked like workers; *tamade*, fucking, was an all-purpose modifier. They had been in middle school when the Cultural Revolution began, and during that decade they had been sent down to the countryside. When they first returned to the city, the older brother got a job at a factory that made springs while the younger brother worked in a lumber factory. Yinqiao, the youngest child, belonged to a different class: She had finished middle school in 1971, after the radical phase of the Cultural Revolution, and she had not gone to the countryside like her brothers. Eventually she got her college diploma; now she held a high administrative position at the university. As in so many Chinese families, birth order had determined the fates of Lijiao's children.

Lijiao's wife, Zhu Shulan, took me into a bedroom. Lying in bed was an old man, immobile, with one eye opened a sliver. He appeared bloated, with a smooth bald head and the flesh on his face and neck as soft and exposed as a hard-boiled egg that has just been peeled. His stomach rose like a mound under the cotton sheet. This was Lijiao.

"He doesn't recognize people," Lijiao's wife said.

"He doesn't know anything," the wife of the second brother said cheerfully. She slapped the old man's face lightly. "Do you recognize me?" she said loudly.

The eyebrow above the open eye flickered. Both women laughed. They treated him like an idiot child—he was just a responsibility now. They did everything for him, feeding him soft foods and cleaning his sheets and monitoring the level on his oxygen tank. He had been this way since he suffered an attack the previous year and almost died.

I asked Yinqiao if they could hire someone to help care for him.

"If he weren't being cared for by family," she said flatly, "he would be dead already."

All that long day I spent with my family, the old man lay in bed. It seemed sad to me, but in fact the man's life was a triumph. Lijiao had brought his family intact through the Cultural Revolution. In the 1980s, he had helped each of his children get jobs at the agricultural university where he worked; all three of them were still employed there now. This was Lijiao's accomplishment, and at the age of eighty-nine he was fated to die peacefully in bed.

THE DINING TABLE OVERFLOWED with lunch dishes. Yinqiao had prepared *chunbing,* my favorite northern dish of floury pancakes stuffed with savory fillings that my mother always made for my birthday. I told them about my visit to Liutai—they were impressed that I had gone.

"None of us has ever been back home," Yinqiao said. Their father had two sisters whom they had met only once, as children.

There were no family members left in the village, I said, but a neighbor had given me a phone number for Zhang Hong.

My cousins looked at each other. "What do you know about Zhang Hong?" the older brother asked.

"I think he's angry at my family about something," I said carefully. My father had mentioned something to me about this "crazy" relative.

"He has mental problems!" the second brother's wife burst out.

Zhang Hong was my father's first cousin. Lijiao and my father were descended from my great-grandfather's first wife; Zhang Hong was from the third, and he had suffered for this connection. In 1957, his father had been labeled a Rightist and lost his university job in Shenyang. During the Cultural Revolution the family had been sent down to the countryside for a decade. After they returned to the city, Zhang Hong's father spent years writing letters and filing appeals to clear his name. He wanted the Communist Party to declare that he had never been a Rightist. He demanded, and won, compensation from his university for lost wages. After his father died, Zhang Hong took up the cause. He researched not only his father's case but also the history of my grandfather and our extended family; he spent all his free time reading old newspapers and copying files. "Everywhere he goes, he carries two huge bags full of documents," Lijiao's wife told me.

I had met this type of person—every reporter in China has. He was the protester, the petitioner, the person so focused on righting a wrong that the effort consumed his life and cast him into a separate universe where he lived alone. In China, such obsessive focus was necessary to fight a legal system designed to bury you with bureaucracy and delay. At a distance, such a person was admirable, but he could be insufferable up close. He spoke for hours about "the 3–7 Case" or "the 12–14 Decision"—people had a tendency to focus on specific dates on which legal judgments had been rendered. But the numbers had a way of overwhelming conversation; they sounded again and again, the petitioner tracing a time line of grievances whose meaning only he knew. At a certain point, you realized that this person was not listening to anything you said. You wanted to sympathize with him, but in the end you only felt numbed by the documents and petitions, the facts and the dates.

One by one, Zhang Hong had broken with everyone in the family. He sent an angry letter to Lijiao and no longer visited after that. He argued with my great-aunt in Beijing. He wrote venomous letters to my father and my uncle, which Yinqiao had saved and gave me reluctantly—she was embarrassed because the language was so hostile.

"He blames being labeled a Rightist on your grandfather," Yinqiao said. "One million people were labeled Rightists. Is it all because they knew your grandfather? Even the country's president Liu Shaoqi could not be protected, let alone a little commoner like you." Her cheeks flushed as she spoke.

"He came to see my father many times," the older brother said. "My father always urged him, saying, 'So many people suffered, not just you. You must put this behind you and look forward.' But he could not."

Zhang Hong cast a shadow over that day. When the family spoke of him, it was always dismissively—*he has mental problems!*—but there was a touch of awe as well. Maybe the grievances he expressed were the same ones they nurtured deep in their hearts; maybe they had suppressed such thoughts in order to get on with life. Maybe they suspected that he was right.

"He feels that he deserves something from your father and uncle," Yinqiao told me, over and over. "He suffered for so many years because of his association with your grandfather, and now he feels that the family owes him something. But we are happy just to be together with you again."

Listening to them talk, I realized that it was amazing there were not more Zhang Hongs in China. Almost everyone you met over a certain age had lost years to political campaigns; many were still paying a price in poor health, or lost education, or family members who had died. But there was a surprising lack of bitterness. When you asked about individual experiences, people tended to retreat into the collective voice. *So many people suffered*—as if that rationalized everything. My cousins repeatedly invoked Liu Shaoqi, who had been China's president and Mao's heir apparent. He had endured two years of beatings and struggle sessions; despite his lofty position, he had died in a Henan prison cell in 1969. The importance of this man, and the ignominy of his end, had deeply impressed my relatives. They seemed to see him as a kind of Chinese Christ, with a perversely nihilistic moral: Because He died in such a way, how could your story possibly matter?

Zhang Hong was different. He was furious at what he had lost and he couldn't get over it; he acted as if his individual sorrows were important. He dared to see his suffering as equal to that of the country's president Liu Shaoqi. Zhang Hong's story mattered and he was determined to tell it. I had always wondered why more people had not been driven mad by the trauma of the Cultural Revolution. Here was one who had, and he was family.

AFTER LUNCH, I sat down with the older brother to ask about the family history. My other relatives jumped in and out of the conversation as they passed through the living room. *What do you know about my grandfather?* I asked.

The best person to answer your question—a silent motioning toward the bedroom where the old man lay, unable to speak, waiting for death.

What do you know about your own grandfather?

He later changed his name to Zhang Shengbo.

He went to Beijing for college. He worked in Beijing.

No, he worked in Harbin.

Over a long day—nine hours, with six relatives talking at me nonstop—I tried, but it was impossible. Every time I asked a question, we were sidetracked into a discussion over someone's other name, or the correct year of his birth, or what someone had said about him once. We drowned in facts; we were lost in a thicket of dates. Nobody could bring it together, combining these details into a coherent story. It was difficult even to figure out what my relatives had gone through, year by year. They glossed over their individual stories; they omitted long stretches and they seemed to have forgotten key events. In a world where so many people had suffered, one person's story did not matter. *Even the country's president Liu Shaoqi could not be protected, let alone a little commoner like you.*

Finally I gave up asking questions. Seven hours into our conversation, I learned that their grandmother—Lijiao's mother—had stayed in Liutai and been killed during the land reform of the late 1940s. Over dinner, Yinqiao turned to me and said, "Our grandfather committed suicide. Did you know that?" I sat and let the conversation wash over me, leaving bits of what I wanted to know like pebbles deposited at the ocean's edge.

*   *   *

Back home in Beijing, I read the letter from Zhang Hong that Li-jiao's daughter had saved for me. It consisted of two typed pages addressed to my father, my uncle, and my aunts. Even somebody who could not read Chinese would recognize it as a rant: The letter was entirely in boldface and marked by urgent underlining, oversize fonts, and multiple exclamation points, as if the typed characters in their neat squares could not contain his emotion. Chinese writing was not supposed to look like this.

> **You said many times that you would not meet with us** . . . *Instead you viewed our troubles with indifference and gloated at our misfortune.*

> *A few years ago, I sent a letter that was virtually a distress call, hoping you would come forward and help my father and your own father at the same time. But you paid no heed, ruthlessly turning away from one in mortal danger.*

> *The Zhang family of Liutai continues the evil practices of the past, riding roughshod over human rights and jockeying for position between the legitimate and concubine branches of the family.*

> *My goal was to revive the tradition of filial piety and fraternal duty passed on from one generation to the next that our grandfather and great-grandfather founded. I*

never thought my father at the end would be victimized
by you, my brothers!!

At the top of page two, he took aim at me:

Does Zhang Tonghe still want to write the family
history? Will she write of these things, too? If she
doesn't, what sort of family history is that?

This letter, I learned from talking to my father, was the culmination of a series of exchanges that had been almost entirely one-sided. In the late 1990s, Zhang Hong had written to my father. He wanted to apply to the Communist Party to seek reversal of the political verdict on my grandfather; this process, known as *pingfan*, allowed people who had been criticized during the Cultural Revolution to restore their reputations. Zhang Hong seemed to think this would help his own father's case, and he asked for my father's support. But it was a bizarre request: My grandfather, my family believed, had been murdered by Communists, and now we should ask the party that killed him to clear his name? My father responded politely that he wasn't interested.

Zhang Hong wrote back an angry letter to my father and uncle. A few years later, he sent another letter, accusing my father's family of causing him hardship and ignoring his troubles. He vowed revenge and sent copies of the letter to my father's and uncle's colleagues at the universities where they worked. "I think Zhang Hong feels that we don't care about him, that we don't care about family matters at all," my father told me. He paused and then added, "Which is probably true."

Zhang Hong had spent years researching the family history. He had been sent to live in Liutai during the Cultural Revolution, where he met many relatives for the first time. He had visited Communist Party archives. He had interviewed the retired director of the Fushun coal mine, where my grandfather was killed. He possessed photographs of the ancestral temple before it burned and diagrams showing the layout of the buildings.

The more I learned about Zhang Hong, the more I realized I would have to talk to him. He was the true historian in my family, even if he was being driven mad by the past. He had the documents and the photographs; he had done the research. I was a latecomer and an amateur, and I would never know what he knew. The thought of meeting him terrified me.

Zhang Hong's last letter to my family had been in 2004, when I was still a reporter in Beijing. I hadn't visited my hometown yet, or thought of writing about family history. Yet in his letter Zhang Hong seemed to know my future.

> **Does Zhang Tonghe still want to write the family history? Will she write of these things, too?**

*   *   *

The Chinese today have a troubled relationship with their past. On the surface, they take pride in it—*China has five thousand years of history,* one is constantly reminded as an American—but there is an aversion to going much deeper than the level of a Qing Dynasty television soap opera. Why did a great civilization collapse so rapidly when confronted by the West? What made people turn so readily on each other—in workplaces, in villages, in families—during the political movements of the 1950s and 1960s? And how could they pick up their lives afterward as if nothing had happened?

The last question is easiest: through forgetting. The Communist Party has not acknowledged the scale of catastrophes like the famine of the late 1950s and the Cultural Revolution. In 1980, Deng Xiaoping ordered that the official history of the past thirty years should be "rough rather than detailed" for the sake of national unity. This approach has fed an aversion to going to the root of things. Thus the Cultural Revolution is commonly blamed on a handful of radical leaders, and the Tiananmen protests were the work of a few "black hands" manipulating the masses. "That is for history to decide," people say when the subjects come up—as if speaking of long ago rather than events they witnessed and participated in themselves.

Forgetting is also a personal choice—a tacit agreement among a great number of people to put the past aside. For my family who left China, it was more beneficial to move on than to mourn the wasted promise of my grandfather's life. For family who stayed behind, it was better to talk about Liu Shaoqi than to ask why their own best years had been sacrificed. The migrants have it easiest of all: Escaping the trap of family, history, and the past is as simple as changing a name or speaking a word aloud. *How do you say "international trade"?*

The past seemed to consist of only painful stories. *A man was assassinated at a train station after the war. A woman was beaten to death in her village. A woman went to the temple and drew a "very worst" fortune.* So much suffering suggests that there will be a historical accounting one day—but the instinct against introspection runs deep in this culture. Perhaps for a long time to come, China will feel the way it does now: a country that is at once tethered to history and unmoored from it, floating, free.

IN THE COUNTY SEAT near Liutai, I visited a ninety-two-year-old man named Guo Dehui. He had bright eyes, shaggy eyebrows, and long fleshy earlobes as curvaceous as question marks; in China big ears were a sign of good fortune. Guo Dehui had been a police officer during the Japanese occupation of Manchuria and later a

KMT legislator, and he had known my family. A local official had accompanied me and he explained to the old man that I was the granddaughter of Zhang Shenfu. Alert as a child, he asked, "Are you the daughter of Zhang Liyu or Zhang Ligang?

"I've been to your house," he said. "It is in Beijing, Xicheng District, Fenzi Hutong, number twenty-five." He rattled off the address, as if just this minute we might grab a taxi and head over. Later I discovered he was only three numbers off on the address—not bad for half a century. He recalled his visit to that house in 1947, the last time he saw my grandmother and my great-uncle. He and my great-uncle had been friends in the 1930s in the Liutai area, where he had served as police chief and my great-uncle had been mayor. "He was very friendly and liked by everyone. That's why he didn't have any trouble after the revolution."

"He came back during the Cultural Revolution," I said. "Did you see him then?"

The old man shook his head. "I didn't see him after that."

In 1954, Guo was accused of being a Taiwan spy during the "Elimination of Counterrevolutionaries" campaign. In the northwestern province of Gansu, he was imprisoned in a shed behind a car factory. He spent his days reading newspapers and tending apple and peach trees—he stayed for twenty years. When he returned to the city in 1975, he was already of retirement age. "The country supports me now," he said. I asked the old man his secret of longevity. "I eat meat, but I don't eat the fat," he said. "Before I turned eighty, I ran half an hour every day. Now I still go for a walk every day. But the most important thing is thinking: Your thinking must be open. When something is past, do not worry about it anymore. You must always think of the good side of things."

*　　*　　*

That fall, I returned to my hometown again. The corn was ripening in the fields and taller than a man already; in a month, it would be harvesttime. I had come back because it wasn't precisely true that there were no more Zhangs here now. After my first visit, a relative named Zhang Tongxian who lived in a nearby town had heard about me and got in touch. He met me in a market town near the village. Tongxian had a long handsome face and he wore a dignified black pinstripe suit—like a country preacher in an old Western, except for the tinted glasses and the red motorcycle. He taught elementary school.

Tongxian took me back to his house, where he and his wife farmed two acres of corn; their two daughters attended school in the city. I sat down on the *kang,* the traditional heated platform that serves as the bed in northern Chinese villages, and he placed a book in my hands. It was our family genealogy, compiled under the direction of my great-grandfather in the twelfth year of the Republic, 1923. The book was bound by string. It had water stains on its cover, and the edges of the pages were frayed and soft. "During the Cultural Revolution, my father wrapped it in plastic and buried it in the ground," Tongxian told me.

The genealogy traced our family back eleven generations to the ancestor who had migrated to Manchuria. An updated version, from 1993, extended the coverage by three generations. Tongxian had taken part in that revision; that was the edition of the genealogy that had been taken from the village and given to my father.

I asked Tongxian what the purpose of compiling the genealogy was.

"It is to handle genealogical relations." He lowered his voice. "Some of the people"—he named a village—"intermarried. This is not something for you to write."

"Didn't they know they were related?" I asked.

"They weren't that clear about it," he said, "and they weren't educated. This is for the sake of educating the younger generation."

He took out a cardboard box. It contained photographs, letters, and diagrams of our family compound and temple that he had drawn based on the recollections of the village elders. The diagrams showed the central rooms where the family had slept, and the sheds along the sides where the servants lived. Symbols marked where the washbasin had been, and the stone tablets, and the Mauser pistols posted at the four corners of the yard—so much detail, painstakingly compiled and put away. Tongxian also gave me a twenty-three-page history of the family that he had written, summing up everything he knew.

It was also on this day that I learned the fate of Lijiao's father, Zhang Feng'en. Soon after the political attacks began, Lijiao had sent his father back to Liutai for safety—believing in the village as a traditional place of refuge. It was a miscalculation. Red Guards were arriving in rural China, and they brought their violent tactics of class struggle. Lijiao's father had escaped such attacks during the land reform of the 1940s. Now he would learn that it is sometimes the people who have known you longest who have the most reason to hate you.

As an eight-year-old boy, Tongxian had seen everything.

> During the Cultural Revolution, Lijiao was given a politically bad label and sent down to the countryside. Feng'en came back to Liutai and lived in the house of his niece.
>
> In 1969, two work teams came to Qitamu. It was summer. They sent an order to have Feng'en brought there. The local saying was, *When you throw a meat bun at a dog, it is gone forever.* Feng'en was the meat bun, and the work teams were the dogs.
>
> That night, he hanged himself from a tree.
>
> Before that, he had already been struggled against. They paraded him around with a pointed hat. One of the people who criticized him was Zhang Lige.

I knew that name. Zhang Lige was the relative my father and mother had met when they visited the village in 1995. They had been guests in his house and they had bowed to him, as the only living representative of the family left. So this man had denounced Lijiao's father and helped drive him to his death.

Zhang Lige was very lazy. He never did any work in his life. Feng'en had helped arrange his marriage so that he didn't have to pay anything. Then during the Cultural Revolution, Zhang Lige accused him. You do something good for someone and this is how he repays you. Zhang Lige and the others shouted slogans: *Down with Zhang Feng'en! Down with landlords!*

I was standing on the edge of the crowd and I saw this. I was crying. Zhang Feng'en came to our house a lot, and I liked him. We called him Sixth Uncle.

I saw him crawling on his hands and knees in the school-yard. The worst I saw was in front of the Liutai commune. He was beaten so that you couldn't see a single spot of skin on his back—it was all blood. That was the worst day.

I was a child then. But none of the adults dared say anything. If you spoke up, you would have trouble.

Before I left, Tongxian said he had something to show me. He took me on his motorcycle to a plain brick house belonging to a farmer who was also a distant relative. At the base of the front gate were two uncommonly grand blocks of marble—stones from our ancestral temple. When the building was torn down during the Cultural Revolution, the old man who lived here had rescued and brought these into his house. Buried in the mud of a peasant's yard was all that remained of my family home—two stones, smooth and snowy white as the columns of a Greek temple. Each was inscribed with the character *shou*, which means "longevity."

*   *   *

In traditional Chinese genealogies, a family traces its lineage back to the *shiqianzu*, the "first migrating ancestor" who came from somewhere else and established himself where his descendants now live. Status-seeking families might claim a connection to a famous person of the distant past, but such spurious links betray themselves in the pages of the genealogy. Only the records after the first migrating ancestor are considered authentic. Migration fixes a person in place and time, and the history of a family begins when a person leaves home.

The Chinese genealogy, which started to appear widely during the Song Dynasty a thousand years ago, is a rigidly Confucian document. Its purpose is to record the merit and righteousness of a clan's members; like Communist Party propaganda, it prefers to emphasize the positive. Widows who remarried after their husbands' deaths—in violation of Confucian propriety—were often omitted from the pages of a genealogy, as were childless concubines and sons who became monks. The list of crimes leading to expulsion from the genealogy was long. According to one set of rules published during the Qing Dynasty, it included: *violating ancestral graves, marrying in disregard of social classes, violent rampaging, whoring, joining armed rebellion, treason or heresy, withholding the truth from the emperor, strangling someone to death without cause, or marrying a prostitute, actress, slave, or servant.* The genealogy reflected the traditional Chinese view that the purpose of history was not to relate facts or record stories, but to establish a moral standard to guide the living. History was not simply what happened, but what ought to happen if people behaved as they should.

First migrating ancestor
Hualong

Married Mrs. Liu jointly buried
in Fengtian Kaiyuan County graveyard
Two sons Yijun Yichen

In the *Jilin Zhang Family Genealogy* given to me by my relative Tongxian, the entry for our first migrating ancestor, Zhang Hualong, was five lines long. Most subsequent entries were equally terse. A man was identified by his name, his wife's surname, the names of his sons, and the location of his grave. Those were the only facts worth knowing: whether a person had continued the family line, and where to pay proper obeisance. Later entries supplied dates of birth and death, and occasionally one would list achievements, though only those conforming to a narrow standard—degrees, titles, and awards. The vast majority of entries continued to list only name, wife, sons, grave. The absence of other details indicated that a man had achieved nothing notable in life: he was a farmer.

The longest entry in the genealogy belonged to my grandfather.

Chun'en
Casual name Xingfu, later changed to Shenfu
National Peking University
Graduated in the economics department
Went to America
Graduated from University of Chicago economics
    department
Graduated from University of Michigan mining
    department
After returning to China served as technical director
    in the Jilin Province Bureau of Industry
(a position higher than senior expert)
And director and chief engineer of the Muling Coal
    Mine
Chief engineer of the Jiaozuo Coal Mine

Taught at Tangshan Engineering Institute
To resist the Japanese, headed the national strategic
    metal production of mercury, tin, and tungsten
Born 1899
Died 1946
Wife Li Xiangheng
Graduated from Peking Women's Normal College
Sons Liyu Ligang

Of my father's generation, there was only a single entry in our branch of the family: *Lijiao. Born 1917.* The rest of the page was blank.

But the genealogy did not describe individual members of the family so much as stamp out anything that made them different. Reading the *Jilin Zhang Family Genealogy* was like going through my grandfather's diary: The individual was missing from the very place I most hoped to find him. So the entry for my grandfather—*Died 1946*—could mention his precise standing in the government hierarchy—*a position higher than senior expert*—but not that he was assassinated when he returned to Manchuria, or that his widow raised five children alone, or that those children would grow up and go to Taiwan and America but always be, like my aunt Nellie:

> *your child wandering on the island in the sea . . .*
> *sending her heartfelt longing to you.*

The entry for my great-uncle, Zhang Feng'en—*Died 1969*—remained silent on how he had died, by his own hand one summer night in the village after being beaten and denounced by members of his own family. It did not mention that Zhang Lige—of the tenth generation, listed on page fifty-five of the genealogy—was chief among his tormentors. Nor did it say that Zhang Tongxian—of the eleventh generation, on page thirty-seven—watched it happen as a child.

But maybe this was the secret of the genealogy, the reason this tradition of private recordkeeping had endured for a thousand years. By sticking to the essentials—name, wife, sons, grave—it imposed order and harmony on human existence. It kept at bay the realities of a world that was not behaving as it should, and perhaps never had. The sense of continuity was amazing: Fourteen generations after our ancestor came to Manchuria, the vast majority of his descendants were still named in the sequence set out by my great-grandfather six generations before.

The genealogy contained one hidden surprise. Our first migrating ancestor had left Wanping County in Hebei Province to go to Manchuria. When I looked this up, I discovered that Wanping is a part of present-day Beijing. My grandfather left Beijing in 1920 to study in America, so he could save his country. My father left Beijing in 1948 on one of the last planes out of the city, when the country was already lost. And from America I came to live in Beijing, the place from which our first migrating ancestor had gone out three hundred years before.

*   *   *

In the winter of 2005, I went to Shenyang to meet the man who had vowed vengeance on my family. Zhang Hong met me at the gate of the Shenyang University of Technology, where he taught computer classes. His face was long and pale, with a high nose and prominent creases tracing the sides of his mouth—a face like my father's, though its deeper lines made him look more sad. He had improbably wavy teen-idol hair, and he wore dark pants and a polo sweater with an alligator on its chest facing the wrong direction. Zhang Hong shook my hand without smiling, his dark eyes regarding me steadily behind an intellectual's glasses. I got the feeling that he didn't smile very often.

He led me across campus into a deserted building and up a pitch-black flight of stairs. His office was drafty, with two wooden desks pushed up against each other.

You viewed our troubles with indifference and gloated at our misfortune.

I never thought that my father at the end would be victimized by you, my brothers!!

Zhang Hong took out a handheld tape recorder. "Do you mind if I tape this?" he asked. "My memory is bad." I must have looked taken aback, because he quickly put the device away.

"From what point of view are you writing your book?" Zhang Hong asked next. "The Chinese people's?"

I pondered the question, which was so distinctly Chinese. "I'm writing this book from my own point of view," I said at last. He was also writing a book, he told me, about the history of our family. It would have three parts: Flourishing, Decline, Revival. He had been researching it for fifteen years.

In the two days I spent with Zhang Hong, he was unfailingly polite. He took me home to meet his wife and son, and he treated me to dinner one night and lunch the next day. Our conversation, he told me, was one of the most important things he had experienced all year. He did not mention the hate mail he had sent to my father over the years, and neither did I.

ZHANG HONG WAS THREE YEARS OLD when his father was labeled a Rightist, and even as a young boy he felt ashamed of that political status. If an adult spoke to him, he would immediately confess the family crime: *My father is a Rightist.* But when no one was around he would shout blasphemies at the top of his lungs. *Down with the Communist Party! The Chinese revolution has been defeated!* "I guess there were two sides of me," Zhang Hong said. "There was the side that did that and the side that told people 'My father is a Rightist.' It's hard to explain what goes on in the mind of a child."

Zhang Hong's father lost his job as a university professor and was sent to do manual labor in the countryside. His mother was committed to a psychiatric hospital with a diagnosis of schizophrenia. "It was brought on by my father's political situation," Zhang Hong said; later his father was hospitalized as well. Looking back, Zhang Hong cannot remember who looked after him and his younger brother for long stretches of time. One semester, the boys boarded at school so their teachers could take care of them, and during a school holiday they were taken to live with the university security guards. When Zhang Hong was eight his parents divorced, and three years later his mother left for good.

When the Cultural Revolution began, his father was arrested and later held for six months on the college campus. In 1970, when Zhang Hong was sixteen, the boys were sent with their father to live in Liutai and work in the fields. Periodic denunciation campaigns alternated with peaceful spells when the villagers, many of them relatives, could be kind to them. Some of them gave Zhang Hong traditional Chinese books—rescued from the library of Xinfayuan, the family estate—and told him what they knew of the family history.

In 1979, the family moved back to Shenyang. Zhang Hong's father returned to the university that had expelled him, and Zhang Hong was later offered a job there too. It is the same school that his son attends now.

AFTER ZHANG HONG HAD TALKED for three hours straight— at which point we had reached only 1968—we went for a walk around the campus. As we passed a three-story building, he pointed to an upstairs window. "That's where they held my father when he was arrested." A doorway: "That's where I went in when I visited him." Zhang Hong had had offers to work elsewhere but he had always declined. Fifty years on, he was rooted to the place where everything bad had happened to him.

More than anywhere else, the Cultural Revolution unfolded on school campuses. Its victims were beaten in classrooms and paraded around athletic fields, denounced by fellow teachers and tortured by former students. Traditional Chinese culture had always held learning in the greatest reverence. That schools became the sites of humiliation and torment was one of the things that made the Cultural Revolution so terrible.

Sometimes now on campus, Zhang Hong ran into people who had attacked his father; like him, they had stayed on. One man as a student had been famous for giving out brutal beatings. After the Cultural Revolution, he came to see Zhang Hong's father and told him he was sorry.

THAT EVENING, I went to a hot-pot restaurant with Zhang Hong's family. His wife had a round fleshy face and tightly permed hair; she worked in the finance department of a real estate company. His son was a junior in college, studying accounting. Over dinner, Zhang Hong spoke at me for two hours about the Communist Party and Confucius, using classical idioms and quotations I did not understand. Shakespeare made an appearance, as did Tolstoy and Beethoven. I remembered that Zhang Hong had had only a seventh-grade education.

The Communist Party is a party of gangsters and hooligans.

Mao Zedong said: If your army is left with just one soldier, then let that one soldier attack.

Beethoven said: There are thousands of princes, but there is only one Beethoven.

Zhang Hong's wife and son did not join the conversation. They ate silently while looking into the middle distance, like people grown accustomed to a relative with an embarrassing medical condition. Zhang Hong's wife spoke only once. When her husband asked if I knew a certain Confucian saying—I didn't—she said quietly, "A person learns the culture of the place where she has grown up."

Zhang Hong's son didn't speak at all. He was a nice-looking boy with round dark eyes and short spiky hair. Every time I met his eyes, he gave me a smile that was sincere but knowing, as if he understood that everything his father and I were talking about was nonsense but he was too good-natured to say so. Later I asked Zhang Hong if he thought his son would one day take up the struggle to clear his father's name. He said no, and he related a conversation between them. "This is an economic era," Zhang Hong's son had told him, "and the Party cares only about business. Your problem is political. If you're looking to the Party for an answer, you will never get it."

NOTHING THAT ZHANG HONG HAD ENDURED during the Cultural Revolution was out of the ordinary. Even the more exotic details of his family story—the divorce, the diagnosis of schizophrenia—were common enough in an era when many individuals and families broke under the stress of persecution. In most ways, Zhang Hong's experience mirrored that of Lijiao's family—the Rightist label, the loss of a university job, the decade spent laboring in the fields. If anything, Lijiao's family had suffered more: Both his mother and father had died violent deaths in their village, while Zhang Hong's parents had survived.

Zhang Hong's family was unusual in one respect: They fought back. When his father was called a Rightist in struggle sessions, he responded: "What crap!" If a Red Guard punched him in the face, he punched back. He wrote letters protesting his innocence, start-

ing with the Shenyang Communist Party committee and moving up
the hierarchy. By the early 1970s, Zhang Hong's father was sending
letters to Mao and his wife, Jiang Qing, and he traveled to Beijing
to file petitions to clear his name.

In 1978, the Communist Party set up commissions to review and
rehabilitate hundreds of thousands of victims from two decades of
political campaigns. In the Party's judgment, the Anti-Rightist movement had been "unnecessarily broad," with many people "mistak-
enly" labeled Rightists. This followed the piecemeal approach to
history laid out by Deng Xiaoping, allowing the reversal of individual verdicts without addressing whether the movement itself had
been wrong. But the numbers said otherwise. Across China, more
than half a million people had been named Rightists—all but
ninety-six, it was eventually decided, had been labeled by mistake.

Zhang Hong's father demanded compensation for his lost salary,
and his university awarded him eleven thousand yuan—more than
$1,300, a large sum of money in the mid-1990s. The school also en-
rolled Zhang Hong in a two-year computer-training program and
gave him a teaching job upon graduation. It tried to remove the
Rightist label, but Zhang Hong's father refused. He wanted the
school to say that he had *never been* a Rightist—an absolute statement that no official was willing to make.

The family's rationale was a strange one. When someone was labeled a Rightist during the 1950s, it had to be confirmed by the
city's Communist Party committee: In China, even witch hunts
were supposed to follow bureaucratic procedure. But in the case of
Zhang Hong's father, the label had not been formally approved. His
argument was not that the verdict had been wrong, but rather that
it had not followed the appropriate protocol. Confronted by one of
the most chaotic periods in Chinese history, Zhang Hong's father
had chosen to tilt at a technicality.

On a 1985 trip to Beijing, Zhang Hong's younger brother drowned
in a canal on the city's northern outskirts, an apparent suicide. Af-

ter his father died in 2001, Zhang Hong pursued his father's case. He wrote letters to the school and the city government, to the Communist Party's history department and the courts and the prime minister's cabinet. He told all of them that his father had never been a Rightist, because he had not been labeled correctly. A few of the offices replied that they couldn't handle the case for one reason or another; most never responded. Zhang Hong was like a prisoner who continued to protest his innocence long after the door was open and the jailers had packed up and gone away.

BEFORE I LEFT SHENYANG, I had lunch with Zhang Hong and a friend of his who worked in the technology department of the Xinhua News Agency. The friend was about to go to Egypt on a three-year assignment. Most of the people sent abroad for Xinhua were said to be government spies, but I decided now was not the best time to explore that particular issue. I asked Zhang Hong how work on his book was going.

"I've written sixty thousand words, but I've only gotten to the Great Leap Forward," he said. "The whole book should be six hundred thousand words."

"The Great Leap Forward," I repeated, suddenly feeling very tired.

The man from Xinhua said with surprise, "You know about the Great Leap Forward?"

I asked Zhang Hong, "Why haven't you finished writing it?"

"My health is bad," he said, "so I work on it when I can." He paused. "To tell you the truth, I don't know from what angle to approach this story. How do I view the past? Do I say that everything that happened then was wrong? Or do I accept it?"

"Don't you regret all the bad things that happened?" I asked.

"It's just that during that time there were also many people who were kind to us," Zhang Hong said. "I have to decide what stance to assume in looking at this era. Or I could combine two stances, but that's not very interesting."

After lunch, Zhang Hong took me back to his apartment. He had some documents about my grandfather that he wanted to give me. In a cramped bedroom that doubled as his office, he took out two plastic shopping bags and shook out their contents: ragged photocopies, newspaper editorials, letters. Paper, paper, paper. As soon as I saw Zhang Hong's filing system, I realized he would never write his book.

The pile contained letters written by his father to various government offices; a document certifying his father's admission to a psychiatric hospital in the mid-1960s; a post-suicide letter from his brother's work unit stating that the dead man had been a hard worker; and a statement signed by an eighty-one-year-old retired official who couldn't remember if Zhang Hong's father had been labeled a Rightist or not. Divorce papers, alimony payments, report cards. Regarding my grandfather, he had some old newspaper clippings—I had them already—and two articles pulled off the Internet with idle speculation about his murder.

Zhang Hong kept a running tally of every time he had sent a letter or made an appeal on his father's behalf. Between 1993 and 2005, there had been fifty-one instances; in 2002 there had been eleven, and twelve in 2003. The most recent letter, to the Supreme People's Court, had been written five days before my visit.

UNTIL I MET ZHANG HONG, it was possible to imagine him as a hero. In a world where almost everyone chose silence and forgetting, he dared to stand up and speak out. Throughout Chinese history, there had been such people—private historians, writing their own accounts of events when the official version fell short. Zhang

Hong believed in the importance of his story, and he told it to anyone who would listen.

But his effort had not led to clarity—instead, it had twisted his mind beyond rescue. He insisted that his father was not a Rightist, yet he failed to see that the entire movement against Rightists had been meaningless. He had instincts of individualism—*There is only one Beethoven and there is only one Zhang Hong,* he asserted—but his ideas were hopelessly confused. *How do I view the past?* he had asked me, as if I could tell him the answer.

In the factory towns of the south, I was meeting young women and watching them learn how to be individuals. They found jobs; they confronted bosses; they tried to learn new skills. Mostly they came to believe that they mattered, despite their humble origins. *Do not feel inferior because we are ordinary migrant workers,* Chunming wrote in her diary. *We have no reason to feel inferior.* In Zhang Hong's world, it was still 1957. He loved himself; he hated himself. He hated Mao; he quoted Mao constantly. He despised the Party; he belonged to the Party. *The Chinese revolution has been defeated! My father is a Rightist.*

12   *The South China Mall*

Chunming's map of Dongguan traced the different people she had been. Over thirteen years, she had lived in seven of its towns and switched residences, by her rough count, seventeen times. In remote Qingxi she rose from factory clerk to department head and got a five-hundred-yuan raise. In Zhongshan she joined the frenzy of direct sales. In Guangzhou she was a reporter with a talent for extortion. In the city's downtown she moved in with her boyfriend and started a company with him—a Dongguan double jackpot—but the venture fell apart, the relationship ended, and she was forced to start again.

Since the late 1990s, she had sold building materials. She spent much of her working day on construction sites and inside industrial shopping malls that traded in paint, pipes, grout, and glue. It was a man's world and she liked that fine; she enjoyed being outdoors and not stuck in an office. Construction seemed to me like the most earthbound of industries, but for Chunming it meant freedom.

Some places she had lived in more than once, but only the latest incarnation stayed in her memory, the way a computer document overwrites older versions of itself. One spring night, she and I took a motorcycle taxi through a district called Humen. We passed a luxury hotel that had eight hundred rooms. From its rooftop, beams of red, blue, and green light swept the sky in wide searching arcs. "I saw this hotel going up," Chunming said. "I sold the water pipes that are in it now." That had been seven years before, when she first entered the building-materials business. Humen was also where she had wandered homeless after fleeing the hair salon. And it was where she had worked when she first came out from her village.

After Chunming had lived in Dongguan a few years, she thought of the city as home. Her past was inscribed in its buildings, in the pipes that delivered water to one of the city's grandest hotels; her personal history was written in plaster and steel and stone.

*   *   *

One afternoon I went with Chunming to an outlying district near the bus station. On a vast construction site, the largest mall in the world was being built. "Only the world's five hundred biggest brands will be here," Chunming told me, "like KFC and McDonald's." But the South China Mall was already causing her headaches. A contractor complained that her company's paint was showing cracks, and he wanted the job redone. Until then, he was withholding 140,000 yuan in payment, or more than $17,000.

Shopping malls—known in Chinese as *mo*, as in *modeng*, modern—were new to the Chinese retail scene. Developers aspired to their Western glamour and cachet, but beyond that they were pretty much at sea; they had no idea how the retail industry functioned in a mall. When it came to planning, the important thing was to make them as big as possible. The South China *Mo* would cover seven million square feet, with a 1.3-mile artificial river equipped with gondolas. A brochure referred to the *mo* as a "Dynamic Entertainment Theme Park" and made special mention of a roller coaster, an IMAX theater with a screen as large as a basketball court, and something called a Teletubbies Edutainment Centre.

Chunming and I waited for the contractor to arrive. Many of the *mo*'s buildings were already up, their facades in clashing architectural styles. There were cupolas, towers, columns; one building was decorated in an apparent Christian motif of crosses. A row of billboards advertising the *mo* lined the sidewalk with one English word per sign, like a word puzzle with no solution.

SPIRIT

STINK

ILLUSIVE

NATURE

SPORT FUL

POPPLE

GLORIOUS

"Are you sure they won't mind my being here?" I asked Chunming.

"Don't you worry about that," she said loudly. "These people are very low-quality."

Just at that moment, as if on cue, a skinny young guy rode up on a mountain bike and skidded to a stop, splashing our shoes with dirt.

"Are you Mr. Mu?" Chunming said, only a little discomfited.

"Yes. I'm the project manager."

"Then who is Mr. Wang? The one who walks a little, you know?" she said delicately.

"He's the chairman."

"Ah, the chairman. And is Mr. Huang the managing director?"

"There is no Mr. Huang. It's just Mr. Wang."

A representative of Chunming's company arrived and took us on a tour. The construction site was a lake of mud, its largest puddles crossed by wooden planks. One building exterior after another showed wide cracks, some extending the length of the facade. But Chunming's colleague blamed the quality of the construction. The surfaces painted in a rival company's product, he said, also had to be redone.

Chunming nodded. "They are just trying to avoid having to pay," she concluded quickly.

Her colleague led us to the corner of a building. "Look at that," he said, pointing to a sizable crack at the base. Chunming knelt and poked at the corner with her fingers. A fist-size chunk of the world's biggest *mo* came off in her hand.

She suspected corruption. Raw-material costs were going up, and many construction companies were cutting corners and defaulting on their debts. In a commercial world that rewarded risk-taking, everyone was overstretched. We circled the complex again. Chunming looked up at a metal tower reaching into the sky; one day soon, an amusement park ride would plunge passengers down its two-hundred-foot length. "I hope the construction of that is better quality," she said. The contractor reappeared on his bike. "I think the problem is with the construction of the building, not the paint," Chunming told him. She glibly repeated something her colleague had said about steel mesh and reinforced concrete and air bubbles.

The contractor could not hide his frustration. Opening day of the *mo*'s first phase, he said, was two weeks away. That seemed extremely unlikely given the current state of the *mo* but perfectly possible considering how things worked around here. "I don't care if it's the factory's problem or whose problem," he said. "If we don't finish, we don't get paid. And we're talking about several million, not several thousand."

At an impasse, they dialed different executives on their mobile phones. Chunming's voice was the loudest. "I have already talked to the cripple!" she shouted at one point. All three of them were young and spoke Mandarin with heavy rural accents; probably none of them had had a day's instruction in business, building, or contracting in their lives. Chunming turned to the contractor and said calmly, "I believe it's not a problem with paint. But if you want to contest it, I will send our technical people by." In the end her company agreed to do some repairs, the contractor paid up what it owed, and the *mo* opened two weeks later, right on schedule.

I STOPPED BY THE SOUTH CHINA MO one weekend afternoon two years later. McDonald's and Pizza Hut were doing brisk business, but the rest of the place was dead. There were only a few stores, which were either deserted or closed. Most of the spaces were empty shells, with glass doors chained shut and walls of bare plaster, as if construction were still under way. Two open areas on the main floor were filled with inflatable bouncy castles; parents paid a few yuan to let their kids jump up and down inside. That looked like an innovation of sorts—the least productive use of indoor *mo* space in the entire retail industry.

The South China Mo felt to me like another Dongguan history museum. Putting up a building was easy; the hard part was figuring out what went inside. In the end, paint turned out to be the least of the *mo*'s problems, and in the afternoon sunshine the building exteriors looked bright and brand-new. There was more than one way for a *mo* to fail.

*   *   *

Corruption seeped through Dongguan life. The motorcyclists who offered rides to pedestrians wore vests that said VOLUNTEER SECU-

RITY OFFICER; this blatantly dishonest job title was used to skirt a law banning for-profit operations involving motorcycles. A regulation limited government banquets to "four dishes, one soup," but officials countered by ordering rare seafood entrees costing thousands of yuan. Driver's licenses were another racket: Aspiring drivers had to take fifty hours of classes at government-affiliated schools, but on test day they still had to bribe their examiners. "In each car there are four people taking the test," a factory executive explained to me, "and if one person doesn't give money, all four may fail."

It was far easier to buy a fake license, as Chunming had done years ago. She had taken a few lessons since—"I know how to drive forward"—and she figured that one day she would learn the rest of what she needed to know. "Driving is not hard," she informed me. "The key is not to get angry at other people."

Kickbacks were universal in her industry. In order to make a sale, she usually had to pay 10 percent under the table to the buyer; that meant the person buying a product often earned more on the deal than the factory selling it. Some potential clients asked Chunming straight out: *How much will you give me?* Others were more discreet. But you could see from their apartments and nice cars, she said, that everyone took kickbacks. Corruption was embedded in the language. The word for "commissions," *yongjin*, meant a legitimate percentage earned by a seller, but it also referred to illegal kickbacks to a buyer. As far as the language was concerned, you couldn't distinguish between legal and illegal transactions, even if you wanted. At the lunar new year, clients were given *hongbao*—red envelopes of cash—and lavish boxes of tea, liquor, and cigarettes, which were called *li*, presents. I never heard the Chinese word for "bribe" used by anyone.

"It's very black," Chunming said. "But even if you don't do it yourself, you won't change anything." She had her own personal code: She refused to sell any substandard product that might harm someone. If she was on the buy side of a deal, she said, "I wouldn't ask for it, but if someone gave me a kickback I wouldn't refuse."

One afternoon, she mentioned that her older brother had moved to Shenzhen. "What does he do there?" I asked.

"His work is not very proper," she said. "He works with other people . . ." She hesitated, then plunged ahead. "Basically what he does is illegal." Her brother resold secondhand mobile phones. Often the phones had been stolen, with their keypad covers replaced to make them look new. Chunming didn't blame her brother; she told me he had tried to do business at home but couldn't make a living there.

"Is Dongguan more corrupt than your hometown?" I asked.

Chunming shook her head. "It's about the same. It's just that there are more opportunities here."

Another day she told me a friend's brother had scored well on the city's civil service exam. I asked her what kind of person aspired to be an official. "The big bosses need the help of officials with the right connections," she explained. "And the officials work together with the companies. It's a form of cooperation. So deciding to be a government official is just another way to go into business." She didn't mention job security, or prestige, or the desire to serve one's country: Being an official was just an alternate route to the market economy. It was the best explanation I ever heard of why anyone in China entered government service.

*   *   *

Chunming's boss parked his forest-green Toyota SUV and walked over to where she and I were waiting. He was in his forties, with a bland square face and glasses, a generic-looking businessman wearing a tan shirt with a gray suit. He said hello to Chunming and ignored me.

"Chairman Chen, this is my friend," Chunming prompted. Chairman Chen's head swiveled fifteen degrees until I entered his field of vision. He smiled and shook my hand, as if I had just become visible that instant. They had come to Shenzhen to negotiate contracts with sales agents. The first stop was a storefront office where they sat and waited amid buckets labeled TILE GROUT and WATERPROOFING SLURRY. And waited. It was ten in the morning, and Boss Xie was already running late.

These were some of the rules of doing business in China: *Never plan ahead. Never turn off your mobile phone. Never be on time.*

Chunming passed the time gathering intelligence from a young woman who worked in the office. "I just saw that big order of Davco go out as we were coming in," she said, naming a rival brand.

"Yes."

"Where is it going? To the construction site?"

"Yes." The young woman named a project.

"It sells pretty well now, doesn't it?"

"Yes."

"You've just arrived, right?" Chunming asked.

"Last month."

Chairman Chen lowered the newspaper he was reading. "How are sales this month?"

"Quite good," the young woman answered.

"But if you've only been here a month," he said, "how do you know if sales are 'quite good' or not?" The young woman blushed and didn't say anything.

Chairman Chen asked Chunming whether she had found a site for a new Dongguan store yet. She described a few possible locations while he continued reading his paper, occasionally flinging questions out of the side of his mouth without looking in her direction. While she was still talking, he took out his mobile phone and started dialing. That let her know their conversation was over.

BOSS XIE ARRIVED AN HOUR LATE, wearing a brown jacket from one suit and black pants from another, and bragging that a client owed him nine hundred thousand yuan. He told Chunming and Chairman Chen that he wanted to pull out of the retail side of the business. Chunming said that first he must hand over a full list of clients. In response, Boss Xie started taking potshots at the products made by Chunming's company. Grabbing a chunk of tile, he scratched a gash across its surface with a small rock. "See? The quality is not good." The performance looked rehearsed; the tile was already riddled with old scratches.

Chunming rushed to the tile's defense. "That's just a sample."

"That's an actual tile."

Chairman Chen sat back in his chair, ostentatiously smoking Marlboros without offering them to anyone. When he did speak, it was often to undercut something Chunming had said.

"We will draw up a contract . . . ."

"The contract is not important. Most important is that we compile the client list."

I imagined what Chunming would say if she had been fixed up with Chairman Chen on a blind date.

He didn't make eye contact the whole time he spoke to me!

He wore a tan shirt with a gray suit!

He is so low-class!

But he was the boss, so she kept quiet.

LATER IN THE DAY, Chunming and her boss visited another sales agent. They had arranged to meet Boss Luo at his store inside a mall selling construction materials, but they had trouble finding him. They were looking in paint stores, but it turned out that his shop sold water faucets and door handles. That was another rule of business: *Diversify like crazy.*

Chunming announced that they were willing to award him the exclusive right to their Shenzhen retail business. Boss Luo was interested.

"Are all your sales entered into a computer?" Chunming asked.

"No," Boss Luo said. "Our salespeople are in the marketplace. Once they go down there, they know right away what's going on."

"Not necessarily," Chunming said. "If you have the precise numbers, you know exactly how your sales are doing."

Boss Luo didn't say anything. *Don't leave a paper trail.*

Chairman Chen spoke up. "How about getting rid of these water faucets?" he asked. "They present the wrong image."

"I can't do that," Boss Luo said, looking pained. "The faucets are a big part of our revenue."

Chunming asked Boss Luo about his sales targets, but again her boss cut her off. "You can figure that out later." Chairman Chen seemed to exhibit many of the traits of unqualified leaders. But when I read the *Square and Round* book, I found that its rules for success described his behavior exactly.

> When you are sitting face-to-face, whoever shifts his line of vision first gains the initiative.

> To maintain a halo around your head and increase your importance, you must appear as little as possible. Let a competent subordinate appear in your place. Only when everything has been resolved do you appear at the end to make a final decision.

The day ended at yet another construction site, where Chunming met up with two colleagues. More troubleshooting: A client complained that their company's base-coat product—which was spread on a building surface before applying paint—was too powdery. More waiting: The man in charge of the project was in a meeting. Someday, Chunming had told me, a forest of luxury apartments would rise on this spot. As the late-afternoon sun stretched their shadows across the lot, she and her coworkers spoke of the rural villages they had come from. It was a country remembered but now gone forever, like childhood.

At home there was a graveyard right behind my house. I'm not afraid of people who have been dead a long time. But the ones who have just been put into the ground . . .

In my village, there is also a graveyard behind my house. I have seen with my own eyes that blue fire that jumps from one grave to another. They say those are the souls of people.

How often do you go home?

I haven't been home in eight years.

The foreman arrived at last. Everyone gathered around a section of wall that had been painted with the base product. It felt smooth and dry, just as it should. Chunming took charge. "Sometimes there may be slight differences from one batch to the next. That may account for slight differences in quality."

"If there are quality problems, it is very important to me," said the foreman, not ready to be appeased.

"And if there are quality problems, it is even more important to us," Chunming said soothingly. "You are very important to us."

"But the date on the bag said it was all produced the same day. How can there be differences in quality?"

Lai Gong, Chunming's colleague from the technical department, explained that a factory produced many batches in one day.

"Your workers must make sure to apply it properly," Chunming said. "You can't wait too long between applying the base and the paint, because the base will get too dry. Right now in Shenzhen it is very dry. Even people feel it." Humanizing the paint surface: brilliant.

The foreman started on a round of elaborate apologies. That was the usual sign that a Chinese business meeting was coming to an end. "My greatest regrets that you had to come all this way!"

"Not at all," Chunming said. "If there are any more problems, just call Lai Gong directly. Lai Gong, give him your card"—the young man fumbled in his computer bag—"and he will help you." Chunming and I walked out to the highway to catch a taxi and meet a friend of hers for dinner. The two young men, who might have been hoping for an invitation, walked down the road in the other direction, looking disappointed and hungry.

CHUNMING AND I SHARED A TAXI back to Dongguan that night. "Sometimes I feel like I need to recharge, like I don't have enough energy," she said. "I lack so many things. I don't know English, I don't know computers. When I joined this company, I told my boss I'd learn English in two years. Now I've been here almost three and I still don't know it." She was thinking of returning to the Assembly-Line English school, where she had taken a few lessons and dropped out. She was also thinking of leaving her paint company.

"What would you do?" I asked.

"My friends, the ones who are all bosses of their own trading companies, are trying to talk me into starting my own company. They make twenty or thirty thousand yuan a month. But if I did that, my life would be just about making money. I want to keep raising the quality of my life. I want to find new kinds of happiness."

It seemed that everything in Dongguan could be reduced to numbers: sales, kickbacks, language ability. The height of a potential boyfriend. You started with numbers—*What year are you? How much a month? How much for overtime?*—and then other numbers charted your progress: salary, the square-footage of an apartment, the price of a new car. But Chunming was looking for something that couldn't be measured. As we sped along the dark highway, the factories of Chang'an zipped past on both sides. "If the lights are still on, it means people are working overtime," Chunming said. "So many people work for years inside the same factory." It was eleven o'clock, but many of the factories were still lit, each one casting a cold blue glow into the night like a dying star.

*   *   *

Two crucial things happened soon after that. Chunming's boss cut her sales commissions without explanation, and a good friend named Liu Huachun bought a Buick. She was twenty-six years old. "She used to be a clerk in a shoe factory," Chunming told me. "Then she started her own factory with investment from her brother, learned everything from start to finish, and within one year she is able to buy a car."

These events spurred Chunming to action. In the spring of 2005, she set up a business with a friend to buy and sell mold parts—the innards of the plastic-injection molding machines that made everything from water pistols to coat hangers. They invested one hundred thousand yuan, about $12,500, in savings and loans from friends. Her new business partner had worked for six months in the finance department of a hardware factory. Chunming's only contact with molds had been on the assembly line a decade before, when she had made plastic toy cars and trains, but she wasn't in the least perturbed. "Doing anything is about knowing how to behave as a person," she told me. "If you can behave well, you will do well."

She didn't tell her boss she was leaving; in fact, she didn't leave. Since she rarely went to the office anyway, Chairman Chen had no way of knowing one of his star salespeople had gone off and started her own company while on his payroll. She continued to keep up with clients and to draw her monthly pay. It was classic Chinese behavior on all sides: He didn't tell her why he cut her commissions. She didn't tell him that she had quit his company.

She also started seeing a dentist. Her two front teeth stuck out slightly and she was considering "teeth beautification," which entailed having the offending teeth pulled and replaced by porcelain fakes. After that you couldn't bite into anything hard, like meat on the bone. Chunming was also considering braces, but that took at least a year—beautification was instant. A friend of a friend had undergone the procedure. "It changed the way she looks," Chunming reported, "and completely transformed her life." The next time I went to Dongguan, Chunming filled me in on all these developments, but she mentioned the teeth first. The molds were a career change, the teeth a cosmetic one, but to Chunming they were part of the same project. She was becoming someone else, again.

THE NEW BUSINESS BEGAN with deception: The partners printed up name cards in Chinese and English that said DONGGUAN YUXING HARDWARE & MOLD PARTS CORPORATION. There was no such entity; at this point, all that existed was a store. " 'Corporation' makes us sound bigger," Chunming explained.

She and her business partner, Fu Gui, were on their way to Shenzhen. It was the first day of the Sixth China International Machinery & Molds Industry Exhibition. In the taxi, Chunming continued to field calls from her old job. "If it says *putty additive* on the label, it means you can use it," she shouted into her mobile phone. "I can show you a price list, but you can't share it with anyone." In between, she called her brother to share bad news from home. "Uncle has stomach cancer," she said in a quieter voice. "We have to send money home right away." The fair was being held at the Shenzhen Convention and Exhibition Center. The center was still under construction and not formally open yet, but its vast floor swirled with crowds. Chunming and Fu Gui joined the mob, like minnows sucked into the mighty current.

"Some of these machines can cost one million!" Chunming said, her eyes big with excitement. She walked up to one that was spitting out plastic coat hangers. "Oh! We used to have these when I worked in the factory." A man proudly handed her a sea-green hanger that was still hot, like a fresh bagel. Chunming and Fu Gui wandered the exhibit booths, handing out cards and picking up product catalogs. Their aim was to meet parts manufacturers or their chief distributors, who bought straight from the factory and offered the lowest price. Everyone claimed to be a chief distributor, but when they quoted a price, you knew they were lying.

"What do you do?" a man at a booth asked Chunming. She mentioned a type of saw blade, hesitated, then said, "We do a lot of things. Look at my card." Occasionally she bargained. "How much?" picking up a drill bit and weighing it in her hand, as if she were buying onions at the market. Then: "So much? When we come, you must give us a better price."

The molds fair was bewildering to me. One booth might display something that resembled an oversize gold battery; another offered a metal cylinder lined with holes, like an old-fashioned hair curler. I saw tangles of brightly colored plastic spirals that looked like Tinkertoy creations. The advertisements around the exhibits didn't help much. Billboards featured metal parts against a backdrop of blue sky or city skyline, or sometimes a bunch of gears grouped in a circle, as if in orbit. Some of the signs were in English, but this was a language almost entirely of nouns rammed forcibly together, like a Mack Truck pileup. TRACTION DRIVE SPEED ACCELERATOR. TURRET PUNCH PRESS. There were ELECTRICAL DISCHARGE MACHINES and CENTERLESS GRINDING and ALLOY QUENCHING FURNACES.

The industry was populated by meaty-looking men who resembled bodyguards, though occasionally a woman from a factory's marketing department had been pressed into service. The hottest booth on the floor belonged to Eva Precision Industrial Moldings. Three young women in tight-fitting shirts handed out flyers while a video featuring gear parts and a disco soundtrack played on a screen behind them.

By midmorning, Chunming and Fu Gui were weighed down with shopping bags full of catalogs, like harried Christmas shoppers. They stowed their loot and continued on their rounds. At noon, Chunming called a friend who also wanted to start a molds business and had asked Chunming to join her. The friend had not even left home yet. That was how Chunming knew that in allying with Fu Gui, she had picked the right business partner.

THEIR NEW STORE was in the Changrong International Machinery and Hardware Center, a mall of machine-parts stores near the Bubugao electronics factory. It was situated in the middle of a long row of stores exactly like it. The downstairs had a meeting area and shelves lined with product samples, while the second floor would be their living quarters; on the floor was a single mattress where Fu Gui slept. Over the next month, Chunming moved in. She and Fu Gui repainted the walls a clean white and stocked the small kitchen with Chunming's pots and dishes and her rice cooker. They moved her double bed upstairs and fashioned a cozy sitting room with shelves, a television, and a sofa. "If the place I live isn't clean and comfortable, I can't work," Chunming said. But however you dressed it up, she was now living in a machine-parts mall. If there was more to life than making money, you couldn't see it from here.

*   *   *

Chunming had one complaint about her new living arrangement—
"I can't bring home lovers anymore"—but her dating didn't seem
to suffer any. She spent a day at a beach resort with a man who
worked in finance; in the course of telling me this story, the man's
marital status changed from "he has been married" to "he is married." She met a good-looking guy in a restaurant and started a relationship even though he had a girlfriend. She cut it off when he
started renovating his apartment, a signal to Chunming that he was
probably getting married soon. She had a fling with someone she
met online.

"He's a surgeon," she told me. "He's very fat, but he has a good
heart. He must be married."

"He *must* be married?" I asked.

"I don't know. He won't tell me."

"Did you ask him?"

She had. "You're married, right?" she asked.

"If you think I'm married," he responded, "then I'm married."

Married men who pretended not to be were the number-one dating hazard of Dongguan. Fu Gui, Chunming's business partner, had
been involved with one such man; Liu Huachun, the friend who
had recently bought the Buick, had been tricked twice. In a place
where people lied reflexively for work, deception naturally seeped
into personal relationships. Lying was often the pragmatic choice
because it got you what you wanted. Eventually your lies might
catch up with you, but few people thought that far ahead.

Chunming had her own rules for such affairs. No one should get
hurt, and neither side should make demands. "Of course, I'd like to
find the right person and get married," she told me. "But since I
haven't, it's fine to be with someone you don't love. You can still enjoy your time together. You can still rest your head on his shoulder
when you're tired and feel a sense of security."

I once asked Chunming if she had ever met a man older than she who wasn't married. The minute I asked I thought it was a dumb question—of course she had—until she answered.

"Very, very few," she said. She thought for a while. "My old boss." Then she made a face. "The ones who aren't married are all no good." Of course, that didn't mean the married ones were any good, either.

WHILE LIVING IN THE MACHINE-PARTS MALL, Chunming and Fu Gui devised a way to trap men. They posted the personal details of an imaginary twenty-four-year-old woman on a local Web site, next to a picture of a beautiful woman they had downloaded from the Internet. "She's 1.65 meters tall, she speaks English and French, she works in international trade, and she likes jazz," Chunming told me. She paused. "I don't even know what jazz is." The men fell over themselves to chat with her. Chunming knew many of them, and one was an occasional lover who told her he never met women online. She cut off relations with him after catching him in the act of flirting with the imaginary jazz fan. The city planner she had been involved with—*He is very ugly*—also came calling. But Chunming had turned against him; she found out that he had bragged about sleeping with her to other people. "We get men to come talk to us and then we attack them," Chunming explained. "But they're very thick-skinned, because they still hope they have a chance with you."

She showed me a recent exchange between the virtual woman and the city planner.

I think you are probably like a pig, she wrote. *A fat pig.*

Actually, I am more like a mouse.

A mouse? Isn't that even more disgusting?

She called him *fat pig* a few more times, while he tried gamely to keep the conversation going. Then I watched as Chunming logged on as two people at once, as herself and as the young woman. The young woman was immediately bombarded with messages.

Are you Hunanese?

What are you doing?

In your picture, you look even younger than twenty-four!

Chunming ignored them. As herself, she was chatting with a possible date, though he was on the far border of possible: forty-two years old, divorced, with a young son.

Are you off tomorrow?

Yes, are you? Can we meet?

I'm going to see friends tomorrow.

How about dinner the following night?

She agreed. *If we meet and have no feeling,* she wrote, *then let's not eat together.*

Chunming took other precautions. She never gave a strange man her mobile-phone number, so he couldn't track her down if things went badly. She didn't even tell him her name, making up one—Ling—instead. After Chunming had explained these rules and detailed her plans, she said, "Now I want to meet a man who has never been online."

"Who has never been online?" Fu Gui said.

"Ever since the Internet," Chunming lamented, "relations between people have become false."

"Ever since mobile phones, relations between people have become false," Fu Gui said. "You can always lie and say you're somewhere you're not."

THE NEXT TIME I SAW CHUNMING, I asked her how the date with the forty-two-year-old man went.

She wrinkled up her face. "Not good."

"What was wrong with him?"

She pointed to the top of her head. "On the top of his head he had a spot . . ."

"What? A bald spot?"

"A spot where the hair was very thin," she said. "I don't like those men who have very little hair. You couldn't see that at all in the picture he sent me." The man also had a seventeen-year-old daughter whom he had not mentioned in their online chats. A bald spot and a grown daughter—both were deal-killers for Chunming. You had to wonder about a man who thought he could hide either of those for very long.

*   *   *

Not surprisingly, Chunming's relations with her boss continued to deteriorate after she stopped doing any work for his paint company. In April 2005—around the time she moved into the machine-parts mall—Chairman Chen cut her salary by five hundred yuan and banned her from signing up new clients in Shenzhen. In May she was formally fired. In June she learned the company would not be paying her commissions she had earned earlier that year. Together with severance pay, the company owed her eleven thousand yuan, more than $1,300. Chunming tried to get in touch with Chairman Chen, but his management strategy in this particular case was not to answer his phone. *To maintain a halo around your head and increase your importance, you must appear as little as possible.* Over lunch with me and a friend, she mulled her options. "Now I just have to see how much money he gives me," she said. "If it's not enough, I'll sue him."

"A lawsuit is too much trouble," Chunming's friend said. "There are other ways to get your money." He had a thin face, with the skin stretched tight over the cheekbones and hair so short it gave him a permanently startled expression. He worked in shipping.

"What other ways?" I asked.

He said a cousin of his had been owed money by a client. "One day I was in the parking lot of the client's company. I saw a Benz parked there. 'Is that the company president's car?' I asked people. It was." Chunming's friend did a little more research and phoned up the company president. "I told him his home address. I told him the ages of his children. The company paid up ninety percent of the money they owed right away."

A few weeks later, Chunming decided to file a legal complaint with the labor bureau in Guangzhou, the provincial capital. "A complaint like this has a big impact inside a company," she told me. "Once the labor bureau starts investigating, all the employees will start thinking, 'What about the money the company owes me?' The company will have to treat them better." She was excited, and so was I. So much of life was unfair; Chunming knew that as well as anyone. Yet she believed her individual suffering mattered, and she was willing to go to court to seek justice. It was the last thing I would have expected.

THE FOLLOWING MONDAY MORNING, we took the bus to Guangzhou. Chunming was dressed, stylishly as always, in a slim black sweater, khaki pants, and high heels. We traveled by subway to the provincial labor bureau and were immediately bounced to the district labor bureau.

The office had a long low counter, with chairs for visitors on one side and a civil servant sitting opposite each chair. The arrangement was supposed to make government more accessible, but there was never one supplicant per official; instead, at least half a dozen people huddled around each chair, maneuvering for an opening. While waiting, they listened in on other cases and periodically offered comments. A middle-aged man was sitting in the chair when we arrived, explaining at great length how his boss had disappeared without paying him. Chunming pushed to the front and crouched low beside him, like a ball boy at a tennis tournament tensed to spring. When the man paused for breath, she bounced up. "Excuse me, I just have a quick question."

The official looked through her documents: her employment contract, letter of dismissal, a copy of her company's registration certificate. The papers showed why it would be almost impossible for ordinary workers to file a complaint. They rarely signed work contracts and they did not have access to a company's registration documents, as Chunming did because her clients sometimes wished to see them. The official told her she must get a copy of the license for the company's branch in Guangzhou.

But by now it was almost noon, and government offices across the city were shutting down. In a world where almost everyone worked nonstop, Chinese officials enjoyed two-hour breaks for lunch and a long nap. When Chunming stopped by one office to ask a quick question, the guard at the gate looked offended. "They are still sleeping."

———

OVER SOUP AND RICE at a self-serve lunchroom, Chunming revealed her Plan B. She opened her business-card case and plucked out a card. GORAN WIDSTROM, GROUP CHAIRMAN. This was the head of her former employer's parent company, which was based in Sweden. He had visited the Dongguan office several years ago and impressed Chunming as a kind person.

"Chairman Chen doesn't know I have the business card of Wei-si-te-ling," she said, using the transliteration of the Swedish name.

She caressed the edge of the card with her fingers. Once Wei-si-te-ling knew what was going on, he would help her get her money back. Chunming asked me if I could call him. I looked at my watch. The Swedes were still sleeping, like the Chinese officials. We lingered and drank several glasses of strong tea.

"Sometimes I wonder what I'm working so hard for," Chunming said. "I read in a book that success is saying the things you want to say and doing the things you want to do. I don't feel like that now."

"What would you like to do?" I asked.

"I'd like to study. I would really like to learn English." Her eyes filled suddenly with tears. She pressed a tissue into them, hard.

As usual, I hadn't seen it coming. "You've already done so much," I said. "Just read your diaries and you can see how far you've come."

"Don't mind me," she said. "I cry very easily. People think I'm strange." She dabbed at her eyes one last time, smiled at me, and stood up to do battle with the bureaucracy.

CHUNMING VISITED three commerce bureaus that afternoon in search of her former employer's branch-office license. The city commerce bureau pushed her to the province, the province to the district. No two officials said the same thing. Finally a woman at the district commerce bureau said she could print up the license for sixty yuan. Once money entered the conversation, there was hope. It was already 4:10 when Chunming, license in hand, ran into the city labor bureau to file her complaint, past the sign that said PLEASE DO NOT MAKE NOISE, SMOKE, OR SPIT. But she was in the wrong place, again. The district, not the city, handled branch offices of foreign enterprises, an official told her. He gave her a brochure explaining this.

Just before five, Chunming returned to the district labor bureau—her third visit of the day. And for the third time, the same official behind the same low counter denied her. "You must go to the city labor bureau. They handle foreign enterprises."

"They don't handle the branch offices of foreign enterprises," Chunming countered, slapping the brochure down on the table. He picked it up; written documents always impressed people in China. The official read the brochure and then put it down. Slowly it was dawning on him that he might actually have to do some work today. He pointed her to the end of the counter to get an arbitration form.

As Chunming filled out the form, she realized that arbitration might be more complicated than she expected. She would have to meet with her old boss to negotiate a settlement, which was the last thing she wanted. She would need to return to Guangzhou for the negotiation and to pay a fee whether or not she got any money. But there was no time to think any of it through, because she was scrambling to fill out the forms, which ran four pages and had to be filled out in duplicate. The government employees were leaving for the day, the women zipping their purses shut with finality.

"Wait, I'm going to file this today," Chunming called out.

The last woman left in the office stood up and shut off her computer. "It's 5:28. Are you going to finish in the next two minutes?" she said caustically.

"Can't you please be more helpful?" I asked. "We came all the way from Dongguan this morning."

"I live far away too," the woman said.

Finally Chunming gave up; she would have to come back another day. "They have absolutely no sense of responsibility in their work," she said to me as the metal gate of the labor bureau clanged shut behind us.

OUT ON THE SIDEWALK, Chunming began to have doubts. Arbitration was so complicated. A legal complaint might bring trouble to Wei-si-te-ling; foreign investors in China were always vulnerable. She had more faith in personal intervention, even from a person living seven time zones away whom she barely knew. "Once I get him on the phone, I'm sure he'll remember me," Chunming said. "And then we can talk about it."

I told her that most likely a secretary would answer the phone. Wei-si-te-ling was probably very busy, I said, and she shouldn't get her hopes up.

"When I met him in China, he didn't behave like a person who was important and busy. I felt like he was someone who really understands how to live." She had such faith in herself and her own importance. When she finally got through to Wei-si-te-ling, the global chairman of a Swedish paint company, she was certain the two of them would talk as friends, as equals. But of course it was exactly the kind of blind confidence that had brought Chunming to where she was today.

I dialed the number on the card. It was an answering service, in a secretary's voice, just as I had expected. I said what Chunming had told me to say.

> I am calling on behalf of Ms. Wu in the Dongguan sales department. She met you at a group meeting in Dongguan at the end of 2003. She has left the company but has always admired you very much.
>
> Now she has been fired for no reason, and the company has not paid the commissions owed her. She wants to file for labor arbitration, but she doesn't know how it will affect you and your company. She is wondering if you can help her.

Wei-si-te-ling never called.

Chunming never returned to Guangzhou to file her arbitration claim. Her former boss offered to pay part of the money he owed, which was enough for her. Too many things in her life were changing. She decided to quit the molds company; she would hand over her stake to Fu Gui, who would pay back her investment at a later date. The company had two regular clients and was already breaking even. "We haven't made big money yet," Chunming said. "But even if I make a lot of money, it won't satisfy me. Just to make money is not enough meaning in life."

She planned to go home for the mid-autumn festival, the lunar calendar holiday that celebrated the summer harvest. After so many years in the city, Chunming still marked time by the traditional holidays, seeing them as natural breaks between the phases of her life. When she returned to Dongguan, she would spend two years studying English. She had made up her mind, she told me. "I want to learn English so I can live a happier life."

Love and Money

Nothing about Min's life satisfied her after she returned from her visit home for the new year. She wasn't learning anything new in her job, and her salary was low. She could see how badly she stacked up: Because she worked in the human resources department, she knew how much everyone else in the factory made. And she was unhappy with her boyfriend. As an assistant on the factory floor, Ah Jie made three hundred yuan more a month than Min, but his was a dead-end job. He was only a middle school graduate, a fact that Min had never mentioned before. At one point he suggested she follow him to Beijing, where he could get a job as a security guard. She turned him down. "Everyone looks down on security guards," she told me. "It's even lower than being an ordinary worker."

Ah Jie's shyness, a common enough country trait, became a liability. At a dinner with Min's friend from a former factory, Lin Jia, and her two sisters, Ah Jie didn't say a word the entire meal. Afterward Lin Jia sent an assessment to Min on her mobile phone: *I've discussed it with my sisters and we all think he is too soft. He is not worthy of you.* From Changsha, where she had found work doing sales for a bank, Min's older sister Guimin weighed in: *In this society, a person who is too well behaved cannot survive.*

Min worried that Ah Jie's lack of ambition was rubbing off on her. "Since I've been dating him, I haven't studied at all," she complained. "I can't go on having fun like this. If I do this for another year or two, that will be my whole life." Ah Jie had reason to be comfortable where he was. Two-thirds of the workers and all the top bosses in the factory were from Henan, his native province. He had many friends at work, while Min was more alone than ever now that her older sister was gone. She had no friends inside the factory, a deliberate choice. "If you get close to someone," she said, "it's easier for them to betray you."

FOR A LONG TIME, I didn't know much about Min's factory. It was Hong Kong–owned, it made handbags—that was all she had said. On the train ride home to her village, she surprised me with a new year's present: a Coach change purse, with the company's signature logo of capital C's, its edges lined in brown suede. I assumed it was fake, like so many things in Dongguan. Only by chance did I learn that Min's factory manufactured for some of the biggest brands in the business: Coach, LeSportsac, Dooney & Bourke, Lacoste. So the purse she had given me was authentic—it probably cost fifty dollars in America.

One night after Min had returned to Dongguan, I asked her and Ah Jie how they got the bags. "If you're friends with the security guards, you can take the handbags out of the factory," Ah Jie said.

"You mean you just steal them?" I asked.

"We work on the factory floor," Ah Jie said, in a matter-of-fact way. "If the production line has filled an order, we can have them make a few extra bags. Then if you're friends with the guards, you can take them out."

"Doesn't the factory care?" I asked.

He shrugged. "As long as we fill the order, they don't care.

"I just took a handbag out of the factory today," Ah Jie continued. "It sells for two hundred U.S. dollars. Do you want it? Why don't you come look at it?"

I said hastily that I didn't need a handbag. "You should give it to your mother as a present," I said.

"His mother lives on a farm," Min said. "What's she going to do with a handbag?"

Min's and Ah Jie's dorm rooms were awash in Coach bags: a purse with the capital-C motif, a black leather billfold with contrast stitching, a dainty wristlet in burgundy suede—"That's for holding makeup," Min ventured. In one of the bags I found a printed card, in English, in an inside pocket:

AN AMERICAN CLASSIC

In 1941 the burnished patina of an all-American baseball glove inspired the founder of Coach to create a new collection of handbags, from the same luxuriously soft, glove-tanned leather. After refining this leather, six skilled leatherworkers crafted twelve signature handbags with perfect proportions and a timeless flair. They were fresh, functional, and women everywhere adored them. A new American classic was born.

In Min's universe, the Coach bags fluctuated widely in value. She gave the purse with the C-motif to her friend Lin Jia, who had lent her a place to stay while she was job-hunting. When Lin Jia's older sister held her wedding in one of the city's grandest hotels, Min brought a luxury handbag as a present. But on most days these purses that sold for hundreds of dollars in America were worthless, because almost no one in Min's circle had any use for them or knew what they were worth. Min stored her keys and ID card in her favorite one—a Lacoste hobo bag in sage-green suede—but it never left the room. Something that nice, she figured, would get stolen in no time at all.

MIN DECIDED to stay put. Summer had come to the Pearl River Delta, with temperatures in the nineties every day. At night the dorms were stifling; on the factory floor, the chemical smell was so strong that periodically a young woman would pass out on the assembly line and have to be carried out. During the summer, personal ambition often lay dormant, like an animal in hibernation.

But there was more to Min's decision than the weather. Over dinner one night in June 2005, she told me she had given notice to her boss, but withdrew it after Ah Jie begged her to stay. "So I've told Ah Jie I'll stay here this year," Min said. "For the new year, I'll go home with him to his family. After the new year, I'll quit and look for a new job. And next new year, he'll come home with me to my house."

As we continued talking, what she had just said slowly sank in: She had mapped out the next two years, and the rest of her life. At the age of nineteen, she had agreed to marry Ah Jie.

"When will you get married?" I asked.

"Probably three years from now."

"Have you told your parents?"

"No. I don't need to tell them until I bring Ah Jie home for the new year, two years from now."

"What about when you don't go home next year?"

"I can just tell my parents our factory is not giving us vacation."

"You mean, lie?"

"Yes." Concealing things from her parents was now second nature to her. Her older sister was living in Changsha with her boyfriend, but when she phoned home she pretended she was still in Dongguan, and she made Min cover for her. Next to that, Min's evasions didn't seem so bad.

*   *   *

Not everyone took Min's engagement seriously. Her friend Lin Jia and her two older sisters continued to bad-mouth Ah Jie. *People from Henan are too poor! He doesn't have any real skills. Find someone else.* One weekend in July, Lin Jia decided to introduce Min to a classmate from home; he worked in the remote district of Qingxi but was in town for the day. "I already have a boyfriend," Min objected. But she was curious enough that she didn't say no.

The night before, she came over to my apartment for a sleepover. Min got off the bus carrying nothing at all, the way country people showed up empty-handed on someone's doorstep. I found a T-shirt and shorts for her to sleep in and took her out to buy a toothbrush. Her phone rang around ten, while we were watching TV, and she answered without a greeting and chatted for a while. "We'll go see Lin Jia tomorrow," she said.

The phone rang again. I had assumed it was Ah Jie both times, but it was actually the potential boyfriend. He hadn't even met Min, and he was already calling her nonstop. "Lin Jia has told him how pretty and smart I am, so he really wants to meet me," Min said. All evening long, Min's phone trilled from the boy's messages to her. Around 11:30, the phone rang as we were getting ready for bed. "We're going to sleep now," Min said. "If you don't stop calling me, I'm going to have to turn off my phone."

———

THE DATE TOOK PLACE in a deafeningly loud dim sum restaurant. Lin Jia was already there with her oldest sister, Lin Xue; Lin Xue's husband and four-year-old daughter; her second sister; the girls' elderly father; and a cousin recently arrived from the countryside. The boy, Zhang Bin, had a narrow face, round dark eyes, and pale cheeks that were flushed with nervousness. He wore a white dress shirt and blue pinstripe suit pants. He had brought a friend from his factory. This was a blind date with eleven people in attendance.

As soon as Min and I sat down, Lin Xue leaned over toward us. "He's a college graduate and a line leader in a factory," she whispered. "He is very diligent."

Lin Xue's husband was sandwiched awkwardly between Min and the boy; the two of them did not say a word to each other the entire meal. From far across the table, Lin Jia giggled and dropped hints. *Why are you so quiet today? What are your plans for later?* Halfway through lunch, the boy left the table and stood by the restaurant window alone, gazing out. He looked like the romantic hero of a Chinese television soap opera, ready to reveal dramatic intimacies. In the soap opera, Min would have gone and stood beside him. Instead she turned to me and said in a low voice, "I don't usually like boys who look like that."

After the meal, Lin Xue's husband spotted someone from work and went over to say hello. The boy gathered up his courage and turned toward us. "I'm happy to meet you and your friend," he said to Min. We lifted our teacups and drank. Min didn't say a word.

SHE CALLED ME AT ELEVEN that night. "We just got back," she said, sounding out of breath. After lunch, she and Lin Jia had gone to the park with the boy and his friend. They climbed the hill to the television tower and then walked around the city.

"How was the boy?" I asked.

"Good. What do you think of him?"

"I don't know him," I hedged. "He seems like a good person."

"Better than Ah Jie?" she pressed.

"What do you think?"

"Good," she said. "He knows how to behave."

Also that night, the boy called her. For the first time, Min told him that she had a boyfriend. "Just give me an opportunity," the boy said.

*   *   *

Things started to move quickly after that. Min bought a new phone card. Since dating Ah Jie, she had shared his mobile phone; getting her own number was a declaration of independence.

Lin Xue was in my neighborhood a few days later, and we met up for lunch. "Min is taken with that boy!" she reported as soon as she saw me. "Now she wants to quit the factory to escape Ah Jie." Lin Xue was triumphant but a little alarmed at her matchmaking success. "I told her not to be so hasty. Is she sure about this?"

Min called me the next day. She had urgent news, but it wasn't what I expected. "I've just spoken with my parents," she said.

"How are they?" I asked.

"I'm going home. I want to get my diploma."

The diploma was a long-standing point of conflict with her parents. Because Min had left school a semester early, she hadn't picked up her diploma before going out. Employers usually wanted to see one, and though Min had talked her way into the jobs she wanted, it was getting harder to explain why she was two years out of school and still had no diploma. She had asked her father to go to her school and get it, but he resisted: He hoped to prevent her from switching jobs again. To her parents, it was enough that Min was employed—they didn't understand that some jobs were better than others. Min tried to explain. "In this job I have no prospects," she said in a phone call home.

"You haven't even gone to college," her mother said. "How can you talk about prospects?" Min was so upset she hung up on her.

Over dinner a couple of nights later, Min told me the boy was twenty-four years old and a chief supervisor in a digital-camera factory. "He's very good," she said. "He has quality and cultivation. He knows the correct way to behave. He takes care of people. In all these ways, he is better than Ah Jie." Min said she would go home later this month after she got paid, pick up her diploma, then return and find a new job near the boy's factory.

I asked why she had to leave her factory right away.

"I don't dare break up with Ah Jie," she said. "I don't know how he would react."

"What do you mean?"

A few days earlier, Lin Jia had gotten a phone call from someone she didn't know. "Don't interfere with what doesn't concern you," a male voice warned her. "Don't tell Min that Ah Jie is not worthy of her." Thuggish threats in the service of relationship maintenance: I hadn't imagined Ah Jie was so enterprising.

"So you don't plan to tell Ah Jie anything?" I asked.

"I'll call him after I leave the factory," she said. "I'll tell him that I'm leaving and he shouldn't try to find out where I am."

"Will he accept that?"

She shrugged. "I don't know. But he won't know how to find me." She planned to leave the factory without taking anything so no one would suspect she was quitting for good. "I'll take a change of clothes and the experience I've gained this year," Min said solemnly. "The other things I can buy again."

THINGS DIDN'T WORK OUT that way. In early August, I got an
e-mail from Min. She was still at the same factory. *My new friend is
fine*, she wrote, *but the situation between us is not very good. Maybe he
and I are more suited to be friends*. Her younger sister Sar had graduated from vocational high school and wanted to work in Dongguan.
Min found someone in her factory's shipping department who was
from the town near her village; he could get Sar a job as a shipping
clerk. There was one problem: Sar was only seventeen, which meant
she was too young to be hired. Min paid thirty yuan to a person
whose specialty was changing the birth dates on government-issued
identity cards. Sar's newly doctored ID said she had been born in
June 1986, while Min was born in February of that year. If anyone
looked closely at the sisters' ID cards, they might wonder. But no
one ever did.

Now I feel much less pressure than I did before, truly, Min wrote to me.

It was late September 2005, and the cooler weather was her signal. A month after Sar arrived, Min jumped again. She found a job
as an assistant in the purchasing department of a hardware factory;
it was a two-hour bus trip from where her younger sister was working. Min left without settling things with Ah Jie. She was no longer
in touch with the other boy. Her solution to these entanglements
was the only tactic she knew: Keep moving.

This time her job hunting was easier because she finally had her
diploma. Her father had gotten it from her school but refused to
mail it to her; he was still trying to keep her from changing jobs.
Min lied and told him her factory had a new rule—anyone without
a diploma would be fired. When her father heard this, he panicked
and paid extra to send the diploma by express mail. Min laughed
when she told me this story.

*   *   *

Min's new factory made metal parts for power supplies, computer monitors, and DVD players. Her workday stretched eleven hours, with every other Sunday off. She made one thousand yuan a month; if she did well, she would be promoted to purchasing supplies on her own. She started reading a book whose title was *Production Planning and Materials Purchasing*.

In the past year, she had sent home five thousand yuan—more than six hundred dollars—but her parents thought that was too little. "Other people's children have much less education," her father said. "How come they send home more money than you?"

"Other people's fathers make enough money so their children don't have to go out to work," Min countered.

Nowadays she saw her parents in a more critical light. When Min's father had worked briefly in the Wenzhou shoe factory in the late 1990s, he had fallen sick and returned home. Her mother had gone out for a year without saving any money either. They had failed where Min was succeeding, and for the first time she recognized this. "They have tasted migrant life. They should know how hard it is," Min told me. "And yet they think that for us to work outside and make money is so easy."

Five months after she was hired, Min was promoted to a job purchasing mold parts for her factory. It was her big break: The young woman who had previously held the job had gone home for a visit and her parents found out she had a boyfriend in the city. "They're holding her at home and not letting her come out again," Min said, "so I have an opportunity." In her new job, she made 1,200 yuan a month in salary and between six thousand and ten thousand yuan a month in kickbacks. In her first six months, she saved thirty thousand yuan—close to four thousand dollars—and sent home about $1,300. For the first time, she opened a bank account in the city, against the wishes of her parents. They wanted her to send all her money home.

"If the company knew I was taking kickbacks, they would fire me right away," Min told me.

"But everyone is doing it, right?" I asked her.

"Yes. But it's something we never talk about."

We were sitting in a McDonald's at a shopping mall near her factory. Min had ordered an iced coffee and fries; she ate out a lot now. I remembered the first time she ever went to McDonald's, two years before, when she brought her face down close to her Big Mac and ate her way through the sandwich one layer at a time. In a low voice, looking around to make sure no colleague was in sight, she told me about her job. Suppliers typically paid 10 percent of a purchase in kickbacks; Min met them away from the factory to collect their payments, in cash. The bank where she opened her account was far from the factory, so she wouldn't run into anyone she knew when making a deposit. People in purchasing were often resented inside a factory because their jobs were so lucrative. When Min ran into her colleagues outside, she would say hello and pick up their restaurant tabs to stay on their good side.

Success brought more pressure. "In the past if I didn't like my work, I would just leave," she said. "Now I worry what happens if the company doesn't want me anymore."

AS SOON AS MIN STARTED making more money, her relationship with her parents changed. They stopped complaining about how little she sent home and started dreaming up ways to spend her savings. They wanted to buy a villa in the nearby city of Wuxue, which would cost 120,000 yuan, about fifteen thousand dollars. Her father hatched a scheme to raise crayfish, which required somewhere between thirty thousand and fifty thousand yuan. He had lost money on last year's cotton crop and had no capital of his own. Min shot down both plans. "You can't make money in one instant," she lectured her father. "You must proceed step-by-step."

It was amazing to me how quickly Min overturned the power

structure within her family. When my grandfather returned home to his village after seven years in America, he had been beaten by his father for changing his course of study without permission. The man had become a modern, foreign-educated person, but he had not gained the slightest status in his father's eyes. In contrast, Min was able to dictate family affairs from afar. She monitored her father's purchases and rejected his business plans, and the fact that she had sent home $1,300 gave her such authority.

There was also a difference in class, which in China is largely cor-related to a person's level of education. My grandfather's father had been an educated man, which gave him stature even though he had never gone far from home. Migrant workers like Min came from the lowest rung of society—if they enjoyed success in the city, they im-mediately rose above all the other members of their family. Soon Min was actively directing the lives of her siblings. She promised her little brother a summer in Dongguan taking English lessons if he did well in school. Her improving finances changed the fate of her youngest sister, Xiu, who had failed the exam to get into high school. When the three older sisters had failed, each had enrolled in vocational school and then gone out to work. But now Min could afford to pay an extra fee that permitted Xiu to enroll in high school—in three years, she would take the college entrance exam.

"How are your grades?" Min asked her sister when she called home.

"I don't know," said Xiu, who was very shy.

"Do you know I'm out here working so you can stay in school?" Min asked. "You better get good grades and not let me down."

"I know," her sister replied. "I will."

Min weighed in on her older sister's situation too. Guimin's job and relationship had fallen apart, and she had returned to Dong-guan to work in a hammer factory. Min thought her sister was too old to be switching jobs so often. "You need to stay in one place and develop yourself," Min told her.

In the summer of 2006, Min paid a visit home. She gave her family a Changhong-brand television set, a DVD player, and five thousand yuan. For her father, she bought a shirt that cost eighty yuan. It was the nicest shirt he had ever owned, and he wore it the whole time Min was home. Min's father had recently celebrated his fiftieth birthday and had gone to see the fortune-teller. After he turned fifty, he was told, his luck would improve. Thanks to his second daughter, this fortune was coming true.

*   *   *

For the 2007 lunar new year, I returned to Min's village. She had gotten two weeks' leave from work because there was to be a wedding at home. Min's cousin and next-door neighbor was marrying a young woman who lived several villages away. During the year, he worked on a construction crew in faraway Ürümqi—forty-four hours by train—and she sewed clothes in a factory in Wuhan, three hours by bus. They had been introduced by a matchmaker the previous year and had gotten engaged right away. In the year that followed, they had *tan lianai*—"spoken of love," or courted—by phone. The process seemed backward to me—first you got engaged, then you started dating—but even so, it was a concession to modern ways because it allowed a couple to get to know each other before marrying.

The night I arrived, Min took me next door to see the cousin. Two years before, the main bedroom of his family's house had been an empty shell with a bare cement floor. Now the room was laid with tile and crowded with furniture: a wardrobe, a couch, a coffee table. A double bed with a pink mattress had the word *Happiness* in English written across it in fancy script. Above the bed was a studio photo of the cousin in an ivory three-piece tuxedo and his bride-to-be in a low-cut ball gown.

"She is so pretty!" Min exclaimed.

"She won't be pretty tomorrow," joked her cousin.

"What are you saying!" Min said. "A bride on her wedding day is at her prettiest."

Though a son traditionally lived in his parents' house with his wife after his marriage, Min's cousin and his new wife would spend only a few days at home before going back out to work. Across the Chinese countryside were countless rooms like these, furnished and decorated at considerable expense, and destined to stand empty almost all the days of the year.

EARLY THE NEXT MORNING, the young men of the village set out for the bride's house, carrying traditional rattan baskets on shoulder poles to bring back the wedding dowry. Peasants had carried loads on their shoulders in this way for centuries, but these young men had spent their working lives as urban migrants, mostly in factories. Only one older man looked comfortable balancing the bamboo pole across his shoulders. The groom, wearing a blue pin-stripe suit and patent-leather shoes, was still denigrating his fiancée's looks at every opportunity. "When you see her today," he told me, "you'll be frightened." Min and her older sister were to accompany the bride back to her new village. They had never taken part in a country wedding before.

At the bride's house, neighbors crowded the muddy yard to watch the proceedings. The main room overflowed with her dowry, looking like a clearance sale at a home appliance store: a refrigerator, an air conditioner, a hot-water dispenser, a washing machine, a high-definition color television, a stereo, and a karaoke machine. In the adjoining room, the bride sat on the bed with her head bowed while her mother, her grandmother, and her aunts wailed and cried—a traditional ritual to mourn a daughter's departure.

The young men took turns running into the house to "steal" the dowry while the bride's family and friends tried to fight them off. It took more than an hour to carry everything into the yard, where it was put into baskets or lashed tightly to bamboo poles. The groom was forced to wear a paper dunce cap, with a mustache and eyeglasses painted on his face and a chamber pot hung around his neck. He marched at the head of the procession out of the village. This was how victims of the Cultural Revolution had been paraded through the streets, except that he was smiling.

THE WEDDING LUNCH at the bride's home followed set rules. There were twelve dishes, and firecrackers were set off between many of the courses. The banquet included a whole fish for each table, a chicken surrounded by a dozen hard-boiled eggs, and sweet glutinous rice balls—their roundness symbolized perfect happiness. The dishes were brought one at a time and cleared before they were finished, to ensure there would always be abundance in this marriage.

In the afternoon, the bride set out for the groom's village. Min and her sister served as her escorts, but many of the wedding guests came along to prevent the bride from being taken away. The group would walk only a few steps before it halted in the road and forced Min and Guimin to sing a song. The procession then inched forward, stopped, and demanded more penalties. Most of the village had come out to join the fun of ganging up on Min and Guimin.

Sing more loudly!

One song is not enough!

It was all playacting, yet it felt serious. Two burly men and several middle-aged women led the attacks. Min and Guimin became flustered; they sang in quavering children's voices, staring at the ground. Suddenly I felt like an outsider—alone, watching from a distance the familiar sight of Chinese people trapped in their groups. Even something as innocent as a communal blind date seemed to point to a flaw in the national character, an inability to break free and take individual action. And now I sensed that the Cultural Revolution was rooted in the dynamics of the Chinese village, with its rituals that enforced the safety of the group. It was dangerous to be alone; in a crowd, you gained confidence and power. When the villagers yelled at Min and Guimin to sing more loudly, or cursed their performances, the most extreme voice always carried the day. The two young women stood at the center of the crowd with their heads bowed, waiting for it to be over.

At last we saw the groom's party on the path ahead. Young men came forward one after another to negotiate the bride's release, offering cigarettes or impromptu performances while the villagers continued their bullying and insults. Finally the groom charged into the crowd, picked up his bride, and carried her off into a waiting black sedan that had been rented for the occasion.

At the groom's house, everyone sat down for another feast even though they were still full from the last one. I kept waiting for some sort of ceremony or declaration to formalize the marriage, but none ever came. In these rituals, marriage had been portrayed with different meanings: an exchange of property between families, a confrontation of rival villages. But none of the traditions featured an agreement between the bride and the groom; the fact that this was a union of two individuals seemed almost incidental. When the liquor was poured, Guimin turned to her cousin and his new wife with a traditional toast: "Give birth soon to a treasured son."

THE REST OF MY STAY passed quickly. Min's family walked up the mountain to kowtow at the graves of their ancestors. She went to admire a three-story tile house that an uncle had built with his earnings as a migrant bricklayer; the house would stand vacant until he returned the next year with money to furnish it. On another day, she visited an aunt who sold clothing in the city to discuss the possibility of investing in a shop together. One evening, another uncle brought home a possible boyfriend for Min's older sister. Guimin did not say a word to him all evening, but after he had gone to bed she pronounced his death sentence: "The wheels of his brain just don't turn fast enough." The boy was gone before breakfast.

On my last morning, Min accompanied me to the bus station—she would not return to Dongguan for another week. She was wearing a belted jacket in watermelon pink, cropped black jeans, and high-heeled boots. Hu Tao, the old boyfriend she had taken out to the city two years before, had gotten back in touch. He wanted to get back together, and he was introducing Min to his mother later that day.

"If I don't find anyone else, I can always marry him in a few years," Min said. Another young man from home who had opened a store in town was also hoping to meet up. Min did not seem too worried about her marriage prospects. The four sisters in the family were expected to marry in order, as in a Jane Austen novel. As long as Guimin stayed single, no one was pressuring Min.

At the station, I bought my ticket and boarded the bus for Wuhan. From my window seat I waved; Min smiled and waved back. It was beginning to rain, so she dashed over to a nearby store for cover. As my bus pulled away, I saw Min intently typing a message into her mobile phone. She was figuring out where she was going next, and as usual she had a plan.

14 *The Tomb of the Emperor*

In the autumn of 1987, my father's cousin Lijiao sat down to write a letter to the Political Consultative Committees of two Northeastern provinces, entitled "Regarding the Issue of Zhang Shenfu's Tablet Urgently Needing an Inscription." Lijiao was hoping to engrave an epitaph on the graveside stele of his uncle, who had been dead for forty-one years.

> *Zhang Shenfu is my uncle. I sincerely hope to solve the problem of his tomb inscription as soon as possible, which will be useful in developing our overseas United Front work.*

A draft of the handwritten letter, which was twelve pages long, had been given to me by Lijiao's children. They had been unable to tell me the story of our family, but on these rough sheets of paper Lijiao had laid out everything—his private history of my grandfather's years in America, his wartime contributions to China's mining industry, his assassination and burial.

> *Before the tomb was a small piece of black marble inscribed with the words* TOMB OF MR. ZHANG SHENFU, *with every character about ten centimeters by ten centimeters. In front of the tomb to the right was a stele. On it was inscribed nothing . . .*
>
> *In the fall of 1948, Shenyang was liberated. In Beiling near the Dismounting Stele was left the tomb of Zhang Shenfu and a stele with no words . . . Li Xiangheng moved with her children to Taiwan . . . Her nephew Zhang Lijiao stayed on the mainland and did not go with them. After January 1949, he had no more contact with them.*

In 1979, Lijiao returned to the grave for the first time in thirty years. The tomb was gone, and my grandfather's remains had been scattered. But the stele with no name had survived—as my grandmother had foreseen, its blankness had protected it from harm. In his letter, Lijiao asked the authorities for permission to repair the tomb and erect a new stele with an inscription. Because the grave was in a prominent site in a public park, this was not something he could accomplish on his own.

> *Zhang Shenfu's second son and oldest son both have deep love for our great motherland and have returned to the motherland many times and devoted their energies to its construction . . . It is said that recently the Party Central Committee has proposed vigorously promoting its United Front work overseas, to make friends and win popular support.*

The "United Front" referred to the Communist Party's policies to win the loyalties of Chinese outside the Party, including those living in Hong Kong, Taiwan, and overseas. As a veteran of political movements, Lijiao knew that a personal plea on his uncle's behalf would not get very far. It was necessary to appeal to patriotism, and it was critical to portray this as an issue of nation, not family. My grandfather's whole life had been forced into such a framework, and now even in death it was the same.

The bureaucracy did not respond immediately. Lijiao wrote a second letter two months later, again asking for the support of the authorities and making clear that he would cover all the costs of the inscription. In November of the following year, after approval had been granted, a new stele was finally erected on the site of my grandfather's grave. Lijiao wrote a final letter, entitled "The Long-Cherished Dream of Me and My Relatives Inside and Outside China Has Been Realized."

> *Because this stele with no words has become a stele with words,*
> *our descendants will have a place to make offerings to their loved*
> *ones. In this, they feel most fortunate.*

Lijiao died in February 2006, less than a year after I visited his family in Harbin. He had lived long enough to see his three children settled in jobs at the same university where he had taught, and a granddaughter enrolled there as well. In 1985, he had been given a provincial-level teaching award, the only person at his university to receive this honor. For the family, it tempered some of the pain he had suffered. "For my father to have lived through that time, I think, means that he had a generous heart," his daughter Yinqiao told me. "People appreciated his decency. Four hundred people attended his funeral. We did not expect so many."

Until the end of his life, she said, Lijiao had believed in the Communist Party. He had never talked about how political attacks had driven his father to suicide. He did not dwell on what he had endured. My father told me that on several occasions he had asked Lijiao about his experiences during the Cultural Revolution, but Lijiao would never say. "I believe that Zhang Lijiao was really brain-washed," my father said. "Whenever he talked about this, he would only say how good things were, how good the Communist Party was. I think until the end of his life he was afraid. A lot of these people who suffered so much thought that the present was just another political movement. They were never sure that things would not go back to the way they were."

Lijiao's daughter had a different interpretation. "My father never told your father about these things," she said to me. "I think he felt that your father had lived abroad, and that this was a nation's own family scandal." In her way of thinking, it was not fear but shame that had kept her father silent.

*   *   *

On the last day of the year in 2005, I visited my grandfather's grave in a Shenyang park. In the frigid morning, the air tingled with the smell of burning coal and the sun hovered cool and pale as a lemon. The park was alive with people, mostly retirees. Old men jogged in a halfhearted shuffle, while old women practiced tai chi. At a foot-bridge, I stopped to look at the lake below, where snowdrifts had been cleared to make a wide oval track. People skated in the crouched pose of champion racers. A woman past middle age had bundled up in many layers; she wore a surgical mask over her face—a common accessory in Shenyang's brutal winters. As I watched, she attempted to glide forward while balancing on one leg with the other stretched out behind her. She almost pitched forward, recovered, and looked around to see if anyone had noticed.

I kept walking until I came to the Dismounting Stelae, a pair of pillars carved with Manchu script that marked the start of the "spirit walk" to the Qing emperor's tomb. Off to the left, I saw the grave in a small clearing surrounded by pine trees.

The tablet marking my grandfather's tomb was about twenty feet high, of gray cement with characters carved in red:

MEMORIAL TO MR. ZHANG SHENFU
AN ENGINEER OF CHINA'S MINING INDUSTRY
FROM JILIN PROVINCE, JIUTAI COUNTY, LIUTAI VILLAGE
1898–1946

I read the inscription slowly, word by word, and felt comforted by it. The epitaph was only four lines long and contained the starkest of facts—but all of it was true. Nothing had been falsified; politics had not intruded on the writing of this text. If you had to describe a life in thirty-five Chinese characters, this seemed a fair measure of a man—his birth and death, his work, his native place, and his name.

I stood looking at the tablet, unsure what I should do to mark the occasion. I didn't kowtow or burn offerings; I simply stood before my grandfather's grave. No one disturbed me. A few men kicked a shuttlecock near the Dismounting Stele, but they paid me no mind. Finally I had to walk away, because it was too cold.

As I was leaving, a man rode by on a bicycle. A tape player strapped to the back of his bike was playing the migrant anthem of that year, a song from a place far away, where every street had a factory and the history museum did not include a single mention of Mao.

> *I love you*
> *Loving you*
> *As a mouse loves rice*
> *No matter how much wind and rain*
> *I will always stay with you*

When I thought about my grandfather's life, it was mostly with sadness at the lost opportunity. As a young man, he had left home—

for Beijing, for America—to pursue his studies and to serve his country. He had lived in foreign environments, and he had struggled to find his purpose, but always he had worked hard. It was his sense of duty that drove him to visit the Fushun mine against all warnings. On that last winter night, when armed men boarded his train and stabbed him with bayonets, all that learning and effort was rendered useless. It had been the crudest type of force; against such weapons, a man's idealism meant nothing. In the years after my grandfather's death, the promise of his China died too.

But it didn't feel like an accident that things turned out as they did. When I read my grandfather's diary, or watched the adults gang up on Min and her sister during a village wedding, I felt as if I were witnessing over and over where China went wrong. The concerns of family and nation were overwhelming, and they trapped a great many people—millions upon millions—in lives they never would have chosen. If it weren't for the sake of the nation, my grandfather would not have become a mining engineer, and he would not have gone to the Fushun mine. But he was born into the burden of being Chinese, and so he did these things. It was the same reason that Lijiao and Zhao Hongzhi stayed behind that autumn of 1948, and it was also why my father suppressed so much emotion. It had led my aunt Nellie to express her feelings through poetry, and it had driven Lijiao's children to diminish the past. Only Zhang Hong had chosen to remember, and for him this memory had become a kind of torture.

And perhaps I, too, am more Chinese than I knew. Because now I understand all of them—understand why a person would choose not to tell her story, or be unable to tell it, or not admit to any feeling, because the emotion would overwhelm you otherwise. I understand the poem my aunt Nellie wrote for her father, in which she tries to contain her emotion, to shape her personal sorrow into something proper and purposeful. In the final verses, she fails—*But*

I hate it! Father—and the emotion floods through, a secret wound suddenly open to the world.

Learning my family story also changed the way I saw the factory towns of the south. There was a lot to dislike about the migrant world of Min and Chunming: the materialism, the corruption, the coarseness of daily existence. But now there was an opportunity to leave your village and change your fate, to imagine a different life and make it real. The journey my grandfather attempted was one that millions of young people now made every day—they left home; they entered an unfamiliar land; they worked hard. But nowadays their purpose was not to change China's fate. They were concerned with their own destinies, and they made their own decisions. If it was an ugly world, at least it was their own.

Perhaps China during the twentieth century had to go so terribly wrong so that people could start over, this time pursuing their individual courses and casting aside the weight of family, history, and the nation. For a long time I thought of Dongguan as a city with no past, but now I realize it isn't so. The past has been there all along, reminding us: This time—maybe, hopefully, against all odds—we will get it right.

*   *   *

The last relative I spoke with about family history was my aunt Irene, my father's younger sister. She had been seven when her father died, and she had only one memory of him: He returned home from a trip with a newly grown mustache, and he kissed her on the stomach and made her laugh.

After he died, my grandfather remained a presence in the lives of his children. When Irene was too tired to study, her mother would say, "Your father died for your country. You must work hard so you can be just like him." Beijing had twelve electric tram lines, all named for martyrs of the nation; my uncle Luke remembers riding the Zhang Shenfu tram when he was a child. A mine in the Fushun complex was called the Shenfu Mine, a street in Shenyang became Shenfu Road, and the isolated station where he had been pulled off the train and killed was renamed Zhang Shenfu. In death, my grandfather was inscribed into the landscape of China. And then the names all changed after the Communists took power.

Once when Irene was in middle school in Taiwan, her class went on a field trip. They saw an exhibit about a person who had been killed, with descriptions of his murder and photographs of his wounded corpse. "I thought, 'the poor man,'" Irene recalled, "and then I saw the name of my dad." She fainted. The pictures were part of the government's anti-Communist propaganda, but Irene had never seen them before. She hadn't even recognized her father's face—only his name.

Of the siblings who had left China, Irene was the only one who knew her mother as an adult. After her older sister and brothers left for America, she spent time alone with her mother and heard many of her stories. Later after Irene had gone to America too, she returned to Taiwan and spent time with my grandmother the summer of her death. Many people shared their memories with me, but Irene's were different. In her telling, her mother was an independent-minded woman who chafed against tradition and longed to travel abroad; her father was a youthful rebel whose patriotic idealism opened up a gulf with his family. The burden of my grandfather's generation had been to see everything in political terms, but Irene's stories restored the personal to their lives.

Holding regret until the end of time. Several people had told me that these words, inscribed on my great-grandfather's funeral garments, expressed his regret for the Japanese occupation of Manchuria. But Irene had another interpretation. When my grandfather returned home after seven years in America, his father wanted him to stay in

Liutai to run the estate; he was angered when the young man decided to leave home anyway. The Japanese invasion cut off communication between father and son without allowing them to reconcile. "It was regret for the way he treated his children," my aunt said. Her story of my grandfather's death was also different. As he lay dying of his wounds, according to several accounts I had read, my grandfather was thinking of his duty to the nation. *I am from the central government,* he had said. *To die for my duty, I have no complaints.* But Irene told me he had tried to write something on a piece of paper, using his own blood. One of the people in his group was able to leave unharmed, and he gave the paper to my grandmother. It contained only a few characters. "My mother couldn't make out much of it," Irene said, "but she could read her name."

In everything I had read and heard about my grandfather, I could find no trace of the individual—his entire being seemed to be focused on saving the Chinese nation. This was the image of the man that was presented in his letters and in his diaries. I wanted to like him, but the more I learned about him the more foreign he seemed. He was like a man disappearing inside his own story, and that seemed terrible to me. But maybe there had been something more— something I could not see, apart from the faintest glimmer in the stories my aunt Irene told me.

I HAD NOT INTENDED to speak with Irene, because she would have been too young to remember much about her father's life and death. I talked with my father, my aunt Nellie, my uncle Luke, Lijiao's family, and many other relatives. All of them had a way of obscuring their tales even as they told them.

We don't know much about family history. We never had a chance to talk about it.

In fact, my experience of China was very shallow.

My grandfather's father. Nobody knew his name.

Months after I spoke with all of them, my aunt Irene called me one day. She had heard I was writing a book, and she wanted to talk about my grandmother.

"Let me tell you," she said, "my older brothers and sister don't know Grandmother the way I knew her." It had not occurred to me to ask about my grandmother. She had never gone far from home; she had left no written record. How much of her life was there to know? But many of the most vivid details of my family history—my grandmother's clashes with her father-in-law, the beating of my grandfather with the *jiafa*—came from my aunt Irene. After our first phone conversation, my aunt sent me an e-mail. In its emotion, it was unlike anything anyone in the family had expressed.

> *My mother (your grandma) came from a very traditional Chinese family, with strict family rules. She has had high education, very unusual for a woman at that time. Later she was very successful in her career. She educated her children very progressively almost single-handed under very difficult conditions with a meager resource. I love her very much and respect her immensely. I got to know her well only after my elder brothers and sister left home.*
>
> *After our short conversation I began to think about the changes, challenges Chinese women had to face, probably that is why Chinese women are very strong. In our family, Grandma, myself, and you, these three generations covered a period of one hundred years of most significant changes around the world, especially in China. We sacrificed, suffered, and we stood up.*
>
> *I am looking forward to hearing from you and talking to you.*
>
> *Love,*
> *Aunt Irene*

My aunt had told me she was "semi-retired" from her job as chief executive officer of an American biotechnology company. But we still had to schedule our phone call a week in advance; her husband, who was fully retired, organized the logistics for her. In China today, women like my aunt are known as *nu qiangren*, superwomen. At the appointed time, I picked up the phone and called my aunt Irene, and this is how she began her story: *I will tell you what I know.*

Sometimes Chunming spoke English in her dreams. She would find herself in a place with foreigners, like the Dongguan library, and she would address them in English and they would respond.

I asked Chunming how it felt to dream in a language you couldn't speak.

"I can't describe it," she said. "All I know is that in the dream I am speaking English."

In the few lessons she had taken at Assembly-Line English, Chunming hadn't yet mastered the alphabet. For pronunciation, she relied on the International Phonetic Alphabet, a system of notation commonly used to learn a foreign language. The queer-looking symbols became her key to English, a row of locked gates behind which language waited to be released like a flood. "I think the secret to learning English is the phonetic symbols," Chunming told me. So many people talked about studying English, but no one I had met invested it with more meaning than Chunming.

If I learn English, I can see more of the world. I can enjoy life more. I want to find new kinds of happiness. If I don't learn English, I will always feel the limits of my life.

In September 2005, nine months after she had gone to the Dong-guan Science Museum, Chunming paid another visit to Mr. Wu. A dozen young women were enrolled at the school, which was still being run out of his apartment. They studied and boarded free of charge and took turns cooking meals; in exchange, they compiled the curriculum for Mr. Wu's textbook project. The students lived in cramped bedrooms behind the classroom. Each room had four bunk beds, with laundry draped over the bed frames and buckets of water on the floor. The rooms felt like workers' dorms inside a factory.

Mr. Wu wasn't there when we arrived; his former student, the English teacher Liu Yixia, showed us around. The power had been cut for the day, and Chunming walked through the sweltering rooms with her lips pursed in judgment.

"We stay here most of the time," said a student named Xiao Yongli. "Teacher Wu doesn't let us go out."

"He doesn't let you go out?" Chunming looked worried.

"He doesn't think it's good for study."

"Once you go outside, you'll begin to have doubts," explained Liu Yixia. "That's why the girls all cut their hair so short."

"Everyone has to cut their hair?"

"Yes, so they won't be distracted by worrying about being pretty."

I chatted with Xiao Yongli in English; she spoke quickly and with confidence. She was twenty years old, from Sichuan Province. She had worked in a Samsung factory and come to Assembly-Line English a year ago. Now she studied ten hours a day.

"Do you study on weekends too?" I asked.

Xiao Yongli had to ask me in Chinese what "weekend" meant. Yes, she said, she studied then too.

I asked her why she had come to Dongguan, and she was silent for some moments. Switching to Chinese, I asked if she understood.

"It's a long story," she said earnestly. "I'm trying to figure out how to say it."

Finally, in English: "I came to Dongguan to work."

She wanted to be a simultaneous interpreter, an odd career choice for Dongguan, where United Nations–caliber translators were not exactly in high demand. "Our teacher says that's the highest level of learning the language," she said. "I want to reach the highest level." Clearly Xiao Yongli hadn't thought much about what she would do with English; that would come later. Right now she was pure determination.

WE MET MR. WU LATER at a coffee shop near his apartment. I half listened as he spoke to Chunming about the cerebrum, the right hand, the left hand, the eyeballs. I noticed that after every sentence he smiled automatically—maybe he had read in a book that this would make people like him more.

"Our students can do six hundred sentences an hour." Smile.

"Six hundred sentences . . ."

"Not all of them, only the best ones," Mr. Wu corrected himself quickly.

"You mean, they can read six hundred sentences an hour?" Chunming asked.

"Read? No! They can read one hundred and eight sentences a minute! I'm talking about writing."

Chunming turned to me. "Can you write six hundred sentences an hour?"

"I'm sure she cannot," Mr. Wu said smugly. Smile.

I considered pointing out that this might not be the skill that mattered most, but I decided against it. My cerebrum was starting to hurt.

"So what you're saying is that most people's potential is not being developed," Chunming said. "I agree with that." She seemed taken by Mr. Wu's sales pitch, and then she asked about his best pupil. "What about Liu Yixia? Do you think she's done well?"

"She's okay," Mr. Wu said. "After all, she studied at my school for a year. But in terms of writing sentences, she cannot compete with my students. That Xiao Yongli can write six hundred sentences an hour."

Chunming asked about the school rules. Mr. Wu locked his students in at night and woke them at six every morning for calisthenics. They were allowed out once a week, on Sunday evenings, to buy personal necessities; each girl could make one phone call home a month. Visitors were forbidden. Of course, Mr. Wu said, an older student like Chunming could rent an apartment nearby and just take lessons during the day. But without absolute devotion, he was skeptical of her chances. "Learning is painstaking work," he said severely, and that time he forgot to smile.

CHUNMING LIKED THE IDEA of dedication and transformation, but she was put off by the school's living conditions and the remoteness of the neighborhood. Meanwhile, she had just invested in a new company. To quit and study English instead—a venture whose payoff was at least a year away—would shock all her friends. On the bus ride home, she mulled it over. "When my friends hear I've started a company and immediately left to study English, they'll think I'm very odd."

"But I bet they'll feel envious," I said, thinking of all the times strangers had gushed over my English.

"I don't know," Chunming said. "But after I learn English and get a new job, that's when they'll see what my achievement is." Outside the bus window, the lights in the factories were coming on. "I could cut off contact with all my friends for two years," Chunming said, "and when I finished I could see them again." She was preparing, perhaps, to renounce the world. But she was outside again, and that was always where the doubts begin.

*   *   *

Two months passed before I saw Chunming again. She went home to see her family. ("Home is always the same. It's even poorer than before.") She had two teeth pulled in preparation for getting braces, which she had finally chosen over porcelain fakes. One night back in Dongguan, she was riding in a friend's car when a Toyota sped toward the intersection where they were stopped, smashed their car on the left side, and roared away. The man in the passenger's seat was hospitalized with stitches to his head. Chunming, who had been sitting in back near where the car hit, twisted her shoulder.

I saw her two days after the accident. She was still in pain and couldn't lift her arm. "When I think about it, I feel really scared," she said. "You must really cherish what you have." We were sitting on the couch in the room above the machine-parts store. "I've encountered a new opportunity," Chunming said. "Whenever I think about it, I feel like my dream has returned to me."

I waited.

In a low voice, she said two words: "Direct sales."

Wanmei, the company she had worked for in 1996, had not died after the government's ban on *chuanxiao*, network sales. It had retooled its business and expanded into a wide range of health products: high-fiber meal, amino acid tablets, pollen supplements. The company was thriving; all three of its Malaysian-Chinese founders drove Mercedes-Benzes. Chunming started eating Wanmei nutritional powder mixed with water every day for breakfast and selling the products to her friends.

Overnight she had become an authority on health. Only 5 percent of the population was healthy and 70 percent "subhealthy," she informed me; the symptoms of subhealth, according to one of her new health books, were *easily tired, has many dreams, excitable, catches colds, lacks concentration*. Much of her conversation revolved around bodily functions, with anecdotes involving personal acquaintances and historical figures such as the wife of Chiang Kai-shek. *I have a friend who did not empty her bowels for four days. Soong Mayling would often wash clean her intestines to remove poisons.*

Chunming had started attending motivational lectures for Wanmei salespeople. She grabbed my pen and wrote:

> To read 10,000 books is not as good as to walk 10,000 miles.
>
> To walk 10,000 miles is not as good as to meet 10,000 people.
>
> To meet 10,000 people is not as good as to have a successful person show you the way.
>
> To have a successful person show you the way is not as good as walking with that person toward success together.

She put the pen down. "That's what the lectures are about."

I asked Chunming how she had re-entered the field. A few months earlier, an old friend from *chuanxiao* days had contacted her. He had rejoined Wanmei and wanted her in his network; salespeople earned a commission on the sales of all their recruits, and he remembered Chunming's talent for selling. He told her that the direct-sales industry was legal now and gave her a Wanmei promotional DVD. She was focused on her new company and told him she wasn't interested.

One day, Chunming heard on the news that the government had passed a law legalizing direct sales; her friend, it turned out, had been telling the truth. She found the DVD he had given her and watched it. "In the 1980s, the people who manufactured tape recorders made a lot of money," the narrator of the video said. "In the 1990s, the Internet made millionaires. The twenty-first century is the era of high growth for direct sales. If you rule out direct sales, you rule out the opportunity for success." The video did not deny that people were suspicious of the industry—in fact, such doubts were central to its arguments. The more people refused Wanmei, the greater the opportunity for those who embraced it first. This was an evangelical appeal, with one difference: If you came late in life to Jesus, you could still be saved. But if you delayed joining direct sales, you would lose out financially to everyone who built their networks before you.

"Today you know about this opportunity in your heart," the man in the video said. "You can no longer pretend that you don't know."

CHUNMING SOLD HER SHARE in the mold-parts company to Fu Gui, her business partner. She moved out of the store and rented a spacious apartment in downtown Dongguan. In the entry, she hung a floor-to-ceiling poster that showed the Wanmei factory complex beneath the slogan "Perfect Cause, Perfect Life." She bought a set of tall glass cabinets and stocked them with shower gel and nutritional meal and powdered drink mix. Posters throughout the apartment advertised aloe vera, bee pollen, royal jelly, health tea, seabuckthorn, and "garlic soft capsule"—"that one is good for overweight people and also fights cancer," Chunming told me. From a machine-parts mall, she had moved to live inside what looked like a product showroom.

She was now taking four of the company's products a day: a high-fiber meal to clean the digestive tract; a health tea; a powder of aloe, minerals, and pollen that was good for the skin; and a nutritional powder for breakfast. She didn't look any more or less healthy than before, but she had finally gotten braces, and permed her hair and dyed it orange, the color of pumpkin pie. Her new bible was *Direct-*

Sell Your Way to Wealth: Major Arguments, and she memorized the food combinations that could hurt nutritional absorption. Under no circumstances, she warned me, should I eat dog meat with garlic. I must never drink sorghum liquor and coffee at the same time. A list of "One Hundred Health Warnings" contained enough symptoms to drive anyone to hypochondria: *skin dry or oily*—"See, I think you have this," Chunming said—*bad breath, bad temper, poor sleep, difficulty concentrating, eyes tear easily.*

After I had endured two sessions of Chunming's proselytizing, I decided that Wanmei's founders—Mercedes-driving Malaysians, or whoever they might be—must be geniuses. Health was a national obsession in China. Most people did not have medical insurance and lived in fear of being bankrupted by illness. And the Chinese loved to discuss ailments and folk cures; questions about fertility or the state of one's bowels were considered perfectly normal, even among people who had just met. A thousand-year-old heritage of traditional medicine was based on adjusting the balance between various foods and herbs, and everyone considered himself an expert. Yet overnight the Chinese had moved into an unfamiliar world of abundance, where junk food was like a virus against which they had not yet developed immunity. Anyone could see what would help them—quit smoking, exercise, eat less fat—but Wanmei's prescription was more appealing, a miracle cure in scientific packaging. And it could make you rich.

"In three years, I'll achieve my goal of financial independence and freedom," Chunming said. "By 2008, at the minimum, I'll have an income of one hundred thousand to two hundred thousand yuan a month. By then I'll have my own car, and freedom in how I spend my time. I'll be able to go wherever I want, whenever I want."

Finally I ventured to ask her: "Why did you choose direct sales instead of English?"

She nodded. This was a new habit: Whenever I asked a question she would nod, because now she had all the answers. "If you don't do this today, you can't do it tomorrow," she said. "If I join today, I get my friends to be in my network. If I wait until tomorrow, I'll be part of their network instead. In one or two years after I make money, won't I learn English even better?" A new idea had entered her world and she reordered her life around it. English lessons, or seabuckthorn and garlic soft capsule—each was just a way to become someone else. And now she had, with seemingly no memory of what had come before.

*   *   *

Soon after joining Wanmei, Chunming attended a company sales convention. Buses from around the country converged on Zhongshan, an hour's drive south of Dongguan, where the company had its headquarters, including a production plant and its own five-star hotel. Only the biggest earners were invited—emphasis on hierarchy was one of the company's organizing principles—but many managers had chartered buses to bring their recruits anyway, so they could "experience Wanmei in person." There are still millions of Chinese who see an overnight bus trip to a factory as a vacation.

None went away unimpressed: Only a highly successful health-products company would have its own luxury hotel. "This is where all the managers stay when they come for training," Chunming said. "Soon I will be a junior manager." She was wearing a stylish twill blazer with her hair in tight pigtails, Pippi Longstocking–style; her eyes were wide with excitement like a girl on the first day of the county fair. The parking lot of the Golden Diamond Hotel swarmed with people: old men with rheumy eyes, migrants in baggy suits, housewives, peasant women with sloping shoulders and leathery skin from long hours in the fields. They were among society's least privileged members, brought together by their devotion to Wanmei. The gathering, it occurred to me, was a kind of anti–talent market.

Chunming walked through the crowd pointing out celebrities. "Oh! I've only seen that woman in photographs! She makes"—a quick calculation—"five hundred thousand yuan a month." She went up to another middle-aged woman. "I heard your talk, 'The Products Changed My Life,' " Chunming said. "I was very moved."

The woman smiled modestly.

Chunming turned to me. "This woman used to be a dishwasher."

We went into the hotel to admire its marble lobby. The wait for the ladies' room was long, and Chunming took the opportunity to meet people—to *duanlian*, or train herself. "Where are you from?" she asked a woman in a pink suit with a flared ruffle at the hips.

"Hunan," the woman answered.

"Where in Hunan?"

"Changsha."

"I've heard that business in Changsha has really taken off!" Chunming said. "And your skin is so good!" The woman went into a stall, and Chunming turned immediately to the woman behind her. "Where are you from?"

By mid-morning, the energy level at Wanmei headquarters was at its peak. Cheering groups posed for photos before the building entrance; crowds flooded the lobby where Wanmei commercials played continuously on TV screens. At 10:30 the top-earning managers walked down a red carpet that had been laid in the middle of the parking lot. It was lined on both sides with recruits, many carrying banners with the names of top salespeople. A great roar went up as the managers marched into the building to begin three days of training on how to sell even more Wanmei products.

I walked into a store and said to the boss, "I'm from Wanmei."

He said, "Out."

I repeated my words.

He said, "Fuck."

(Laughter.)

I walked out. I thought, the next person will not be so low-class. So I went into the next store, and I talked to the boss. He became a customer, and he has bought sixty thousand yuan of products from me.

(Applause.)

Later that day, Chunming attended a "sharing" session for Wanmei salespeople. More than a hundred people had gathered to hear inspirational speeches in a drafty auditorium whose stage was hung with leftover new year decorations. A woman in a cream-colored pantsuit took the stage. She had joined Wanmei in 1996, quit after the government ban, and returned, just like Chunming.

> I want to ask the women in the audience: Are you satisfied with the way your life is now? Do you want to change your life?
>
> Yes!
>
> Are you satisfied just to marry a good husband?
>
> No!
>
> I don't believe you. I know some women in the audience think it's enough to marry a good husband. But if you don't have knowledge and cultivation, can you hold on to your husband?
>
> No!
>
> That's right. We live in a very pragmatic society.

The speakers all spoke without notes. They used hand gestures and made eye contact and smiled. They knew how to repeat sentence patterns, to establish a rhythm, and to excite a crowd. Their hands didn't tremble. A retired music teacher went up and disappeared behind the lectern but for a cloud of permed gray hair. She was sixty years old and she spoke in a gentle, even teacher's voice.

In the past I looked much older than I was. I caught a lot of colds. I was always tired. From head to foot, I had many health problems: congestion, intestinal problems, lung problems, skin conditions, sleeplessness, heart disease, tired eyes. I couldn't walk half an hour without getting tired.

In November 2003, a colleague introduced me to Wanmei. My first week taking Wanmei, one side of my nose cleared. The second week, the other side cleared.

(*Applause.*)

In two weeks, Wanmei got rid of all my colds. After a few months, I could walk for a whole day.

(*Applause.*)

I could sleep through the night.

(*Applause.*)

I am grateful to Manager Chen. My medical problems are very serious. He taught me how to use the various products and in what amounts.

In China, people from such humble backgrounds rarely spoke in public. But here they were, each person unapologetic and full of faith that her personal story was interesting. They were better speakers than most Chinese professors and officials I had seen—better, by far, than their country's top leaders, who appeared once a year for a live press conference looking like wax figures wheeled in from a museum.

A woman wearing a down jacket with the ruddy skin of a farmer took the stage. She spoke in a raspy voice, with such a thick Cantonese accent that she was almost impossible to understand.

In the past, my health was very bad. I went to the hospital every week with colds, dizziness, headaches. A friend introduced me to Wanmei, and I started to go to lectures. Through Wanmei's training, I have changed myself.

In the past, I couldn't speak Mandarin. I would never

dare to stand up here and share my experience. I felt too inferior. We are all ordinary people. But through Wanmei, we
have become healthy, we have done training, we have made
friends. These are things that money can't buy.

*   *   *

In the months after the sales convention, Chunming waited for the
government to issue Wanmei's business license; without it, she
couldn't recruit the network of salespeople who would help her earn
a lot of money. But she started to hear troubling rumors: Wanmei's
top managers earned money not by selling products, but by charging exorbitant fees for training sessions. It looked like Wanmei—
"Perfect Cause, Perfect Life"—might not be much better than a
pyramid scheme.

Once again, direct sales had trapped Chunming. She had borrowed money from friends to rent and furnish her downtown apartment, so she took a job as a salesperson at a family-owned factory
that made glue used in shoes and handbags. She moved into a single room in a tile building next door to the glue factory. With this
latest life change came yet another hairstyle: Chunming grew out
her perm and had her hair cut in a sharp asymmetrical line in back.

But she had no time to be disappointed. A new man entered her
life, an American in his mid-fifties named Ha-wei Dai-meng-de.

YOU ARE ABOUT TO COME *face-to-face with what you have been looking
for all these long years.*

Harvey Diamond was an American health guru who believed
that most drugs were toxic and that the human body had the ability to heal itself. He advocated regular "monodieting"—eating only

fruits, vegetables, juices, or raw foods for a number of days—and cutting back on animal products, as a way to cleanse the body and combat disease. His *Fit for Life* series of books, according to promotional materials, had sold more than twelve million copies and had been translated into thirty-three languages.

In the summer of 2006, Chunming came across his ideas in a Dongguan bookstore. She was immediately entranced by the story of Ha-wei Dai-meng-de, who had been plagued by ill health until he discovered the medical precepts that changed his life. Chunming read Ha-wei's latest book straight through twice. She began consuming fruits or fruit-and-vegetable juices every day for breakfast; for lunch and dinner, she ate only vegetables and rice. She drank three quarts of water a day and carried a water bottle everywhere she went, in accordance with Ha-wei's prescriptions. His underlying philosophy appealed to her. *Take charge of your health*, he wrote. *Remake your life. Your actions carry consequences.* These were the tenets of the American self-help movement, which reflected a fervent belief in second chances; they were well suited to young migrants from the countryside who were just getting their first chance. Aside from the fruit-and-vegetable fasts, much of what Ha-wei had to say was standard knowledge for any American schoolchild: Eat fruits and vegetables, cut back on meat, exercise. But for Chunming, basic nutrition was a revelation around which she could shape her whole life, just as Ha-wei had done.

CHUNMING'S NEW LIVING QUARTERS were humble. A bed draped in mosquito netting took up most of the room, with a desk and a bookcase squeezed to one side. The apartment had a small bathroom but no kitchen; a low table by the door was stacked with celery, carrots, oranges, apples, and tomatoes. When I visited her now, the first thing Chunming did was grab a handful of fruit and cut it up in the bathroom sink for me. Suddenly a fruit-and-vegetable diet was the natural order of the universe, and she had become an expert in evolutionary biology.

Sharp teeth are intended to eat meat, but we have only two sharp teeth. That means that we're supposed to eat mostly vegetables and very little meat.

Anyone I meet, I tell them, "Drink more water." Now I can look at someone and just from the quality of their skin I can tell if they have health problems.

Chinese people are overly addicted to medicines. When a child has a fever, they give it a shot. But the fever is the body's way of fighting illness. Fever is good for a person.

I found myself agreeing with a lot of what she said. Chinese people did rely too much on medicine, and they had a morbid fear of drinking water. The whole country seemed to me permanently dehydrated. It was common to be told that a woman shouldn't drink cold water because it would damage her womb, while drinking water at night caused stomach trouble. But as usual Chunming had gone to extremes. "After I read that book, I didn't eat rice for one week," she told me. "I just ground up fruits and vegetables into juice and drank them." On that particular day, she had consumed two glasses of tomato juice and an apple.

Ha-wei counseled his readers to build up gradually to raw-food diets. *Your effort to improve your health and prevent becoming sick needn't be a stress-filled journey. It can be a joyous one. This is not a race!* Maybe he had not met anyone like Chunming. She was already seeing the benefits: Her nose wasn't oily anymore; she no longer suffered from constipation and eyelash loss. Her moles were getting smaller, a scar on her leg was fading, and her teeth were getting whiter. She had stopped using toothpaste.

Chunming's quest for perfect health proved to be a boon in her new job. At the end of the workday, she would stand outside the gate of a shoe or handbag factory and ask the workers the last name of their factory's boss and the head of the production department. Then she called up those executives and pretended to have done business with them or to have a friend in common. In the disorganization of the Dongguan workplace, no one questioned her and almost everyone agreed to a meeting. After she made her sales visit, Chunming would send a letter of thanks along with a few health books as a gift. In the letter, she wrote:

> *I know you are very busy. I recommend this set of health books to you and hope you can look them over in your spare time. I think you will benefit a great deal from them. I recommend these books from the bottom of my heart. I believe these are the best books I have ever read about health.*
>
> *Whether we do business or not doesn't matter. We can be friends just the same. Every company must make its own choice. Of course, if you wish to give me an opportunity, I will value it and do my best to provide your company with the most satisfactory service.*

She had met close to a hundred potential clients this way and had already landed four regular ones.

I tried to picture Ha-wei's typical American reader. Perhaps it was an overweight man fed up with years of yo-yo dieting, or a middle-aged woman who worried about the breast cancer that ran in her family, or a retiree who woke up every morning to a cocktail of medications. All of these people, you could say, were victims of modern living, of technology and medical advances and processed food. They longed for a way of life that was healthy and simple and pure. Chunming had grown up in a rural village, where people ate vegetables and rice and almost no one went to the hospital or ate food that had been bought in a store. And now she wanted the same things the Americans wanted. For better or worse, that was one measure of how far she had traveled.

*   *   *

Almost everyone I knew in Dongguan was a striver. To some extent, this was self-selecting: A person with ambition was more likely to be open to new things, and that included talking to me. I can't say that Min and Chunming were typical of China's vast population of migrant workers. They were only the young women I ended up writing and caring about, the ones I came to know best. But their lives and struggles were emblematic of their country today—and of the China of my family, too, who strived to make up for everything they had lost or left behind. In the end, across time and class, this is the story of China: leaving home, enduring hardship, and making a new life. They did so against daunting odds, but perhaps these challenges were no more intimidating than those that faced newcomers to America a century ago.

Successful or not, migration changes fates. Studies of recent migrants suggest that most of them are not destined to return to the farm. The ones who do well will likely buy apartments and settle in their adopted cities; the others may eventually move to towns and cities near their home villages and set up stores, restaurants, and small businesses like hairdressing salons or tailoring shops. Such enterprises, in turn, tend to employ returned migrants, who are seen as more capable than those who have never gone out.

As I got to know the factory girls, I couldn't help worrying about them. They took such risks, and they were surrounded by corrupt or dishonest people. They contained tragic flaws: The same fearlessness that had helped them rise in the world could be their downfall. Min made major life decisions with a snap of her fingers; Chunming embraced every fad that passed her way. Liu Yixia moved too fast to improve her English the way she wanted. In some ways, I probably knew them better than their own friends did. Being an outsider helped—I was so removed from their universe that they felt comfortable confiding in me. They were hungry to know about my world too, asking me how Americans ate, and dated, and married, and made money, and raised children. Perhaps my presence was encouraging to them, a promise that someone knew and cared what they were going through. But in all the time I knew them, the migrant girls never asked me for help, and rarely even for advice. Life was something they faced alone, as they had been telling me from the first day we met. *I can only rely on myself.*

The first time I met Wu Chunming, she was working for a foreign company, making a thousand dollars a month, and living in a three-bedroom apartment in downtown Dongguan. The last time I saw her, two and a half years later, she was working for a Chinese company, making $150 a month, and living in a single room in a part of the city known for small shoe factories with poor working conditions. By every calculus that mattered, she had fallen a long way. But she was more serene than I had ever seen her. In a city where a Mercedes was the measure of all things, Chunming had somehow broken free and developed her own personal morality.

"Before I was always hungry," she told me. "If I saw a sweater I liked, I would have to get it immediately. Now if I don't eat the best things or buy the nicest things, it doesn't matter so much. If I see a friend or a family member happy, then that is meaningful." She was no longer panicked about being single at the age of thirty-two, and she had stopped having affairs with men she met online. "I believe I'll become more and more beautiful, and more and more healthy, and my economic circumstances will get better and better," she said.

Chunming hoped to have children someday, and she often asked me about American attitudes toward child-raising. "I would like a

child to grow up to have a happy life and make a contribution to society," she said.

"A contribution to society?" I asked her, startled. "What do you
mean?"

"I don't mean to be a big scientist or something like that," Chunming said. "How many people can do that? I think if you live a
happy life and are a good person, that is a contribution to society."

*   *   *

The last time I went to Dongguan was in February 2007. The air
tasted smoky and cold, and the streets were full of workers heading
home to the village to celebrate another new year. A driver in
Chunming's factory was going to deliver a *hongbao*—a red envelope
containing eight hundred yuan—to a client and attend their new
year's banquet. He convinced Chunming to go with him because
she knew how to talk, and she invited me. The dinner would probably be in a fancy restaurant, she said, which was how most factories did things nowadays.

When we arrived at the Wonder Fashion Leather factory, she was
disappointed. The workers were already eating in the factory cafeteria at large round tables under fluorescent lights. This was where
they ate all their meals, although on this day there was a whole fish
at each table. The dishes were greasy; Chunming picked at the vegetables, which were also coated with oil. At the front of the room,
the factory boss led workers through games of musical chairs and
telephone. He knew his employees by name and teased the ones
who had boyfriends and girlfriends already. "I can see this boss is a
good person," Chunming said.

After dinner came the lucky draw. The workers left their free
food and beer and moved forward as one, like a battalion given the
signal to advance. There were more than a hundred of them, mostly

teenagers wearing short-sleeve factory shirts. Some of the boys were so young they looked like girls. In every factory, the lucky draw was the highlight of the new year's banquet. To me, it was a game of terrible odds; to the workers, it was the amazing possibility that for once in this world, you might get something for nothing. The top prize tonight was wool blankets, and then comforters, hair dryers, and thermoses. There were also cash awards of fifty, one hundred, and two hundred yuan. Those who didn't win anything could claim a consolation prize, a face towel and a scoop of clothing detergent out of a giant bag. When the workers heard that, they cheered just as loudly as for any of the other prizes.

As one of the factory's suppliers, Chunming was invited to draw the winning tickets for the one-hundred-yuan prize. She walked to the front of the room, grabbed the microphone, and effortlessly took over the proceedings.

> Do you all hope that the factory does well in 2007?
> Yes!
> Do you all hope that the boss makes a lot of money, so you can have higher salaries and more prizes?
> Yes!
> Do you all pledge to work very hard this year to make those wishes come true?
> Yes!

In her factory days, Chunming told me, it was rare to meet anyone from the outside world. When you did, it felt fresh and new, and you tried to learn everything you could. Now she spoke to these young people as if she had known them all her life; her voice rang out through the hall. *I am the same as you.* The workers pressed forward, cheering their visitor and dragging out their applause, as if they too did not want this night to end.

SOURCES

I wanted to learn about the factory world as the migrants did—from the bottom up and the inside out. But in the course of researching this book, I have also benefited from written materials that provided context and background to the things I saw firsthand. I have listed the sources that were most useful to me.

Throughout the book, I have used China's standard romanization system, *hanyu pinyin*, for the names of people and places. During the era of Kuomintang rule, a different system was used—Beijing was known as Peking or Beiping, the wartime capital Chongqing was spelled Chungking, and so on. For the sake of clarity, I have used the current spellings, with one exception: In China today my family name is spelled Zhang, but I retain the older form of Chang—a name that signals to anyone who grew up on the mainland that my history is not quite their own.

Chapter 1: GOING OUT

The figure for minimum wage is for Guangdong Province in 2004, when Min and the other young women I knew in Dongguan were starting out. The minimum wage in that region has since increased to between $70 and $110.

The number of migrant workers in China, as of the end of 2006, comes from the National Bureau of Statistics. It counts rural Chinese who are living away from home.

The yuan-dollar exchange rate used throughout the book is 8:1.

For background on migration in China:

Du Yang and Albert Park. "Qianyi yu jianpin: laizi nonghu diaocha de jingyan zhengju" [Migration and casting off poverty: empirical proof from a survey of rural households]. *Zhongguo renkou kexue* [Chinese Journal of Population Science] 4 (2003): 56–62.

Gaetano, Arianne M., and Tamara Jacka, eds. *On the Move: Women and Rural-to-Urban Migration in Contemporary China.* New York: Columbia University Press, 2004.

Jacka, Tamara. *Rural Women in Urban China: Gender, Migration, and Social Change.* Armonk, N.Y.: M. E. Sharpe, 2006.

Lee Ching-kwan. "Production Politics and Labour Identities: Migrant Workers in South China." In *China Review 1995.* Edited by Lo Chi Kin, Suzanne Pepper, and Tsui Ki Yuen. Hong Kong: Chinese University Press, 1995.

Li Qiang. "Zhongguo waichu nongmingong jiqi huikuan zhi yanjiu" [Research on migrant workers' remittances]. *Shehuixue yanjiu* [Sociological Research] 4 (2001).

Ma, Lawrence J.C., and Biao Xiang. "Native Place, Migration and the Emergence of Peasant Enclaves in Beijing." *China Quarterly* 155 (September 1998): 546–581.

Murphy, Rachel. *How Migrant Labor Is Changing Rural China.* Cambridge, U.K.: Cambridge University Press, 2002.

Pun Ngai. *Made in China: Women Factory Workers in a Global Workplace.* Durham, N.C.: Duke University Press, 2005.

Tan Shen. *Funü yu laogong* [Women and Labor]. Internally circulated edition. 2002.

West, Loraine A., and Yaohui Zhao, eds. *Rural Labor Flows in China*. Berkeley, Calif.: Institute of East Asian Studies, 2000.

Zhang Hong. "China's New Rural Daughters Coming of Age: Downsizing the Family and Firing Up Cash-Earning Power in the New Economy." *Signs: Journal of Women in Culture and Society* 32.3 (2007).

Chapter 2: THE CITY

There is no official number for the percentage of the Dongguan population that is female. I have used the figure of 70 percent, based on estimates from talent market executives, the deputy mayor's office, and surveys in local newspapers.

For background on the economic development of Dongguan:

Vogel, Ezra F. *One Step Ahead in China: Guangdong Under Reform*. Cambridge, Mass.: Harvard University Press, 1989.

Chapter 3: TO DIE POOR IS A SIN

For background on China's direct-sales industry:

Ho, Herbert H. *The Developments of Direct Selling Regulation in China, 1994–2004*. Washington, D.C.: U.S.-China Business Council, 2004.

Chapter 5: FACTORY GIRLS

The farming instructions from the traditional Chinese calendar given in this chapter apply to Hebei Province on the North China plain.

For background on the new generation of Chinese migrants:

Lin Xue. "Liangdai dagongzhe de bieyang rensheng" [The different life experiences of two generations of migrant workers]. *Dagongmei* [Migrant Women] 4 (2004): 24–25.

Wang Chunguang. "Xinshengdai nongcun liudong renkou de shehui rentong yu chengxiang ronghe de guanxi" [Characteristics of the new generation of flowing population from rural china]. *Shehuixue yanjiu* [Sociological Research] 3 (2001): 63–76.

For background on the athletic-shoe industry:

Vanderbilt, Tom. *The Sneaker Book: Anatomy of an Industry and an Icon*. New York: New Press, 1998.

Chapter 6: THE STELE WITH NO NAME

For the early history of my family, I relied on an unpublished account by my relative Zhang Tongxian, as well as:

Zhang Dianjun, ed. *Jilin Zhangshi zongpu* [Jilin Zhang Family Genealogy, revised edition]. Unpublished. 1993.

For the history of Manchuria:

Elliott, Mark C. *The Manchu Way: The Eight Banners and Ethnic Identity in Late Imperial China*. Stanford, Calif.: Stanford University Press, 2001.

Gottschang, Thomas R., and Diana Lary. *Swallows and Settlers: The Great Migration from North China to Manchuria*. Ann Arbor, Mich.: Center for Chinese Studies, 2000.

Hosie, Alexander. *Manchuria: Its People, Resources and Recent History*. Boston: J. B. Millet, 1910.

Lee, Robert H. G. *The Manchurian Frontier in Ch'ing History*. Cambridge, Mass.: Harvard University Press, 1970.

For background on the traditional education of Chinese children:

Saari, Jon L. *Legacies of Childhood: Growing up Chinese in a Time of Crisis, 1890–1920*. Cambridge, Mass.: Council on East Asian Studies, 1990.

For the history of Peking University:

Weston, Timothy B. *The Power of Position: Beijing University, Intellectuals, and Chinese Political Culture, 1898–1929*. Berkeley, Calif.: University of California Press, 2004.

For background on Chinese students in America:

Ye Weili. *Seeking Modernity in China's Name: Chinese Students in the United States, 1900–1927.* Stanford, Calif.: Stanford University Press, 2001.

For background on the Kuomintang era:

Eastman, Lloyd E., et al. *The Nationalist Era in China, 1927–1949.* Cambridge, U.K.: Cambridge University Press, 1991.

Sheridan, James E. *China in Disintegration: The Republican Era in Chinese History, 1912–1949.* New York: Free Press, 1975.

For background on Manchuria during the civil war and on the assassination of Zhang Shenfu, my grandfather:

Chang Kia-Ngau. *Last Chance in Manchuria: The Diary of Chang Kia-Ngau.* Edited by Donald G. Gillin and Ramon H. Myers. Stanford, Calif.: Hoover Institution Press, 1989.

Levine, Steven I. *Anvil of Victory: The Communist Revolution in Manchuria, 1945–1948.* New York: Columbia University Press, 1987.

Nie Shiqi. "Jingdao Zhang Shenfu xiansheng" [In respectful mourning of Mr. Zhang Shenfu]. *Central Daily News*, March 13, 1946: 5.

Su Lin. "Shei zhi 'Zhang Shenfu' xiangxi qingkuang" [Who knows the detailed circumstances of Zhang Shenfu]? *Huashang chenbao* [Shenyang Chinese Business Morning View], June 29, 2001: 1.

Tao Gang. "Yizuo bei—yituan mi" [A stele—a mystery]. *Liaoshen Evening News* [Shenyang], May 29, 2000: 2.

Tung Wen-ch'i. *The Reminiscences of Mr. Tung Wen-ch'i.* Comp. Chang Yu-fa and Shen Sung-chiao. Taipei: Institute of Modern History, 1986.

Zhang Lijiao. Drafts of letters to the Heilongjiang and Liaoning Provincial Political Consultative Committees and the Heilongjiang Office for Overseas Chinese Affairs. October 1987.

"Zhang Shenfu beihai shi yubu yinmou" [Zhang Shenfu's murder was a prearranged conspiracy]. *Xinhua Daily News*, March 9, 1946: 2.

"Zhang Shenfu deng yunan jingguo" [Events surrounding the murders of Zhang Shenfu and others]. *Central Daily News*, March 5, 1946: 3.

"Zhang Shenfu deng zao cansha" [Zhang Shenfu and others are murdered]. *Central Daily News*, February 10, 1946: 2.

Chapter 7: SQUARE AND ROUND

Ding Yuanzhi. *Fang yu yuan* [Square and Round]. Guangzhou: Guangzhou Publishing House, 1996.

Guangyi Teaching and Research Section. *Liyi suzhi* [Etiquette and Quality]. Unpublished. 2003.

————*Shejiao koucai* [Social Interaction and Eloquence]. Unpublished. 2003.

Xiao Jin. "Zhuanxing shiqi de Zhongguo jiaoyu gaige zhuanxiang hefang" [China's educational reform in transition: Is it transforming?] *Hongfan yanjiu* [Legal and Economics] 3.2 (2006): 144–83.

Xiao Jin and Mun C. Tsang. "Human Capital Development in an Emerging Economy: The Experience of Shenzhen, China." *China Quarterly* 157 (March 1999): 72–114.

Chapter 8: EIGHT-MINUTE DATE

For background on the impact of migration on Chinese rural women's attitudes toward marriage:

Chen Yintao. "Dagongmei de hunlian guannian ji qi kunrao" [Rural working women's attitudes toward love and marriage and their dilemmas]. *Renkou yanjiu* [Population Research] 21, no. 2 (March 1997): 39–44.

Connelly, Rachel, et al. "The Impact of Migration on the Position of Women in Rural China." Paper presented at Population Association of America Annual Meeting. 2003.

Zhang Hong. "Labor Migration, Gender, and the Rise of Neo-Local Marriages in the Economic Boomtown of Dongguan, South China." *Journal of Contemporary China*, forthcoming.

Zheng Zhenzhen. "Guanyu renkou liudong dui nongcun funü ying-xiang de yanjiu" [A study on the impact of migration on rural women]. *Funü yanjiu luncong* [Collected Studies on Women] 6 (2001): 38–41.

————"Impact of Migration on Gender Relationships and Rural Women's Status in China." UNESCO Research Project. 2006.

Chapter 9: ASSEMBLY-LINE ENGLISH

For background on the Ladder English company:

"Jiazhang zhiyi Jieti Yingyu" [Parents are suspicious of Ladder English]. *Xinwen chenbao* [Shanghai Morning Post], February 2, 2005.

Mu Yi, Zeng Le, and Liu Jun. "Lao yuangong tibao 'Jieti Yingyu' pian-cai shu" [Old employees expose fraudulent tactics of "Ladder English"]. *Xinkuaibao* [Guangzhou New Express Daily], February 2, 2005.

Chapter 11: THE HISTORIAN IN MY FAMILY

For background on Chinese historical writing and traditional genealogies:

Beasley, W. G., and E. G. Pulleyblank, eds. *Historians of China and Japan*. London: Oxford University Press, 1961.

Jing Jun. *The Temple of Memories: History, Power, and Morality in a Chinese Village*. Stanford, Calif.: Stanford University Press, 1996.

Meskill, Johanna M. "The Chinese Genealogy as a Research Source." In *Family and Kinship in Chinese Society*. Edited by Maurice Freedman, 139–61. Stanford, Calif.: Stanford University Press, 1970.

Van der Sprenkel, Otto Berkelbach. "Genealogical Registers." *Essays on the Sources for Chinese History*. Edited by Donald D. Leslie, Colin Mackerras, and Wang Gungwu, 83–98. Canberra: Australian National University Press, 1973.

Chapter 15: PERFECT HEALTH

For background on Harvey Diamond's health and diet plan:

> Diamond, Harvey. *Fit for Life: A New Beginning*. New York: Kensington, 2000.

For background on returned migrants, I relied on the work of Gong Weibin at China's National School of Administration, as well as:

> Ma Zhongdong. "Urban Labour-Force Experience as a Determinant of Rural Occupation Change: Evidence from Recent Urban-Rural Return Migration in China." *Environment and Planning* A 33 (2001): 237–55.

ACKNOWLEDGMENTS

Writing a book, as a friend once reminded me, is not a group activity. Just the same, I owe a large debt of gratitude to many people who helped me see this project through.

My thanks go first to those I knew in Dongguan, who taught me so much about this city in which we were all outsiders. Lu Qingmin and Wu Chunming generously opened up their lives to me, granting me their trust, patience, time, and lasting friendship. Zhang Qianqian and Jia Jimei showed me life on the assembly line, while Jiang Haiyan and Chen Ying shared their struggles to rise above it. Liu Yixia opened my eyes to the ways English is learned in a factory town.

Luke Lee and Allen Lee of Yue Yuen illuminated the workings of a shoe factory and gave me unfettered access to their company's Dongguan compound. Thanks also to William Anderson and Kitty Potter of Adidas for paving the way for those visits. Deng Shunzhang and the other teachers at the Zhitong school kindly allowed me to sit in on their White-Collar classes. The Dongguan Making Friends Club opened its doors and membership files to me. Ben Schwall accompanied me on an extended tour of the karaoke underworld. Lin Xue shared numerous insights into factory life and became my first good friend in Dongguan. Tan Shen at the Chinese Academy of Social Sciences gave invaluable advice on navigating the factory towns of the Pearl River Delta. And Min's parents were generous hosts when I visited their village.

Researching this book gave me the opportunity to get to know members of my far-flung family. Nellie Chao, Luke Chang, and Irene Chow were generous with their time and their memories; thanks especially to Aunt Nellie for sharing her poetry. Zhang Lijiao's widow, Zhu Shulan, and their children Zhang Song, Zhang Ji, and Zhang Yinqiao welcomed me into their home as a younger sister and shared letters and recollections over my favorite Dongbei dishes. Zhang Hong devoted the better part of three days to telling me everything he knew of our family history. In Beijing, my great-aunt Zhang Lian offered home cooking, newspaper clippings, and her memories of growing up in Liutai. Zhao Hongzhi took me to our family's old house at no. 6 and remembered so many details everyone else had forgotten. In Liutai, Zhang Tongxian was a knowledgeable guide—one of many private historians I was privileged to meet along the way.

I was fortunate to work with gifted and dedicated colleagues in my years at the *Wall Street Journal*. Marcus Brauchli taught me how to write a leder; I have appreciated his friendship and support since the day we met in a Prague movie theater. Ian Johnson was always generous with his knowledge and insights, and he was kind enough to review the manuscript and supply helpful—and humorous— comments. Jonathan Kaufman was an enthusiastic champion of my early articles about migrant workers, and Mike Miller gave those pieces the space that every reporter feels she deserves. Sophie Sun,

Kersten Zhang, and Cui Rong provided invaluable research assistance; I thank them for their good humor and their patience with my endless inquiries. Urban Lehner, Reg Chua, and John Bussey supported my career at the *Journal* and granted me leave to start working on this book. Lily Song, Dou Changlu, and Yue Dingxian provided help in many ways over the years. I benefited greatly from friendship and conversations with my fellow reporters: Kathy Chen, Charles Hutzler, Karby Leggett, Peter Wonacott, Matt Forney, Matt Pottinger, Jason Dean, David Murphy, Joseph Kahn, Craig Smith, and Rebecca Blumenstein.

I am indebted to Doug Hunt, whose thoughtful reading of an early draft helped me resolve major problems with the book. Susan Jakes suggested myriad improvements and guided me to useful reference works after reading the manuscript—I thank her for that and for her friendship over the years. I appreciated the comments of Michael Meyer, Terzah Becker, and Zhang Hong of Colby College, all of whom reviewed the manuscript with great care. He Hongling and Guo Daoping patiently deciphered my grandfather's diaries, and Travis Klingberg gave invaluable advice on the book's visual elements. Thanks to Jane Lee and Jen Lin-Liu for their friendship and encouragement from the day I decided to write this book.

I am grateful to Cindy Spiegel, my editor at Spiegel & Grau, for her sympathetic and insightful readings—no writer could wish for better. A big thanks to Chris Calhoun, my agent, for his early faith and continuing support, and to Marcy Posner for her expert handling of the foreign rights.

My greatest debt is to my parents, who taught me Chinese and told me about China, then left me free to learn so much on my own. My father patiently endured many rounds of questions, and my mother made helpful corrections after reviewing the manuscript. The work that has taken me so far from home has also brought me closer to them. I am grateful to my brother Justin, who always encouraged and understood me despite having chosen such a different path through life.

And to Peter Hessler—thank you for showing me the possibilities, in life and in writing. Every writer should have a reader such as you.